STRATEGIC ACQUISITIONS:

A Guide to Growing and
Enhancing the Value of
Your Business

STRATEGIC ACQUISITIONS:
A Guide to Growing and Enhancing the Value of Your Business

Bruce R. Robinson

Walter Peterson

IRWIN
Professional Publishing
Burr Ridge, Illinois
New York, New York

Senior sponsoring editor:	Amy Hollands Gaber
Project editor:	Jean Lou Hess
Production manager:	Pat Frederickson
Designer:	Mercedes Santos
Art studio:	The Wheetley Company, Inc.
Compositior:	The Wheetley Company, Inc.
Typeface:	11/13 Times Roman
Printer:	Book Press

Library of Congress Cataloging-in-Publication Data

Robinson, Bruce R.
    Strategic acquisitions : a guide to growing and enhancing the
value of your business / Bruce R. Robinson and Walter Peterson.
        p.   cm.
    Includes index.
    ISBN 1-55623-853-3
    1. Consolidation and merger of corporations.   2. Strategic
planning.   I. Peterson, Walter.   II. Title.
    HD2746.5.R624   1995
    658.1'6—dc20   94–21386

Printed in the United States of America

1 2 3 4 5 6 7 8 9 0 BP 1 0 9 8 7 6 5 4

To Arthur W. and Doris E. Robinson
and
Marithé Peterson

Preface

This book gives business managers a step-by-step guide to taking charge of strategic acquisitions. It not only explains how to plan and execute acquisitions but also details who does what and when. Rather than "deal" issues, we emphasize business operating issues—strategic, people and financial matters—which we show to be the key elements that must be controlled to assure a successful acquisition program. Before, during, and after completion of the deal, we place the acquisition process in the hands of the business manager who is in the best position to develop winning business strategies, select and motivate employees, and accurately establish financial forecasts for business valuations.

The responsibilities of the deal specialists—investment bankers, lawyers, and accountants—are defined and distinguished from the responsibilities of business managers. The book gives a time perspective to the strategic acquisition process which forces decisions to be made on the basis of the underlying business opportunity rather than on the timetable established by deal specialists. The book shows that the deal is not completed when a closing takes place but continues until the acquired company is fully integrated into the acquiring company and meets the buyer's performance expectations.

The authors were prompted to write this book after successfully implementing this type of program and witnessing the failure of so many financially driven acquisitions. More than 200 business managers have been trained in the process described in this book. It has been used by Bruce Robinson to acquire his own businesses. As a security analyst, Walter Peterson has worked with the chief executives and chief financial officers of companies that have used strategic acquisitions in achieving their growth objectives. Some of these companies are profiled in this book.

Business managers in the 1990s will confront a challenging and potentially hostile global economic environment, one which is likely to be characterized by anemic growth in the industrialized nations. We explain how to survive and prosper in this treacherous environment by combining a merger and acquisition program with strategic planning to build sustainable competitive advantages.

We expect that readers of this book will approach acquisitions with different objectives in mind: the senior executive in a large company who wants to be CEO of his own business; an entrepreneur who needs to make acquisitions to build a small business into a larger company; a business manager who needs to acquire a competitive advantage; the owner of a privately held business who wants to retire; or managers who want to divest divisions in order to focus on core businesses. All these individuals share a common characteristic—they are not involved in doing deals on a full-time basis.

Because they are not full-time deal makers, business managers often make the fundamental mistake of evaluating acquisitions primarily as financial decisions, much like a manager of a diversified stock portfolio. They get caught up in details of the deal structure and lose sight of strategic, operating and people issues, which ultimately determine the success or failure of any business. Just the reverse is the appropriate order of priority in examining a potential acquisition. If an acquisition does not help realize strategic goals, financial models, however sophisticated, will not transform a poor strategic fit into a good arrangement. This is why we insist that business managers, not financial executives or outside deal specialists, take charge of the acquisition process.

The business manager will learn how to control the merger and acquisition (M&A) process and how to best utilize deal specialists, whether they be investment bankers, lawyers, accountants, or other professionals. There are many relatively arcane legal, tax, and securities regulation issues that are best left to outside experts who can be hired as needed. These specialists can make a valuable contribution to the optimum structuring of a deal, but the business manager must always remain in charge of the process and not become a captive of deal makers who may be driven by transaction fees.

The primary objective of strategic acquisitions is to enhance the proprietary value of a business unit by building competitive advantage. The most frequently used word in corporate announcements of acquisitions is "synergy," but one plus one will not be greater than two unless the acquisition flows from a detailed strategic planning and competitive analysis process. By structuring merger and acquisition activity within a company's overall business development and strategic planning process, the business manager will avoid the trap of pursuing acquisitions as ends in themselves rather than means to an end. Managers can easily get caught up in the excitement of doing a deal and rationalize an acquisition that makes no strategic sense but may appear to represent an attractive financial opportunity.

By adopting the strategic planning methods and four-step acquisition program advocated in this book, operating managers will benefit from a better understanding of competitive forces and the dynamics of growth even if an acquisition is never consummated. A strategic acquisition program develops many of the benefits of a benchmarking study. The business manager will become keenly aware of elements that build and destroy the value of a business.

The book is addressed primarily to strategic acquirers, but sellers must also understand the strategic acquisition process if they are to realize maximum selling prices. Sellers will learn what strategic buyers are looking for and when and why they will pay a premium price. A business guided by a sound strategic plan will be viewed with greater confidence by a potential buyer.

We believe that mergers and acquisitions should be part of a company's strategic planning and business development functions. While staff specialists can assist in developing and implementing these functions, the business manager must "sign off" on the program and communicate the importance of the goals to employees. The strategic acquisition process provides a mechanism whereby a company can effectively measure its performance against that of its principal competitors and thus understand its competitive strengths and weaknesses.

The Overview explains why so many of the financial acquisitions of the 1980s failed and why the economic environment and conditions in financial markets will favor strategic acquisitions in the 1990s. The first four chapters describe the strategic planning and competitive analysis methods which must underpin acquisitions. The main sources of synergy are discussed: access to new markets; cost reductions; new technology that gives products and services a proprietary advantage; and new products, which can be sold through existing distribution channels.

The next seven chapters describe the four key steps in the acquisition process: Search, Screen, Critical Evaluation, and Integration. Complete forms and formulas assist the reader in implementing the process steps. Then companies that have successfully used acquisitions to achieve strategic goals are profiled. Finally the Appendices provide detailed instructions for implementing a strategic acquisitions program.

Acknowledgments

We want to express our appreciation to the executives of the Profiled Companies who agreed to share their views on strategic acquisitions: Diane Harris of Bausch & Lomb; John Kucharski of EG&G; Bernard Schwartz of Loral; Horace McDonell of Perkin-Elmer; John Woodhouse of Sysco Corporation; and Peter Pantazelos of Thermo Electron.

Our colleagues Bob Waugh, John Hoover, Mark Decker, Jim Chambers, and Jack Dallman, read early drafts and provided valuable comments.

We especially thank Charlotte Norwood for her editorial review, and our editor, Amy Hollands Gaber, for her confidence in our project. She gave us the guidance and encouragement needed to finish the book.

Overview

DEMISE OF DEALMAKERS—
RISE OF STRATEGIC ACQUIRERS

By taking charge of strategic acquisitions, a business manager will gain a powerful weapon in the battle for competitive advantage. The business manager must never relinquish control of acquisitions to deal specialists who can assist in the technical details of the process, but lack a specific grasp of how businesses work. Strategic planning combined with a four-step acquisition program will build sustainable competitive advantage— the fundamental basis for building the value of a business.

Strategic acquirers will dominate M&A activity in the 1990s. We define strategic acquisitions as those transactions undertaken for the primary purpose of building enterprise value by strengthening a company's competitive position in a segmented market. Adoption of the techniques advocated in this book will give the business manager the ability to overcome anemic economic conditions and earn above-average financial returns while avoiding the pitfalls of leveraged acquisitions made primarily for financial reasons.

We have witnessed the demise of dealmakers like Michael Milken who reached superstar status in the 1980s, rivaling rock stars and athletes in terms of media attention and earnings. Leveraged buyouts (LBOs), management buyouts, hostile takeovers, and junk bond funding, which were the favored techniques of financial buyers, are out of favor. The shift to strategic acquisitions is well under way as evidenced by the marked drop in the total number and dollar value of leveraged buyouts in the early 1990s.

Three essential conditions, which are no longer present, allowed the dollar value of mergers and acquisitions in the 1980s to eclipse the value of transactions in prior decades and dealmakers to dominate merger and acquisition activity: 1) stock market valuations that were well below intrinsic values in the aftermath of the severe recession of 1981–82 and the accompanying bear market for equities; 2) readily available financing for takeover artists from junk bonds and other sources of leveraged financing; and 3) a deterioration in credit standards and excessive valuations typical of a bull market in equities, which was fueled in part by record corporate stock repurchases. In the 1990s, however, the availability and cost of long-term capital will remain a major constraint on acquisition financing.

HOW CHANGES IN CAPITAL MARKETS WILL IMPACT M&A ACTIVITY

In the United States, mergers and acquisitions have gone through major waves of activity, with each wave punctuated by a particular type of merger and unique conditions in the capital markets. In the early part of the 20th century horizontal mergers dominated the scene in which companies bought both competitors and suppliers, as J. P. Morgan and other financiers put together the great industrial and railroad trusts. In the roaring bull market of the 1920s, the merger movement was characterized by holding company acquisitions using inflated stocks as the medium of exchange. A similar exchange of paper was the principal medium in the conglomerate merger wave of the 1960s. Accounting excesses of the conglomerate era caused the Accounting Principles Board in 1970 to issue Opinions No. 16 and No. 17, which severely restricted the use of pooling of interests accounting for business combinations and forced writeoffs of goodwill.

Leveraged financing dominated merger activity in the 1980s. Total M&A transaction value peaked at $336 billion in 1988, of which LBOs accounted for $94 billion, including the mother of all LBOs—the $23 billion takeover of R. J. Reynolds. The dollar value of mergers and acquisitions dropped to $153 billion in 1992. Activity rebounded strongly in 1993 to $275 billion as buoyant stock prices were reflected in a growing percentage of strategic deals done for stock.

Corporate bankruptcies, which usually rise significantly during a recession, began to climb well before the official July 1990 beginning date of the last U.S. recession. Some of the well known LBOs, which ended in Chapter 11, included Macy's, Federated Department Stores, TWA, Southland, Revco, and Jim Walter. The bankruptcy of the Executive Life Insurance Company resulted from its heavy concentration in junk bonds. Some commercial credit companies, notably Westinghouse Credit, suffered heavy losses from real estate and LBO financing. Failures of S&Ls and commercial banks were other casualties of excessive leverage.

Reaction to excesses in the capital markets typically ushers in a new era. Fallout from excessive debt financing will continue to have a tremendous impact on M&A activity in the years ahead. Bankruptcies of LBOs and the conviction for securities fraud of Michael Milken and other players in the takeover binge, such as Ivan Boesky, Dennis Levine, and Martin Siegel, signaled the demise of dealmakers in the M&A market. This financial reality check will result in mergers and acquisitions being driven primarily by strategic goals established by business managers.

A combination of excessive purchase prices and insupportable leverage ratios caused junk bond defaults to rocket to a historical high. Whereas for the period 1980 to 1988, default ratios on junk bonds averaged 2.5% per annum, defaults climbed to 9.7% in 1991. While the worst is over in terms of junk bond default ratios, it is clear that the major activity in the high-yield market for the next several years will be for the purpose of restructuring and refinancing. In contrast to the 1980s when an estimated 70% of the proceeds from junk bond issues were used for LBOs and recapitalization, public financing for buyouts will be virtually nonexistent for the next few years. The good news for the strategic buyer is that the demise of the dealmaker results in more realistic pricing.

The recovery in the stock and junk bond markets beginning in 1991 allowed some companies that had previously gone private in leveraged buyouts in the 1980s to re-emerge as public companies by issuing common stock to pay down debt. In 1993 new issues of junk bonds totalled $54 billion, compared with $38 billion in 1992, $10 billion in 1991 and $1.4 billion in 1990. However, most proceeds from junk bond issues were used for refinancing and expansion, not for LBOs.

Common stock will become the most important medium of exchange for mergers and acquisitions in the years ahead, reflecting the revival of equity markets, particularly initial public offerings (IPOs). Acquirers without a publicly traded stock available will be at a disadvantage. Whereas the takeover activity caused a substantial reduction in the net equity issued by U.S. corporations between 1985 and 1991, the buyback trend reversed dramatically in 1992. Companies that went private in LBOs re-emerged as public companies, high cost junk bond debt was refinanced from equity offerings, and a record number of companies completed IPOs. The result was the issuance of $72 billion in new equity in 1992, including a record $39 billion for IPOs. The trend accelerated in 1993 as equity offerings totalled $102 billion, of which IPOs accounted for $57 billion.

GLOBAL ECONOMIC CONDITIONS
WILL SPUR STRATEGIC ACQUISITIONS

Strategic acquisitions can help companies overcome the restraint of slow economic growth. Anemic growth expectations for the United States throughout the 1990s stem from the long-term need to correct a debt binge by all sectors of the economy, of which LBOs and takeovers were only one of the more visible signs of distorted economic values. Measured as a percentage of GNP, total government, consumer, and corporate debt rose from 1.4 times GNP in 1980 to more than 1.9 times GNP in 1991.

Although consumers and corporations have markedly improved their financial positions since the 1990 recession, government borrowing will continue to make gargantuan demands on credit markets and pre-empt credit available to the private sector for financing acquisitions. Despite the much ballyhooed federal budget accord of 1990, the U.S. Government budget deficit reached a record $292 billion in fiscal 1992. Congress tried again in 1993 with the Budget Reconciliation bill, which projects a reduction in the budget deficit to $170 billion in fiscal 1996 before beginning to rise again.

The process of reducing excessive debt burdens of consumers, corporations, and the U.S. Government will take many years to complete and will be reflected in slow growth. During the four years of the Bush administration, GNP grew at only 1.0% per annum, adjusted for inflation. GNP in the 1991–1993 recession recovery period expanded at only 2.5% per annum, the slowest recovery rate in the past 50 years.

Foreign sources of capital cannot be counted upon to supplement inadequate U.S. savings. Downturns in the Japanese real estate and stock markets and Germany's internal capital requirements have removed capital exports from these countries. The former Russian republics and the Eastern European nations have an insatiable demand for credit to rebuild their economies.

The contraction of credit available to business borrowers was evidenced by a dramatic shift in the composition of bank assets between 1990 and 1993. During this period total industrial and commercial loans declined from $654 billion to $587 billion and holdings of government securities climbed from $449 billion to $626 billion. In effect, while the private sector was starved for funds, commercial banks were financing the growing federal budget deficit. During this credit crunch, banks basically made no loans for highly leveraged acquisitions. In order for the commercial banking industry to finance economic expansion, there must be a serious reduction in the government deficit in the years ahead. Otherwise, as banks reduce their holdings of government securities and expand private credit, there will be a very rapid rise in interest rates, which will hinder a recovery.

THE GLOBAL MARKETPLACE
FOR MERGERS AND ACQUISITIONS

Brutal global competition will force businesses to limit their acquisitions to those companies that provide a competitive advantage. Strategic buyers and sellers will increasingly recognize the link between financial markets and M&A valuations in the United States and economic and financial trends in foreign markets. A strategic plan should include an analysis of the company's global competitive position.

The value of U.S. businesses purchased by foreign corporations and the value of foreign corporations purchased by U.S. companies have declined in recent years. After reaching a peak of $70 billion in 1988, the value of U.S. businesses purchased by foreign buyers dropped to $15 billion in 1992. A large part of the drop reflected a withdrawal by Japanese companies from the U.S. market. The $6.1 billion purchase of MCA in 1990 by Matsushita Electric was the last hurrah.

Even when competition is strictly within the United States, for example a regional supermarket chain, sellers conducting a full search will contact foreign companies that may be seeking expansion in the United States. Whatever the shape of regulations and treaties governing trade relationships between nations, companies without local representation are likely to be at a competitive disadvantage. Thus, strategic acquirers will be eager to enter foreign markets and may be willing to pay a premium price to gain access to a new market.

U.S. corporations will encounter a myriad of laws and restrictions when acquiring foreign companies and should seek expert financial and legal counsel. To date, mergers and acquisitions of foreign companies have been made primarily for cash due to problems involved in issuing shares in foreign markets. We expect that situation to change over time as global equity markets become more closely linked, the volume of shares traded in markets outside of the headquarters country increases, and securities regulators make it easier for foreign countries to comply with domestic securities regulations.

The message is clear: A company's strategic plan must address segmented markets on a global basis; acquisitions must be pursued as a way to enhance a company's worldwide competitive position. Failure to do so can have disastrous consequences.

MEASURING THE BENEFITS FROM STRATEGIC ACQUISITIONS

The pitfalls of an acquisition program motivated mainly by financial considerations should be evident by now. The case against leveraged buyouts and financially driven transactions is supported by the failure of many of these transactions in the 1980s and divestitures by conglomerates and other companies in order to focus on core businesses. There is a fundamental difference between a financial buyer who is essentially a manager of a portfolio of assets and the business manager who makes an acquisition decision on the basis of competitive strengths and weaknesses, possible savings from consolidation, and other operating measures.

What are the benefits of a strategic acquisition program? Our approach is to study companies that have successfully implemented strategic acquisition programs and examine specific transactions to identify the underlying causes of success and failure. These companies are profiled in Chapter 12. Of course, financial measures cannot be ignored. Ultimately a dollar value is attached to the cost of an acquisition and financial projections are critical. But the basis for these calculations is the responsibility of the business manager, not outside dealmakers.

The first step in achieving benefits from strategic acquisitions is to develop a strategic plan.

Contents

List of Figures

Chapter One

A Business Manager's Strategic Acquisition Process

The Strategic Acquisition Process starts with a Strategic Plan and uses an acquisition or divestiture to facilitate that plan. This chapter will give you an overview of the process that will let you control acquisitions in a way that will enhance your ability to compete in the markets your business serves.

As a business manager responsible for implementing a strategic acquisition, you are immediately faced with many issues:

1. How do I find suitable acquisition candidates?
2. How much should I pay for an acquisition?
3. How long does an acquisition take?
4. How do I maintain secrecy?
5. How do I integrate the new company into my present business?
6. What assistance should I expect from my accountant, lawyer, investment banker, and broker and what should it cost?

These are only a few of the questions you may have regarding a strategic acquisition. They will be answered in the next few chapters. The most important issue is whether you can control the acquisition process in a way that assures success in facilitating your strategic business plan.

The acquisition process is complex, often directly involving up to a hundred people. Transaction specialists and dealmakers such as investment bankers, brokers, accountants, lawyers, and staff specialists usually have the most experience with acquisitions. They each have their own unique perspective on what is to happen, when it should happen, and who should make it happen. Unless you, the business manager, are in control of the acquisition process, it is likely to be taken over by deal specialists focusing efforts on their own area of expertise. If that person is a lawyer, the process is likely to be regulation driven; an accountant will be accounting-rule driven, and the financial structure of the transaction will be the driving factor in the case of an investment banker. These transaction specialists are essential to completing the acquisition but won't assure success in meeting your business objective. You *must* control the acquisition process since you, the business manager, are responsible for directing the business strategy and it is your money being spent to accomplish this task.

But you have limited experience—or no experience—in doing an acquisition. So, where do you begin? You need a step-by-step process, a road map to guide you from the beginning of the acquisition process to success in achieving your business objective.

BREAK THE STRATEGIC ACQUISITION PROCESS DOWN INTO MANAGEABLE STEPS

The chart in Figure 1–1 gives you an overview of the strategic acquisition process. This chart shows how you can break down acquisition activity into four distinct process steps: SEARCH, SCREEN, CRITICAL EVALUATION, and INTEGRATION. Each step defines a period of time when specific issues are addressed and decisions made that will help you in making successful strategic acquisitions. The SEARCH step begins with a Strategic Plan that leads to a strategic acquisition objective and ends with identification of target buyers or sellers. This step typically takes 30 to 120 days and deals primarily with searching for suitable acquisition candidates. The SCREEN step begins with initial contact with target businesses and ends when you prepare a letter of intent or offer letter to the selected target. This step usually takes 60 to 120 days and involves a preliminary evaluation and negotiation with targets to determine if an acquisition is feasible. The CRITICAL EVALUATION step begins with an agreement in principle (offer letter) and ends with a definitive agreement and "closed deal." This step usually takes 60 to 90 days and involves a detailed investigation of the selected acquisition candidate and definitive negotiation. The INTEGRATION step begins with the transfer of the company to the new owner and ends when you have accomplished your strategic objective. This step can take a year or more to accomplish and involves integration of the acquired business into the acquiring entity to accomplish the strategic business objective. The first three steps (SEARCH, SCREEN, CRITICAL EVALUATION) can consume five months to a year, but the acquisition is not complete even when you reach a definitive legal

FIGURE 1–1
Strategic Acquisition Process

Strategic Acquisition Process
Process Steps

		Search	Screen	Critical Evaluation	Integration
Business Management Issues	Strategic Issues	CHAPTER 5	CHAPTER 7	CHAPTER 9	CHAPTER 11
	People Issues				
	Operating Financial Issues				

	Initial Contact	Offer Letter	Definitive Agreement
Deal Issues	CHAPTER 6	CHAPTER 8	CHAPTER 10

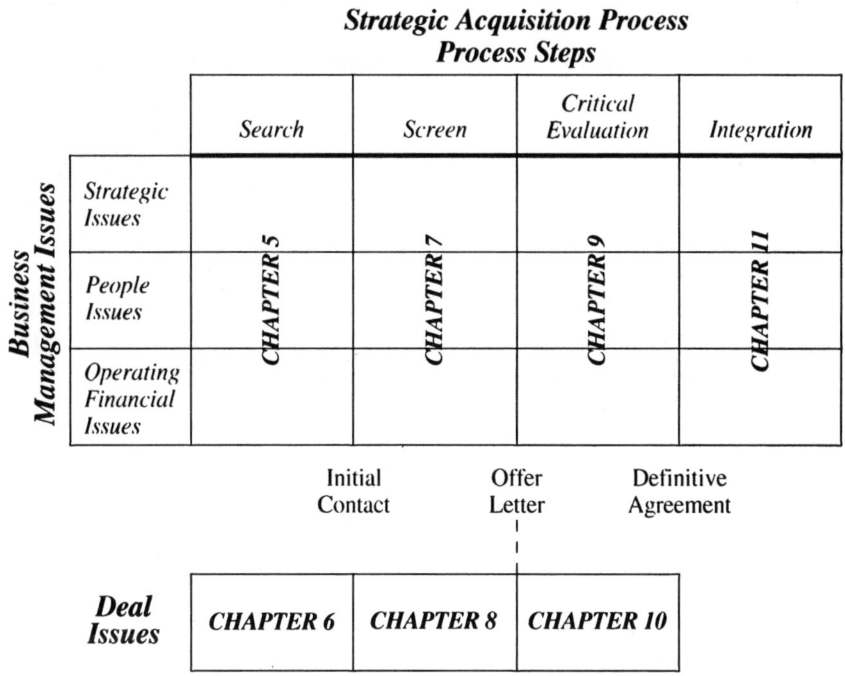

agreement. It is finished only when you have fully integrated the acquired company into your business and met your business objective. The transaction specialists depart when the legal agreement is reached leaving you, the business manager, to complete the INTEGRATION step. If you have addressed the business management issues along with the transaction issues during the first three steps in the acquisition process, the INTEGRATION step will flow naturally and successfully from the process.

SEPARATE THE BUSINESS MANAGEMENT ISSUES FROM THE TRANSACTION ISSUES

Defining the acquisition process helps you separate the Business Management issues from the Transaction issues. The Business Management issues are the Strategic issues, the People issues and the Operating and

Financial issues associated with making the right business decisions to accomplish the acquisition's strategic objective. The Strategic issues address the initial direction for acquisition activity, continuous evaluation of the feasibility of achieving the strategic objective, and translating the business strategy into a post-acquisition implementation plan. The People issues address the role of the business manager in selecting individuals who will champion and facilitate acquisition activity, evaluating the capability of acquired personnel to effect the business strategy, and integrating the acquired personnel into the post-acquisition business. The Operating and Financial Issues address the process of developing a suitable operating plan with financial forecasts and key decision milestones, testing that plan to assure financial objectives will be met, and converting the financial reporting systems to be comparable to the acquiring company's. Acquisitions begin and end with these Business Management issues, not with Transaction issues.

The Transaction issues are the one-time legal, accounting, and finance issues required to reach a definitive legal acquisition agreement. They begin when you have identified a target company that meets your business strategy needs and end when you sign a definitive agreement to close the acquisition transaction. Legal issues involve structuring the transaction to assure compliance with local, state, and federal laws. The accounting issues focus on compliance with generally accepted accounting principles to meet FASB and SEC rules and regulations and tax issues. The finance issues deal with paying an appropriate price relative to comparable transactions and the financial structure of the consideration paid in the transaction, that is, stock, notes, deferred payouts, etc. There are a few legal, accounting, and finance issues to be considered after the transaction is complete, but those issues are considered part of operating the business and thus the responsibility of the business manager.

Why is it important to separate Business Management issues from Transaction issues? If not separated, you may get caught up in the transaction-related deal structure and overlook a critical deficiency in the acquired business. Or the transaction specialists may structure a deal that costs you a key strategic advantage. If not separated, you may forget that the acquisition is not over with the signing of a definitive purchase agreement. It is only beginning. Successful INTEGRATION of an acquisition may take longer than doing the deal. The roles of business managers and transaction specialists can be clearly understood by separating their respective responsibilities during the acquisition process.

HOW DO YOU USE THE STRATEGIC ACQUISITION PROCESS?

Begin with a Strategic Plan as described in Chapters 2 and 3 and determine if a Strategic Acquisition may be the appropriate business decision. If it is, identify the team of business managers and transaction specialists who will work with you in the acquisition process. Show this team what your strategic objectives are and how you intend to use the process described in this book to manage the acquisition. You may experience resistance from your business managers or transaction specialists. Be mindful the process is not intended to be a substitute for their good judgment. However, this process will provide a road map that will let you, the business manager, take charge of the strategic acquisition process.

Chapter Two

Strategic Planning for Acquisitions
Defining the Market Battlefield

At the beginning of the Strategic Acquisition Process, you must identify a clear business objective. If you already have a strategic planning process through which you have identified a clear strategic objective that can be achieved by an acquisition, proceed to Chapter 4 for the first step in a strategic acquisition. If you are wondering what we mean by a strategic business objective and how to do a strategic plan, Chapters 2 and 3 will walk you through a step-by-step process to develop your plan and identify a strategic objective. First you will develop a conceptual model for strategic planning (The Market Battlefield Model) then translate that model into reality through the use of two planning forms (Market Battlefield and Strategic Battle Plan forms) to create a written Strategic Plan for your business. This Plan will identify your strategic business objective.

WHAT IS A STRATEGIC BUSINESS OBJECTIVE?

Merriam Webster defines STRATEGY as, "the science and art of military command to meet the enemy in combat under advantageous conditions." This might be translated into relevant BUSINESS STRATEGY as "the science and art of meeting your market competitors in the market battlefield under advantageous conditions." A STRATEGIC BUSINESS OBJECTIVE thus will either give your business a competitive advantage or remove a competitive disadvantage in the markets you serve. For example:

1. Acquiring a superior distribution system for your products may give you an advantage in your markets.
2. Acquiring a unique production capability that lowers your product costs will give you a competitive advantage.

3. Divesting an irrelevant or inferior product line may remove a competitive disadvantage in your markets.

Notice that strategic business objectives relate to actions taken in defined markets, usually those you are presently serving.

These defined markets will be visualized and described using a Market Battlefield Model as a conceptual basis for written strategic plans that will define your strategic business objectives.

VISUALIZING THE MARKET BATTLEFIELD, THE FIRST STEP IN A STRATEGIC PLAN

All businesses in a free market economy are fighting on a market battlefield—many on more than one. These businesses must visualize their market battlefield in terms of Products or Services offered, Customers, Customer Needs, Market Alternatives, and External Market Forces—factors that identify the market battlefield terrain within which they compete. The shape of the battlefield will vary according to customers' needs. Businesses must also define how their competitors are positioned on the market battlefield and identify their own position relative to those competitors. In the military analogy, businesses who have not clearly delineated these positions are entering combat without knowing the particulars of the battlefield, their competitors' position and strength, or their own competitive advantages. Failure to accurately visualize the market battlefield for your business is, quite simply, suicidal. On the other hand, an accurate concept and definition of the market battlefield is the basis for developing winning business strategies.

The simplest Market Battlefield Model would show your business against a single competitor fighting for a few uncommitted or transient customers (X). This can be diagrammed:

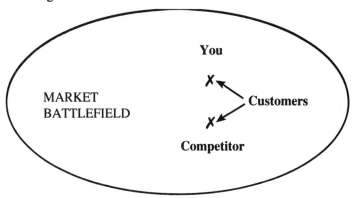

This model tells you very little about customer needs, how your competitor is positioned relative to those needs, or customer loyalty.

Customer Loyalty and the Market Battlefield

You could show customer loyalty by adding to the simple model loyal customers (customer C) behind the market competitor to whom they are loyal:

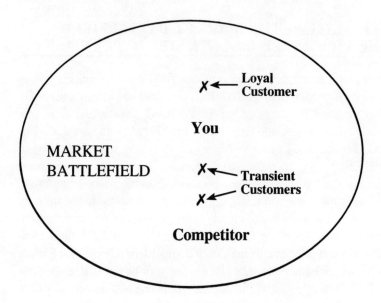

This model can then be expanded to include many customers (Xs) and competitors as shown in figure 2–1. This model allows you to contemplate the difference between a loyal customer and a transient customer in developing your business strategy. How loyal are your customers? How loyal are your competitors' customers? The loyal customer is typically tolerant of minor differences in product price or performance and will be difficult for the competitor to attract away from your business. Markets with a high degree of supplier loyalty require overwhelming competitive advantages to win new loyal customers and are marked by some degree of market inertia. The transient customer may be easier to attract to your business but is usually a one-time buyer who will move to the competitor offering the slightest advantage in price or performance. Are your markets

FIGURE 2–1
Market Battlefield

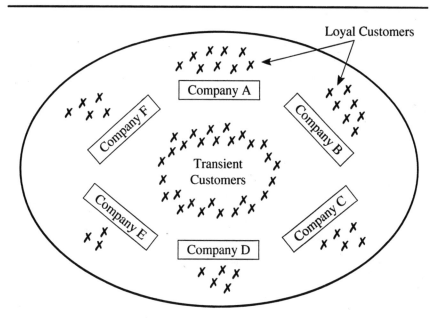

characterized by a high degree of supplier loyalty? Are transient customers the only ones you attract upon entering a new market? These are questions you must resolve in describing your market battlefield in order to develop a winning business strategy.

Customer Needs and Their Effect on the Shape of Market Battlefields

But market battlefields take on different shapes based on the characteristics of customers' needs in that market. For example: purchasers of commodity products, such as minerals, may be very price oriented in their purchase decision while purchasers of custom jewelry may be primarily performance oriented. To avoid errors in strategy development, a market that includes primarily price-driven customers should be viewed differently from a market that contains mostly performance-driven customers. As a first approximation of market battlefield shape as a function of customer need, you can envision three distinct shapes:

FIGURE 2–1A
Price Market

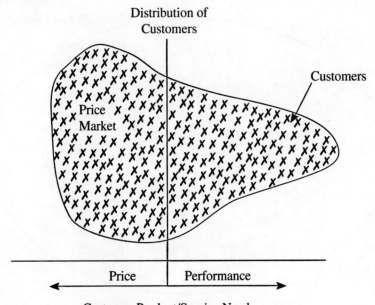

Customer Product/Service Needs

The Price Market (Fig. 2–1a) has a battlefield shape showing the majority of the customers grouped to the left of the model where price is the deciding factor in their purchase decision. Typically, commodity products such as salt, iron, and sand are sold into Price Markets with customer need for lowest price dominating their decision process. Winning strategies in a price market are based on achieving the lowest possible costs. There is very little strategic opportunity based on a performance advantage.

The Performance Market (Fig. 2–1c) has a battlefield shape showing the majority of customers grouped to the right of the model where performance is the deciding factor in their purchase decision. Typical products and services for these markets would include premium jewelry, race cars, and cosmetic surgery. Winning strategies in a Performance Market are based on offering better quality or unique capabilities. There is little opportunity for those suppliers offering low prices and low performance.

FIGURE 2–1B
Value Market

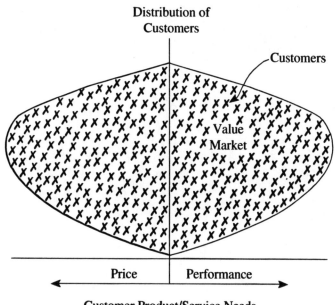

Distribution of
Customers

Customers

Value
Market

Price | Performance

Customer Product/Service Needs

We have shown a Value Market (Fig. 2–1b) as one in which price and performance figure equally in the customer's purchase decision. Typical products sold into Value Markets could include midsize automobiles, standard telephones, and temporary secretarial services. Distribution of customers in a Value Market is centered between Price and Performance needs and is typified by products or services having differentiable product features but that are sold to a set of customers who treat price and performance needs equally in their purchase decision. Winning strategies in a Value Market are based on market leaders offering the best combination of price and performance while smaller competitors provide niche price or performance advantages.

What is the shape of your market battlefield? How is the shape of your market changing? Many markets start in a Performance shape, transition to a Value shape and eventually end up as Price-shaped markets. You have seen this occur in the last five years in certain segments of the personal computer market. If you are in a market where your Performance

FIGURE 2–1C
Performance Market

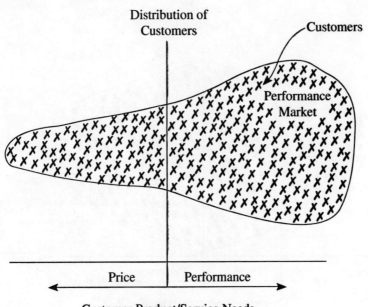

Customer Product/Service Needs

advantages are recognized less and less by Price-oriented purchasers, how tenable is your market position? What are the implications in developing your strategic plan?

Would you expect to find more loyal customers in a Performance Market? Generally, Performance purchasers are more loyal to suppliers than Price-oriented purchasers. For example, suppliers of custom products (art, jewelry, or tailored clothing) generally have a high degree of customer loyalty. This is usually due to the intricate nature of advantages in a Performance market and the complexity of the purchase decision process. In a Price Market, populated by purchasers driven primarily by cost, the decision is simpler. Suppliers of commodity products like salt, oxygen, or sand, are selling into a Price Market and enjoy little customer loyalty. Their market battlefield is characterized by a preponderance of transient customers.

Figure 2–2 shows the nature of customer loyalty for each of the three shapes of market battlefields. Price Markets are shown with primarily transient customers. Performance Markets are shown with a preponder-

FIGURE 2–2
Market Battlefield—Customer Loyalty

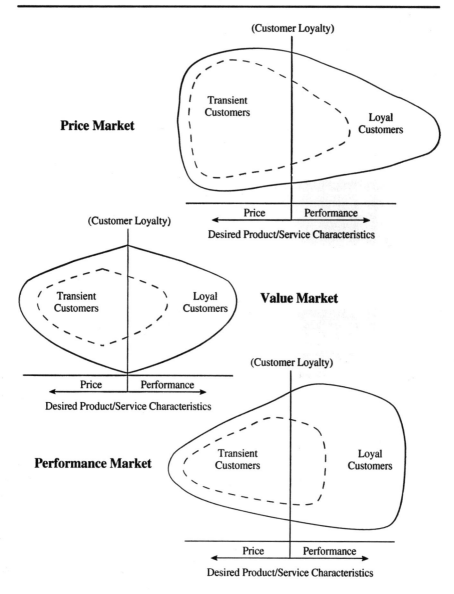

ance of loyal customers. What are the implications of this Market Battlefield visualization to your strategic decision process?

1. It is easier to enter or change market share in a Price Market populated by transient customers but difficult to hold market position.
2. It is more difficult to attract new customers in a Performance Market but they tend to be loyal customers and it is easier to hold market position.
3. Positioning your products or services on the price or performance end of a Value Market may be essential to the success of your business strategy.

The recent crises in the air travel market battlefield were precipitated by the airlines' employing continual fare wars to fight for the transient customer. While chasing this price-driven customer, the airlines decreased the loyal customer base by diminishing the level of service (performance) to all passengers. Southwest Airlines, positioned at the Price end of the market battlefield with lower cost and quality of service is the only winner in the airline passenger market (and the only profitable airline during the last year). The loyal airline customers have been held by programs like frequent flyer mileage bonuses, which make changing air carriers less attractive to customers. But has the airline industry market battlefield changed to a Price Market? Has customer loyalty been permanently or only temporarily affected by frequent flyer programs?

In contemplating the fate of the airline industry and developing winning strategies it is important to understand that the shape and composition (transient versus loyal customers) of the market battlefield is established not by the airlines, but by customer characteristics. The customers' needs define the terrain of the airline market battlefield. The winners will be those airlines best positioned to satisfy those needs.

To define the market battlefield you must first define the Product or Service, the Customers, and those Customers' Needs. This will limit the extent of the market to purchasers of the defined goods and services. It will tell you the shape of the market battlefield based on needs (Price/Value/Performance) driving the customer purchase decision. Understanding those needs will indicate the difficulty of entering or holding a position based on potential customer loyalty. This will let you take the first step in visualizing the market battlefield. But you also must know whom you are fighting against in order to develop winning strategies.

Market Battlefield, Whom Are You Fighting Against?

The Customers define the terrain of the battlefield, and competitors fight for positions as shown in Figure 2–3. Competitors (A through H) are arranged around transient customers who constantly move from one competitor to another. The battle for transient customers is continuous as they define market terrain similar to "no mans land" in the battles of WWI, which was of little strategic value but cost many lives. The valuable customers in the market battlefield lie behind each competitor; they are well-defended loyal customers. Weapons used in the market battlefield are shown as competitive strengths (X, O, –, etc.); competitive weaknesses are shown as gaps between competitors and absence of strengths in competitors' positions.

These competitive strengths may be price, as shown on the far left of the battlefield, a combination of price and performance as shown in the middle of the battlefield, or as specific performance advantages (such as a patented product) as shown with the competitors on the far right of the battlefield.

Competitors are arranged on the battlefield model according to their market share and the market needs they serve. Market share in this market battlefield model is defined as those loyal customers directly behind each competitor as shown in Figure 2–3. Transient customers are shown in the middle of the battlefield model and must either be converted to loyal (repeat) buyers or will remain one-time buyers who shop for marginal product differentiation (either price or performance) with each purchase. Market leaders typically offer both price and performance products and services that let them hold the middle of the battlefield model. Specialized performance competitors are usually smaller and hold the far right side of the battlefield servicing customers with performance needs. Competitors specializing in the lowest price products and services hold the far left of the battlefield servicing customers driven primarily by low-price needs.

The market battlefield model helps you visualize your position relative to your competitors and answer the following questions:

1. Where is your business positioned in your market battlefield?
2. Are you a market leader trying to defend a broad range of customers with products and services covering the range of offerings from low priced to high performance?
3. Are you a specialized supplier of high performance products?
4. Are you a specialized low cost and low price supplier?

FIGURE 2–3
Market Battlefield, Competitors

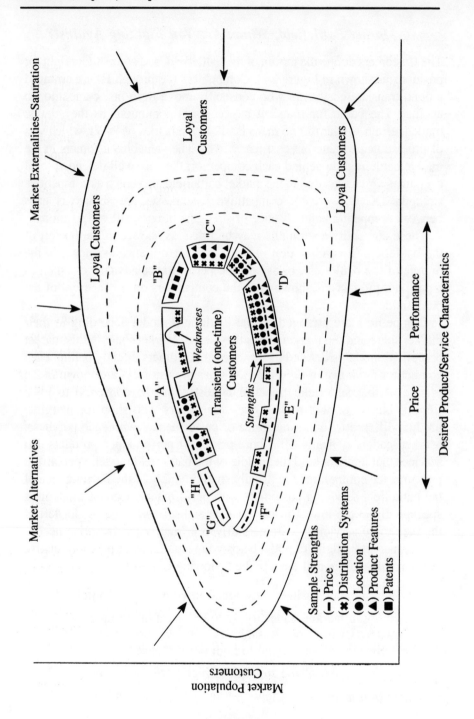

16

5. Where are your competitors' weaknesses and strengths?

6. Where are your weaknesses and strengths?

You will see that this conceptual model for the market battlefield can be translated into a concise one-page description (The Market Battlefield Form) that will form the basis for a strategic plan and let you develop winning business strategies with well-defined objectives. Unfortunately, however, markets and battlefields are not static as shown in this model. They are dynamic, changing all the time.

Along with changes in competitors and customers' needs, as we have shown, there are changes in the overall size of the market battlefield.

ANTICIPATING CHANGES IN THE SIZE AND SHAPE OF MARKETS

What makes the size and shape of the market battlefield change? We know that markets are continuously changing (dynamic). If you develop your strategic plan around a static model of the market battlefield, you will fail to anticipate future changes and adjust your strategy accordingly. Three major forces that change the size and shape of the market battlefield are:

1. Market Alternatives—Those alternative products or services that fill the same customer need. An automobile, for example, is a market alternative to a motorcycle.

2. Market Externalities—These are factors beyond competitive activity that can change the size and shape of the market such as government regulation, natural catastrophes, wars, etc.

3. Market Saturation—Customer needs that are satisfied and will not require additional products or services. For example, once a customer has acquired a set of fine silverware his (her) needs are satisfied.

Looking back to the Market Battlefield Model in Figure 2–1 you can see how these forces change the size and shape of the market battlefield. Although they may act randomly to change your market battlefield, they normally act in a predictable manner described as market maturation. If you can predict their impact on your markets, you can anticipate the appropriate strategy.

MARKET MATURATION

Is your market battlefield new and poorly defined or are customer needs satisfied by long-established competitors with well-defined positions? A strategy that will succeed in the new market battlefield will not necessarily succeed in the more mature market.

You must know how Market Alternatives, Market Externalities, and Market Saturation affect the future of your markets to develop the appropriate strategy. The Market Maturity diagram of Figure 2–4 shows how markets normally mature from their New phase to their final Residual phase in five identifiable stages: New, Growth, Mature, Decline and Residual. How mature are your market battlefields and how fast is the progression from New to Residual?

First, let's understand the characteristics of each phase of market maturation. A market is characterized as a NEW market when products and services are taking on definition and a distinct market is emerging. In this

FIGURE 2–4
Market Maturity

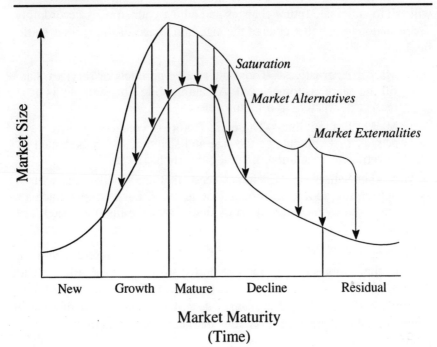

Market Maturity
(Time)

phase of market maturity significant changes are seen in products and services as competitors maneuver for market position and definition. Once a clear expansion pattern is established, a GROWTH market emerges with market leaders and product differentiation established. When market growth slows, it becomes a MATURE market as it is impacted by market saturation, market externalities, and market alternatives. This peak in demand is easier to recognize in hindsight than in foresight and is often more gradual than shown in Figure 2–4. It is followed by the DECLINE phase of market maturity where rapid decrease in demand is often experienced as the market saturates or market alternatives rapidly capture demand for products or services or externalities seriously impinge on the market. When the rate of decline in the market slows or levels out, it enters the RESIDUAL phase of market maturity characterized by a consistent level of demand for mature products and services.

Recognizing Market Battlefield Maturity

Looking at the entire Market Maturity curve of Figure 2–4 it is easy to identify the various phases of market maturity. In real market battlefields you have only part of the data shown in the Market Maturity curve and must predict the rest of the curve. During the Growth phase of a market, how do you predict the timing of the Mature phase and the Decline phase? If at the Mature phase, how do you predict the Decline phase? There are two ways to identify the current state of market maturity and project the future:

1. Carefully analyze the historical growth in total sales revenue for the entire market.
2. Analyze trends in Market Forces: Saturation, Market Alternatives, and Market Externalities.

Historical growth in market sales revenue is the best indicator of current market maturity, and trends in market forces are the best indicators of where the market may be going.

There are many ways of analyzing historical market growth. You can look at total units sold, total sales revenue, total number of customers and come up with three different answers. As a practical matter, estimating total sales revenue by competitor is the best approach to estimating historical market growth. The information is most readily available through industry associations, market research reports, and independent market research firms. You may want to normalize the historical sales revenue to eliminate the effects of inflation, where inflation rates are significant compared to changes in sales revenue. From a careful analysis of the last four or five years of sales revenue data you can usually determine if your market is growing or declining and at what rate. But you need to carefully analyze trends in Market Forces (Saturation, Market Alternatives, and Market Externalities) to more precisely understand market maturity.

How do trends in Market Alternatives, Market Externalities, and Market Saturation indicate market maturity? The following chart summarizes how you can interpret these trends in estimating the maturity of your market:

Maturity Stage (Market Size)	Market Alternatives Trend	Market Externalities Trend	Market Saturation Trend
New (Small, Growing)	No Growth, Begin Decline	No Major Barriers	None
Growth (Rapid Growth)	Rapid Decline	No Major Barriers	None
Mature (Slowing Growth)	New Alternatives Emerging	May Have Negative Barriers Emerge	May Start
Decline (Shrinking)	Alternatives Taking Large Market Share	Negative Externalities May Drive Decline	Started
Residual (Slow Decline)	Dominate Customer Need Satisfaction	May Determine Rate of Decline	May Be Dominant Factor

With an analysis of these trends and historical market revenue analysis you still must estimate the future growth and size of your market to see how it will affect your market strategy within the changing market battlefield.

Looking at some well-known market battlefields will give you some insight into how this process works for each phase of market maturity to develop appropriate strategic initiatives:

NEW: The emergence of teleconferencing is defining a New market battlefield, replacing mature market alternatives such as mail, telex, telephone calls, fax and possibly business air travel. External market forces, such as deregulation of the telephone industry, are trends that support the growth in this market. Strategic initiatives focused on applying new technologies to entice customers away from more traditional market alternatives will dominate near-term competition.

GROWTH: The laser printer market battlefield is characterized by rapid growth as personal computer users replace mature market alternatives such as dot matrix printers, impact printers, and ink jet printers. There are no market externalities impeding the growth of laser printers and the market is a long way from saturation. Strategic initiatives are focused on establishing market position through broadening product offerings to include a wide range of price and performance products with clear market leaders defining the market battlefield.

MATURE: The four-passenger automobile market (in the United States) characterizes a mature stage market battlefield. Rapid transit, low-cost air travel, and telecommuting are growing market alternatives to travel in the four-passenger automobile. Market externalities such as growing pollution control regulation, congested highways, and higher fuel costs are negative trends that indicate a maturation of this market. Market Saturation is a well-defined trend that also indicates market maturity. Strategic initiatives are focused on differentiating product offerings with the introduction of four-passenger sport utility vehicles, trucks, and high-performance vehicles.

DECLINE: The medium-size central computer market characterizes a Decline stage market. Market alternatives, such as personal computers and distributed processing, are growing rapidly and replacing the medium-size computer that dominated small business applications in the 1970s. Market externalities, including rapid advances in CPU electronic chip technology, have made low cost PCs a replacement for these products. Market Saturation is clearly underway. Strategic initiatives are focused on finding niche applications and exiting the market battlefield.

RESIDUAL: The black-and-white television market characterizes the residual stage in market maturity. The color television market alternative is now the dominant product satisfying customers' needs. Market externalities, such as opening up low-cost foreign manufacturing markets, may continue to drive down costs to produce color television alternatives. Market saturation is nearly complete. Strategic initiatives are focused on exiting this market and finding niche related markets such as computer monitors.

In a dynamic market battlefield you can use market history and trends in Market Saturation, Alternatives, and Externalities to define the future market battlefield, which is critical to selecting the appropriate strategy. The above examples show how strategies appropriate for one phase of market maturity are not appropriate for a different stage.

How do you translate this Market Battlefield Model into a clear, concise description of your market battlefield that can be used as a basis for formulating business strategy?

THE MARKET BATTLEFIELD SUMMARY

As a business manager, you must translate the Market Battlefield Model into a working description of your own markets to form the conceptual basis for formulating a business strategy. The Market Battlefield Summary Form in Figure 2–5 is designed to help you describe your market battlefield in a concise manner and provides detailed information necessary for strategy formulation.

Precise instructions for the use of this form are found in Appendix A. The amount of space available for each item of information may seem limited. However, this limitation will require you to distill your thoughts into the essential information describing your market battlefield. With the information on this Market Battlefield Summary, you will be able to develop your business strategy as described in the next chapter.

How should you use this form? What information is required in each box? You should start with Box 1, describing the product or service and complete each box in order. The precise information required in each box is described in Appendix A. In general you will see that each piece of information is an element in a precise description of your market battlefield.

We can describe each of these elements, which relates to numbered sections of the form, as follows:

1. PRODUCTS AND SERVICES should be described to differentiate them from market alternatives. This means if you own an airline, you would not define your product or service as transportation; rather, you would define it as air passenger transportation, or air freight transportation to differentiate from the market alternative of rail or ship transportation. You may further refine your definition to eliminate services outside the scope of your business, that is, coach class air transportation selling for less than $.15 per passenger seat mile. This would eliminate charter air transportation from your market battlefield definition. This task requires a judgment as to the scope of your product or service offering, which in turn defines the size and character of your market battlefield. It is not that simple.

2. CUSTOMERS should also be described to eliminate those you are unable to serve. Typically there are geographic limitations on most small companies since they are unable to satisfy worldwide demand for their products or services. You should limit your customer identification to those you now serve or will be able to serve in the foreseeable future and

FIGURE 2–5
Market Battlefield Summary Form

Market Battlefield Summary

1. Products and Services	2. Customers
3. Customer Needs	Shape of Battlefield ☐ Price ☐ Performance ☐ Value
4. Market Alternatives	5. Externalities	6. Saturation (%)

7. Competition	Target Priority	#	Strategic Initiative	Strengths	Weaknesses	Sales This Year $ / Last Year $	Change $ / %
1.							
2.							
3.							
4.							
5.							
6.							

Total of _____ Others

8. Market Size (Sales $)											9. Market Maturity
– 5 Yr	– 4 Yr	– 3 Yr	– 2 Yr	Last Yr	This Yr	Next Yr	Yr 2	Yr 3	Yr 4	Yr 5	

Form A

_____ Date   _____ Subunit   _____ Strategic Business Unit   _____ Company to those you know well enough to understand their basic needs in purchasing your products or services.

3. CUSTOMER NEEDS should be thought of in terms of the customer's underlying requirement to purchase your goods or services. You should refine this statement to include the driving force behind the customer's desire to purchase, that is, what drives that particular customer to sign a purchase order today.

SHAPE OF BATTLEFIELD should describe the overall characteristic of customers' needs: Price, Value, or Performance.

4. MARKET ALTERNATIVES should describe those products or services that will satisfy customers' needs but are not defined in Box 1 (PRODUCTS AND SERVICES). For example, train transportation is a market alternative to air passenger transportation. Indicate whether the market alternative is growing or shrinking in order to help forecast changes in market size.

5. EXTERNALITIES are those forces outside your market that cause the total market to rise or fall. It may include government regulation, catastrophic weather changes, or other events beyond your control or that of your competition. Indicate whether externalities will cause your market to grow or shrink. Limit these externalities to those currently affecting your market or will affect it in the foreseeable future.

6. SATURATION is the estimated percentage of customers who have acquired the products or services offered and have satisfied their need for that product.

7. COMPETITION is a detailed summary of those with whom you compete, how they compete, their market strengths and weaknesses, sales into this market battlefield (market share), and changes they have made in market share. You should include your own business in this summary for comparison.

8. MARKET SIZE is the total sales ($) revenue of products or services sold into this market battlefield. You may elect to adjust this data for inflation.

9. MARKET MATURITY describes the current phase of market maturity as either: New, Growth, Mature, Decline, or Residual consistent with the prior definitions of these terms.

Once you have completed this form you will be able to reflect on your market battlefield and how you are positioned to compete. The next chapter will show you how to use this Market Battlefield Summary as a basis for business strategy formulation.

Chapter Three

Strategic Planning for Acquisitions
Developing the Strategic Battle Plan

You have defined the Market Battlefield: your competitors and their strengths and weaknesses, the customers and their needs, the market factors affecting future size and shape. How do you translate this information into a plan of action, a Strategic Battle Plan—a plan that lets you translate your competitive position on the market battlefield into the right strategic initiative, a plan that considers competitor reaction to your initiative and leads to maximum possible return on your invested capital while anticipating market maturity? This chapter will show you how to translate your Market Battlefield position into the appropriate Strategic Battle Plan.

As we have stated, business strategy is the science and art of meeting your competitors in the market battlefield under advantageous conditions. The starting point for developing your strategic battle plan is careful analysis of your competitive advantages and disadvantages versus the competitors in your market. Can you take advantage of existing strengths or competitor weaknesses or must you add to your competitive strengths or remove a competitive weakness? Next, you need to analyze which competitors will offer the least resistance to a competitive initiative, estimate the cost of such an initiative, and select the target competitor(s). Then review the potential financial returns should your strategic initiative be successful. Based on this analysis you should be able to select the appropriate type of strategic initiative for the Strategic Battle Plan.

SELECTING THE APPROPRIATE STRATEGIC INITIATIVE

There are five types of strategic initiatives: BUILD, HOLD, HARVEST, RETREAT, and PROBE initiatives, which are defined as follows:

BUILD—To invest in a strategic initiative to increase market
share.

HOLD—To invest only in strategic initiatives that help hold and
defend market position (share).

HARVEST—To withdraw from a market battlefield making no
additional investment or gradually reducing investment.

RETREAT—To exit a market battlefield as fast as possible while
attempting to minimize losses.

PROBE—To make a small investment to explore market
battlefield strategic opportunities. This investment is
limited in amount and terminated at a specific date.

Each type of strategic initiative will yield maximum return on investment when appropriately selected. Knowing which type of initiative is
likely to result in appropriate strategy is the first step in defining the
market battle your firm intends to wage. After you have carefully characterized the market battlefield you may be inclined to overestimate the
opportunities available for you to build your market position. As you will
see, there are very few market battlefield situations that lead to financial
success with a BUILD type of strategy. Selecting a BUILD strategy with
no advantage when facing overwhelming competition can be compared to
the famous "Charge of the Light Brigade." It may be exciting and filled
with the sort of short-term bravado that great stories are made of, but
ultimately it will result in disaster. *The appropriate strategy does not necessarily imply defeating your competitors.*

STEPS TO DEVELOPING THE
APPROPRIATE STRATEGY

First, in step 1 of Figure 3–1, you should evaluate your position and
determine if you have a significant competitive advantage over a target
competitor or competitors. By "significant" we mean the competitive
advantage can pass the following test:

1. It is recognized by the targeted customers as a significant factor
   in their purchase decision.
2. It is meaningful enough to attract loyal customers, not just
   transient customers.
3. It is unique to your business.

FIGURE 3–1
Strategic Initiative Selection Chart

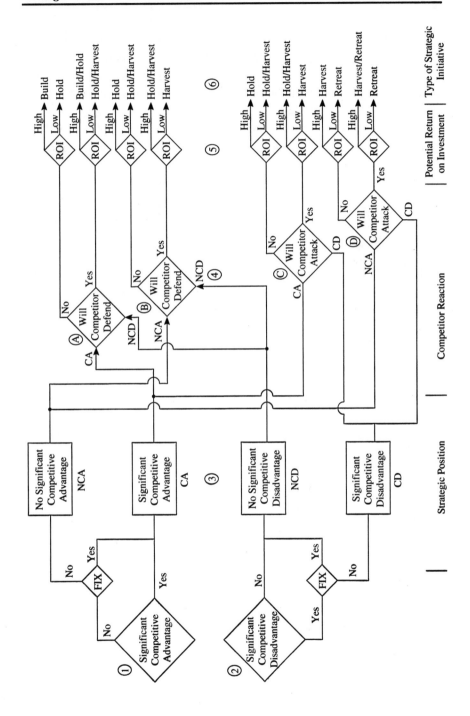

27

If you do not already have a significant competitive advantage, you can fix this situation by either internally developing or acquiring the necessary advantage. The first step in developing the right strategy is to determine whether your strategic position already has a significant competitive advantage or if one can be attained.

Next, in step 2 of Figure 3–1, evaluate your competitive disadvantages against your target competitor or competitors. By significant competitive disadvantages we mean those with the following characteristics:

1. They are currently resulting in some loss from your loyal customer base.
2. They are recognized by your customers in their purchase decisions.

If you have a significant competitive disadvantage, you can either fix it internally or acquire resources from outside your business.

The third step in Figure 3–1 in developing a strategy is to establish your competitive position. You will occupy one of four:

a. Competitively advantaged (CA) with no competitive disadvantages (NCD)
b. No competitive advantages (NCA) with no competitive disadvantages (NCD)
c. Competitively advantaged (CA) with competitive disadvantages (CD)
d. No competitive advantages (NCA) with competitive disadvantages (CD)

The fourth step in developing the right strategy is to assess likely competitor reactions. It is generally true (though not always) that competitors will defend against your strategic advances and attack where they see a competitive disadvantage. For example, if you are competitively advantaged with no competitive disadvantages, a competitor may or may not be able to defend against a strategic initiative. If you have no competitive advantage and are competitively disadvantaged, a competitor will very likely attack your market position. Your estimate of competitor reactions should not only be based on your competitive position but on the history of competition in your markets. In some market battlefields, like commodity products, competitors will react very swiftly to a competitive disadvantage. Other market battlefield competitors, like custom nuclear power plant manufacturers, take many years to react to competitive disadvantages. Your market battlefield analysis will help you assess how your competitors will react to your initiative.

The fifth step is to assess the potential return on investment in the markets defined by your market battlefield. Markets that are yielding a high return on invested capital and are projected to continue to yield a high return generally encourage higher-risk strategic initiatives than do low-return markets.

Once you have considered the potential market returns on invested capital, you should be able to select the most appropriate strategy for your position in light of assumed competitor reaction. As you can see in Figure 3–1, few winning strategic initiatives are BUILD-type initiatives. In fact, this analysis would lead to the following distribution of outcomes for various types of strategic initiatives (if all events were equally likely):

Type of Strategic Initiative	Frequency of Selection
Build	9.4%
Hold	37.5%
Harvest	37.5%
Retreat	15.6%

This analysis may explain why so many BUILD strategies are inappropriate and result in a significant number of business failures. Only 9.4% of the likely strategic initiatives are appropriately BUILD strategies. It is much more likely that a HOLD or HARVEST strategic initiative will be beneficial for your business. Even a RETREAT strategy is more likely to be the right strategy than a BUILD strategy. In fact, our experience leads us to conclude that effective HOLD and HARVEST strategies can lead to significant financial benefits, and even a well-executed RETREAT strategy can save a business and preserve financial resources for more opportune market battlefields.

ADJUSTING STRATEGIES TO MARKET MATURITY

Unfortunately market battlefields are continuously changing as markets mature, necessitating periodic changes to your strategy. As was shown in Figure 2–4 on page 18, most market battlefields progress through five

distinct phases of maturation: *new, growth, mature, decline* and *residual.*
Market saturation, market alternatives, and market externalities are the
forces that cause markets to mature and decline.

Figure 3–2, "Type of Strategy vs. Market Maturity," describes how
market maturity will influence your selection of market strategy. The suggested types of strategic initiatives are only intended to be guidelines, not
hard and fast rules, for modifying strategies as you assess market battlefield conditions.

New Market Battlefields

In a *new* market battlefield, customer loyalty is not firmly established and
all competitors will be investing to gain market share by winning customers to their products and services. These investments will often exceed
near-term financial return requirements of rational competitors but it is
the price of entry in new market battlefields. As we have seen, if you do
not have a significant competitive advantage and few, if any, competitive
disadvantages, you should not employ a BUILD-type strategy. It follows

FIGURE 3–2
Type of Strategy vs. Market Maturity

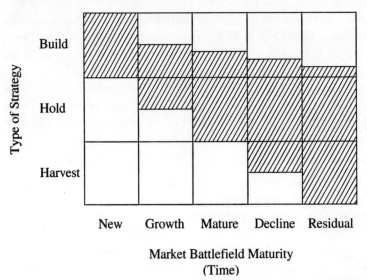

Market Battlefield Maturity
(Time)

Note: Probe or Retreat Strategy may be appropriate as special actions at any phase of market maturity.

that you should not enter emerging market battlefields unless you have the requisite competitive advantage. Unfortunately in new market battlefields most of your competitors will believe they have a significant competitive advantage but the customers will mostly be transient customers in a rapidly changing market. These customers probably have not established a price/performance criteria for purchase decision-making, and this leads to considerable market instability.

The new personal computer market battlefield was flooded with a variety of products using software that was incompatible from one manufacturer to another. Apple, HP, Tandy, DEC, TI, Compaq and others introduced products that were incompatible with each other but each tried to force customer loyalty to their unique product offering by spending millions of dollars to build market position. Only after IBM entered the PC market and Apple established the Macintosh did price-performance standards emerge that would stabilize consumer purchase decisions and provide for a sustained market growth opportunity.

Growth Market Battlefields

In *growth* market battlefields, market competition will be more orderly as customer price/performance decisions become better established, market leaders emerge, and customer loyalties solidify. Customers begin to make repeat purchases, or at least comparative purchases, and will establish standards for price and performance. Market leaders will have emerged, and competitors will posture around these leaders in the market battlefield. As repeat purchases are made, customer loyalties are established. Competitors will be looking for financial returns while holding market share and investing less vigorously in BUILD-type strategies. This does not imply that substantial growth won't occur for those competitors who hold market share in a growing market.

You will obtain maximum financial return if your competitive position in the market battlefield permits you to BUILD or HOLD market position (share) during the growth phase of the market battlefield.

The survivors of the new market battlefield entered the growth phase of the PC market battlefield and initiated BUILD strategies around IBM and Apple products or HOLD strategies around niche market positions. Tandy and Compaq built around the IBM product line as did several low-cost late-market entrants. HP held on to a unique piece of the scientific and industrial PC market. DEC lost its initial position in the standard PC market battlefield. (RETREAT-type strategies are always appropriate whenever you have lost your shirt.)

Mature Market Battlefields

When market battlefields reach the *mature* phase they are characterized by established customer loyalty, well-defined price performance characteristics, and competitive equilibrium. Customers have had time to develop confidence in their suppliers and will change only if suppliers fail to adapt to their changing needs. That is to say, there is a significant level of market inertia with only transient customers moving from supplier to supplier. Price-performance characteristics of products are clearly defined and compared in trade publications and consumer magazines. A rational purchase decision is possible by each purchaser. The competitors have reached a more stable relationship (equilibrium); opportunities for building market share exist only when established competitors ignore changes in customer needs. Most competitors are investing to HOLD market share as it is difficult to attain a significant competitive advantage. Many competitors should be able to realize significant financial returns on their investment at this phase of market maturity. Market saturation, market alternatives, and external market forces are slowing the growth in the mature market battlefield. Competitors who have not achieved an acceptable market share may exit the market as clear market leaders tend to HOLD their market positions and leave little opportunity for building adequate sales volume through market share growth or market growth.

In the case of standard PCs, market alternatives like laptop computers and computer networks have started to slow the growth. Mistakes made by market leaders have let low-cost PC clone manufacturers capture significant market share as designs become stabilized in the mature market and price competition emerges. Customer loyalty remains high for manufacturers like Apple, and they have successfully defended their strong market position.

Building market share can only happen when IBM or Apple makes a mistake like failing to respond to new and faster software applications or not reducing price with production volume. Some competitors have been able to achieve strong financial returns in this mature market while others (like Compaq) have had to invest substantial amounts to defend their market position. This market battlefield is just beginning to mature and may not peak for several more years. It does, however, show us some of the characteristics of a maturing market battlefield.

Decline Phase of the Market Battlefield

The *decline* phase of market maturity often brings intense rivalry for loyal customers with little product differentiation. This leads to severe price competition and a shakeout of all but the strongest market battlefield competitors. The market leaders may be able to realize an acceptable return on investment, but higher cost competitors will be forced to retreat from the market battlefield to minimize their financial losses. It is very difficult to build market share as product or price advantages are difficult to sustain and products or services tend toward commodity-type market battlefields.

Typical successful strategies in declining markets are either HOLD strategies or HARVEST strategies.

The decline in the airline industry has given us a clear example of what can happen when a mature market battlefield begins to decline even a little and for short periods of time. Only the larger or niche competitors are likely to survive, by HOLDING-type strategies with the smaller, high-cost competitors forced to RETREAT from the marketplace. Recently AMR, the parent of American Airlines, announced plans to invest less in its airline business (HARVEST strategy) and build its more profitable businesses. This industry will stabilize once the shakeout is complete (the bankrupt companies retreat) and it reaches a more stable residual phase in market maturity.

Residual Phase in Market Maturity

The *residual* phase in market maturity is characterized by a more stable commodity market battlefield-type relationship between competitors. It is a period when competitors who have established a strong market position with loyal customers can HARVEST their business and produce good financial returns on their investment.

For those companies that develop significant competitive disadvantages during the residual phase of market maturity, competitors will quickly force them to RETREAT from the business. In most cases competitors will not invest heavily to gain share in residual markets as potential incremental returns on new investments are likely to be too small. In fact most competitors are withdrawing cash to invest in other market battlefields consistent with a HARVEST type of strategy.

The residual market for light general aviation aircraft has been characterized by HARVEST or RETREAT strategies over the last ten years.

Driven down to one-tenth the annual sales volume of a decade ago by market externalities (product liability costs), many of the competitors have dropped out of the market. Those few manufacturers remaining are making only those investments necessary to HARVEST or RETREAT from the business. Beech Aircraft has not developed a new general aviation aircraft in ten years but continues to sell a twenty-year-old design. Mooney Aircraft has made only modest improvements to its twenty-year-old design; Piper Aircraft attempted to introduce new aircraft into this residual market and met with financial disaster (now in Chapter 11). Until those external market forces (product liability costs) are removed, winning market battlefield strategies will remain either HARVEST or RETREAT strategies.

TRANSLATING STRATEGIC POSITION IN THE MARKET BATTLEFIELD INTO A PLAN OF ACTION

To win in the market battlefield we have shown that you must choose a type of strategic initiative appropriate to your position in the battlefield relative to your competitors. You must now carefully identify those competitors whom you will engage in your strategic initiative (or those most likely to engage you) and allocate your business resources to obtain specific defendable strategic objectives. The Strategic Battle Plan of Figure 3–3 will help you translate your strategy into a plan of action; Appendix B will give you detailed instructions.

First you must rank order your strengths and weaknesses as they relate to the customers of your target competitor(s). You may have significant performance strength against one competitor but if his customer needs are primarily price driven your performance strength may be of little value in winning over his customers. If your customers are primarily performance oriented and a competitor is attacking against a performance weakness in your product or service, price strength may be of little value in defending your market position.

Next, categorize your proposed strategic initiative by "TYPE." The TYPE of strategy you select has been determined based on market battlefield analysis as shown in Figures 3–1 and 3–2.

You will then select well-defined and measurable strategic OBJECTIVES. Good strategic objectives include a specific market share objective, market position objective, and financial return objective. They should be defendable objectives. You can attempt to gain more market share

FIGURE 3–3
Strategic Battle Plan

Strategic Battle Plan

10. Competitive Strengths (vs. Target Competitor)

11. Competitive Weaknesses (vs Target Competitor)

12. (T)ype / Strategic Initiative

Strategic Initiative	Now	Future
Build		
Hold		
Harvest		
Retreat		
Probe		

13. Objectives

14. Strategic Plan

15. Tactical Plan

16.

	History					17. This Yr	Future				
	– 5 Yr	– 4 Yr	– 3 Yr	– 2 Yr	Last Yr	This Yr	Next Yr	Yr 2	Yr 3	Yr 4	Yr 5
Market Size $											
Market Share %											
Sales $											
OP/Sales %											
ROI											

Form B

Date   Subunit   Strategic Business Unit   Company

35

than your resources can support only to lose to more substantial competitors at a later date.

Your STRATEGIC PLAN should then be succinctly summarized in terms of strengths and weaknesses that have been considered and how they will be focused against specific competitors to establish your strategic objectives.

A brief summary of your TACTICAL PLAN should describe the specific actions you will take to implement your strategic initiative. The expected results of the market battle will then be contrasted with your historic results in the selected market battlefield to determine if the invested effort is financially feasible.

SUMMARY

Appropriate Strategies Come from Careful Assessment of your Position in the Market Battlefield, Adjusting to Market Maturity and Successfully Executing the Market Battle.

The right strategic initiative does not mean gaining market share, attracting transient customers, or increasing profits. Appropriate strategic initiatives maximize return on investment from your business at an appropriate level of risk. If you attempt to gain market share through a BUILD strategy when you don't have a clear competitive advantage, you will lose the market battle. If you do not fix your competitive disadvantages, you cannot HOLD your competitive position in the market battlefield. If you increase prices excessively without increasing product performance, you will gain near-term profit improvement and HARVEST your business at the expense of long-term market position. The decision model of Figure 3–1 will help you select the appropriate type of strategy based on your position in the market battlefield and its financial opportunities. You must MODIFY your COMPETITIVE POSITION (advantages & disadvantages) to CHANGE STRATEGIC INITIATIVES.

MARKET MATURITY will force you to CONTINUALLY ADJUST your STRATEGY as the market battlefield changes over time as shown in Figure 3–2. Strategies that work in new and growth phases of market maturity are unlikely to work in mature or declining phases. How often have you seen great market innovators fail to capture long-term market positions? Your business can't afford to sit still in the ever-changing market battlefield. Picking the appropriate "type" of strategy in the face of changing competitive advantages, disadvantages, and market conditions is essential to sustaining business success.

Successful EXECUTION of the Market Battle depends on several basic elements:

1. Surprise (timing)
2. Overwhelming competitive advantage
3. Minimizing a competitor's ability to retaliate
4. Adequate resources to defend market position

The appropriate strategic initiative based on a careful analysis of competitive position and market maturity will fail unless it is properly executed.

In the next chapter you will see how strategic acquisitions can be the keys to obtaining the above elements for winning Market Battles. In fact, you will see how acquisitions can be used to change the very structure of the market battlefield.

Chapter Four

Strategic Acquisitions
Using Acquisitions (Divestitures)
to Facilitate a Strategic Plan

After reading Chapters 2 and 3, you understand how to define market battlefields and develop strategic battle plans. But how can acquisitions be used to facilitate a strategic plan? There are many types of acquisitions that can be used to facilitate a strategic plan. For example, you may acquire a product line that substantially enhances your existing competitive advantage or corrects a competitive disadvantage. You may divest a business in a maturing market because of predatory pricing. You could acquire the largest regional distributor of your products, upset market equilibrium, and hence execute a strategy competitors couldn't duplicate. Thus, you can use acquisitions in one of three ways: to MODIFY your COMPETITIVE POSITION on the market battlefield, to REACT to market battlefield MATURITY, or to EXECUTE market battlefield INITIATIVES.

As you saw in Chapter 3, the essence of a successful strategic plan is having a competitive advantage on the Market Battlefield. Acquisitions can be used to MODIFY your COMPETITIVE POSITION to give you a competitive advantage or to eliminate a competitive disadvantage. You also saw that strategies must consider market maturity in order to be effective. Acquisitions can be used to REACT to MARKET MATURITY. Finally, Chapter 3 revealed the importance of successful execution of strategic battle plans. Acquisitions can be used to assure successful EXECUTION of MARKET BATTLE INITIATIVES.

A strategic acquisition is one that facilitates a Strategic Battle Plan. A machine-tool builder who purchases a fast-food franchise restaurant has probably not made a strategic acquisition as it does not affect the machine-tool business. But if you own a real-estate business and purchase the same fast-food franchise restaurant because you know where the best competitive locations for new restaurants are, it is a strategic acquisition.

Why? Because strategic acquisitions help you win market battles based on implementing a strategic plan. The machine tool company is unlikely to augment the restaurant's ability to compete in the marketplace. The real-estate business, on the other hand, brings a critical competitive advantage to the restaurant—a great location. The expected return from a machine-tool company's acquisition of a restaurant would be similar to any other investment; the real-estate company's acquisition, however, can generate exceptional financial returns since the addition of a great location to the franchise restaurant represents a significant competitive advantage.

WHEN DO YOU USE STRATEGIC ACQUISITIONS?

Only after you have developed a strategic plan and identified a clear strategic need should you initiate a strategic acquisition. Then you must identify suitable candidates and have adequate financial and management resources to carry out their acquisition. Too often we have seen business people pursue strategic acquisitions when they do not have adequate financial resources to complete them. Likewise, good strategic acquisitions have failed because there was not adequate management available even to support existing business and none to support acquisitions. A real strategic need, suitable acquisition candidates, and adequate management and financial resources are prerequisites for successful strategic acquisitions.

A genuine strategic need is one that permits you to achieve real strategic plan objectives and produce substantial financial returns. Acquisitions are significant, one-time expenditures and are difficult to reverse. They must satisfy strategic needs that are "real," not imagined, in order to justify the expenditure. The change made by a strategic acquisition in your market battlefield position must be considerable. The need to react to changing market maturity must be obvious. The need to execute a new battlefield initiative must be pressing in order to warrant the cost of an acquisition. Acquiring a company is a lot like jumping over the Grand Canyon—you can't do it in small steps and failure is a painful experience.

How to Succeed at Strategic Acquisitions

To succeed at strategic acquisitions you must have both adequate management and financial resources, but you must focus these resources on a clear strategic need. You must find suitable candidates that satisfy a clear strategic need to:

1. MODIFY your COMPETITIVE POSITION on the market battlefield,
2. Help you REACT to MARKET MATURITY caused by externalities, saturation, or market alternatives, or
3. EXECUTE a STRATEGIC INITIATIVE in a way not possible except through acquisitions.

Strategic acquisitions are used to facilitate a strategic plan based on your market battlefield assessment.

MODIFYING YOUR COMPETITIVE POSITION WITH STRATEGIC ACQUISITIONS

How can you use acquisitions to capitalize on a clear competitive advantage or fix a competitive disadvantage? How can acquisitions help you posture your business to match changing market needs? How can acquisitions help you to face changes in competitor market positions or to counter new competitors? When should your business become an acquisition? All of these questions deal with the use of acquisitions to *modify* your position on the market battlefield to win market battles.

Using Acquisitions to Capitalize on a Clear Competitive Advantage

When you recognize a clear competitive advantage, acquisitions let you quickly capitalize on that advantage. Sysco Corporation, a food wholesaler serving the foodservice market (see Chapter 12), recognized its economies of scale were a significant competitive advantage in new geographic markets. Instead of building warehouses and sales forces in new markets and waiting years to win customers from local established competitors, it elected instead to acquire those local food wholesalers. By adding more product lines to the acquired businesses and improving their warehouse efficiency, Sysco was able to significantly expand them. A competitive advantage, broad product lines, and warehouse efficiency combined with strategic acquisitions let Sysco become the largest and most profitable food wholesaler in the United States.

Using Acquisitions to Fix Competitive Disadvantage

Occasionally your market battlefield summary will reveal competitive disadvantages that must be fixed. USAir recognized it could not compete with American, United, and Delta Airlines in the international market. British Airlines recognized that it would be difficult to expand its services into the U.S. market. The two companies have petitioned to merge their businesses to overcome their market disadvantages. This transaction would resolve the competitive disadvantage of limited international market access for USAir and improve their market battlefield competitive position. The three large U.S. competitors, however, have tried to maintain their market battlefield position by asking U.S. federal regulators to block the merger. We are currently waiting to hear whether the regulators will approve the transaction.

Using Acquisitions to Match Your Business Posture with the Market

Your market battlefield summary may show your business is poorly postured for the market it serves. For example, you may offer high cost and performance products in a price-driven market. You may be a value competitor like Sears Roebuck and Co. and find that a poor economy has shifted your primary market to a price market. This means your products offer good performance and service at a reasonable price while the customer wants the lowest possible price. In the 80s, Sears lost considerable market share to Kmart, Walmart, Price Club, Target, and other retailers offering less performance at a lower price. Sears took years and lost millions of dollars trying to convert to a price competitor to match the demands of the marketplace. Possibly Sears would have been better off buying one of the low-cost chains and renaming it Searsmart while downsizing value-driven older stores to satisfy the smaller number of value-driven customers. Acquisitions should be used to quickly reposition a business such as Sears to meet changing customer needs.

Using Acquisitions to Face Changes in Competitor Positions

You may find your Market Battlefield Assessment reveals a significant change in your battlefield position relative to your competitors. Perkin-Elmer recognized that its Japanese competitors (allegedly with government support) were gaining significant market share in its semiconductor manufacturing equipment market. It reacted by selling these businesses to a consortium of U.S. manufacturers of semiconductors and similar equipment. This is an example of how you can use divestitures as part of a strategic acquisition process to respond to changes in competitor position on the market battlefield.

Using Acquisitions to Counter New Competitors

When you develop your battlefield summary, you may discover new niche competitors have entered your market. Harley Davidson, a U.S. manufacturer of motorcycles, found Japanese competitors entering its market with motorcycles that were more fuel efficient, started with an electric starter, and were easier to operate. By failing to respond quickly to these niche competitors, Harley Davidson lost the majority of the motorcycle market in the United States. In fact, these competitors eventually redefined the U.S. motorcycle market, leaving Harley Davidson holding only a performance segment for large motorcycles. Had Harley Davidson acquired the small engine, electric starter, and small motorcycle capabilities, the Japanese entry into its U.S. market might have been thwarted early. The Harley Davidson example demonstrates how strategic acquisitions could be used to keep niche competitors out of your markets through acquiring competing capabilities.

Your position on the market battlefield is continually changing as competitors' capabilities change, the shape of the market (customer price and performance needs) changes, new niche competitors enter, and old competitors merge or leave the market battlefield. Strategic acquisitions can help you MODIFY your POSITION on the MARKET BATTLEFIELD.

When Should Your Business
Become a Strategic Acquisition?

Your strategic plan may foretell your company's demise in the market battlefield. It may identify buyers who could use your competitive advantage to strengthen *their* market position. Thus, your company may be more valuable as an acquisition by a strategic buyer than as a stand-alone business entity. PSA, a West Coast U.S. airline, was unable to sustain its competitive position in the West Coast battlefield for air travelers. Its strategic plan would have revealed a cost disadvantage relative to South-

West Air and a performance disadvantage relative to the larger carriers (American and United) who had a high volume of connecting traffic. It would also have shown USAir as struggling to gain a position in the West Coast market. PSA's management wisely sold it to USAir under favorable terms, giving USAir a large West Coast presence. The price paid by USAir would have been difficult to justify by a buyer from an unrelated market. Subsequent performance of the former PSA segment of USAir's business has reinforced the wisdom of selling PSA. The competition ultimately faced by USAir in the West Coast market has exceeded its expectations and it has reduced the acquired PSA business in the face of this competition. So, as you see, your business's strategic plan can also help you decide when to sell, to whom to sell, and how to get a maximum price.

REACTING TO MARKET MATURITY WITH STRATEGIC ACQUISITIONS

How do you react to opportunities for your company's skills and resources in a rapidly growing new market? Or to alternative products or services that use new technology to satisfy your customers' needs? What about market externalities, such as government regulations, that reduce demand for your products or services? If you have enough time and money, you can use your existing resources or build new resources internally for your existing business. However, there is often inadequate time or money to develop internal capabilities to react to market maturity. Acquisitions and divestitures can provide immediate solutions to these strategic issues of market maturity.

Reacting to New Market Growth Opportunities with Acquisitions

You may identify very attractive new market growth opportunities that can use your company's capabilities but present significant barriers to entry. Acquisitions can enable you to jump into those growth opportunities and will often provide immediate returns on your investment. For example, EG&G Inc., a Boston-based high technology instrument manufacturer, realized that airport security instruments represented a new growth opportunity. Even though EG&G made radiation measuring instruments and understood the technology of airport security instruments, it had no products serving this market. Furthermore, there were several competitors with government approved products already available who were continuously improving their products. Rather than start from scratch with development of its own products, EG&G acquired Astrophysics Research Corp., the largest manufacturer of airport screening instruments. EG&G was able to bring its technical know-how in radiation measurement to the acquisition and enter a related fast-growing market through this strategic acquisition.

Reacting to Market Saturation with Strategic Acquisitions

Often we find our existing market share approaching saturation while investors and shareholders demand growth in sales and earnings. Provided you don't run afoul of the antitrust regulations, you can continue to grow in a saturated market by acquiring competitors that give you an added strategic advantage. This can result in lower costs to your customers through economies of scale or new capabilities in your existing business, allowing growth in a declining or flat market, which still holds promise for the future.

Chrysler Corporation's acquisition of the Jeep product line gave it a new recreational vehicle capability when its standard four-passenger vehicle market was saturated. Sales of Jeep recreational vehicles are credited in part with keeping Chrysler in business until it could redesign its four-passenger autos to replace the older designs. The Jeep acquisition permitted Chrysler to spread its costs over a broader product offering and return to profitability in a saturated market.

Reacting to Market Alternatives with Strategic Acquisitions

How will you react when a clear market alternative to your products and services threatens to force you out of business? How should video stores react to pay-per-view television, which will eventually offer consumers a more convenient method of renting movies? The stores could sell their video store assets and redeploy them into pay-per-view television services. Strategic divestitures can save your capital when a market alternative appears on the horizon. A strategic acquisition in the emerging market alternative may let you continue to benefit from your accumulated market knowledge.

Reacting to Market Externalities with Strategic Acquisitions

How do you react to market externalities, like changes in government regulations or currency fluctuations, which threaten your market position? The German and Japanese auto manufacturers have recently seen their currencies strengthen to the point where autos built in their countries are no longer price competitive. They could build new manufacturing facilities in the United States or they could acquire existing U.S. auto manufacturing capability. The faster they begin manufacturing in the United States, the faster they will regain their lost market share through reduced manufacturing costs and product pricing. Acquisition of existing manufacturing capabilities will hasten their cost reduction effort and help them overcome the market externality of currency exchange differential. This is one example of how strategic acquisitions can be used to react to market externalities.

In summary, market maturity will force you to continually adjust to a changing market battlefield. All phases of market maturity—New, Growth, Mature, Decline, and Residual phases—present strategic challenges in the management of your business. Acquisitions and divestitures provide a management tool to let you react to continuously changing market maturity. In New and Growth markets, acquisitions can provide a means of jumping into new related market opportunities.

As market saturation, market alternatives, and market externalities force market contraction, acquisition of competitors, new technologies, or new capabilities may let you continue to prosper in maturing markets.

USING ACQUISITIONS TO ASSURE SUCCESS IN EXECUTING A STRATEGIC INITIATIVE

You may have identified a "Winning Strategy." You may see an opportunity to upset market equilibrium and significantly improve your market battlefield position. You may face a competitor who is in financial trouble. You may have recognized a serious deficiency in your products or services. All these situations require successful execution of a strategic initiative.

Tactical success in executing a strategic initiative occurs when you accomplish your strategic objective. As seen in Chapter 3, the chances for success can be enhanced if you apply the following tactics:

1. The Element of Surprise
2. An Overwhelming Competitive Advantage
3. Minimize a Competitor's Ability to React
4. Maintain Adequate Reserves

These tactics are as old as the military teachings of Clausewitz and apply to market battlefields as well as to military battlefields.

The Element of Surprise

Developing new products or markets can take years, and it is very likely your competitors will know about your activities well in advance of your initiative, giving them sufficient time to react with a defense to counter your initiative. An acquisition gives you an immediate change in your ability to compete and can be executed in a way that will surprise your competition and give you a tactical advantage in achieving your strategy. Thermo Instrument acquired Finnigan Corporation in 1990 to broaden its analytical instrument business and give it a world leadership position in mass spectrometers. It would have taken five or ten years to design, manufacture, and market products that would give Thermo Instrument an equivalent portion of the mass spectrometer market. In order to have achieved this position internally, Thermo Instrument would have had to maintain continuous competitive pressure on the Finnigan product line and would have given all competitors time to react to their product offerings. With the acquisition of Finnigan, Thermo Instruments instantly established a position in the mass spectrometer market, surprising competitors and assuring the company a position in the market battlefield before its competitors could react to the strategic initiative.

An Overwhelming Competitive Advantage

Too often, your competitors will match each small strategic initiative with a defensive response. How do you get significantly ahead of the competitors and establish an advantage that they cannot or will not match? Sysco Corporation, in its growth through regional acquisitions, brought automated warehouse technology and broad product lines to the acquired food distributors. The smaller local competitors were overwhelmed by the resources brought into their markets by Sysco. This competitive advantage introduced to the acquired regional distributor assured the success of Sysco's strategic initiative.

Minimize the Competitor's Ability to Retaliate

Acquisitions often can be used to secure a scarce resource and minimize your competitor's ability to duplicate your action. Should Sysco Corporation acquire the largest regional distributor of food products in a specific geographic market, its national rival would be left with only the second or third largest distributor. This would give Sysco Corporation the best economies of scale and minimize its national competitors' ability to successfully retaliate through a comparable acquisition.

Maintain Adequate Reserves

Running out of money is the quickest way to lose a market initiative. If you start to develop a new product and underestimate the cost of development (you can probably remember a few of these situations), you may not be able to execute a strategic initiative. Any new business initiative involves risk of cost escalations due to inflation, design problems, retaliation of competitors, or market resistance to change. Acquisitions must be financed as single stand-alone transactions leaving you with adequate reserves to continue financing your day-to-day operations.

How Can a Potential Strategic Acquisition Run into Trouble?

You should carefully assess the strategic need to be sure that making an acquisition is the right answer. Then take charge of the acquisition process to ensure that the strategic need will be satisfied after the deal is closed. Faulty execution by outside dealmakers can cause a company to lose the strategic opportunity represented by an acquisition. If your primary strategy in an acquisition is surprise and the dealmakers drag out a transaction, you will lose this important element. If the competitive advantage acquired is in the new management team and the dealmakers scare them away, you lose the strategic opportunity. If the competitive advantage acquired is a low-cost manufacturing facility and you wind up with unforeseen environmental restoration costs due to post-transaction discoveries, you lose the advantage. In order to preserve the strategic opportunity, strategic acquisitions must be guided by the business manager who is responsible for the strategy and not by investment bankers, lawyers, accountants, or corporate staffers.

Suitable acquisition candidates are not always available. When you identify acquisition candidates, you may find that none is for sale or that there are other reasons why an acquisition is not feasible. In our own experience, we have on occasion tried to acquire businesses with specific technical expertise to improve our company's competitive position only to find these businesses were closely held and the owners lacked interest in a sale. You may believe any business is for sale; it's just a matter of price. We have found more than half the companies contacted will not even discuss selling, let alone pricing. So don't be surprised; your target acquisition may not be available and no existing suitable alternatives may meet your strategic needs.

Inadequate management resources to facilitate an acquisition and support its integration have destroyed many good strategic opportunities. An acquisition may instantly increase the size of your business by a significant percentage. If your management is not ready for the changes and challenges this will generate, your initiative will fail. As Dean Freed, former Chairman and CEO of EG&G Inc., told his management team, "If you don't have solid management control over your existing base business, don't even think about an acquisition."

This means you must have extra management capability and time to deal with the uncertainties (surprises) of an acquisition. It means you must be able to devote management time to a rigorous analysis to make certain the acquisition will meet your strategic objectives. It correctly implies you can't fix a poorly managed business with a strategic acquisition or any other kind of acquisition. Acquisitions will only amplify problems of an inadequate management team.

To have available adequate financial resources for an acquisition means that you must have the financial capacity to both acquire a business *and to sustain its operation.* How often have you seen acquirers destroy good strategic acquisitions by cost cutting them out of business to service the transactions debt. Commonly you will find transaction costs creeping up during the acquisition process. If, in the end, you do not have the financial reserves necessary to implement the post-acquisition strategic initiative, you have not made a strategic acquisition as you will not be able to meet your strategic objectives. You will fail. Therefore, you must accrue sufficient financial resources for post-acquisition costs and surprises. You must accurately analyze an acquisition candidate to estimate the post-acquisition costs and maintain adequate financial reserves to cover these costs in addition to the purchase price and transaction costs. (See Chapter 9 for a perspective on valuing companies.)

When Would You Not Want to Do a Strategic Acquisition?

Using in-house resources, such as your engineering team, manufacturing plant, existing distribution or advertising capability to implement a strategic plan is called internal development. Is this the best way for you to implement a strategic plan? Perhaps no viable acquisition candidates to meet your strategic criteria are available to buy. Or the owner of the acquisition candidate may not wish to sell or will sell only at a prohibitively high price. Sometimes the appropriate acquisition may violate antitrust laws. Often, there is no way to satisfy the seller's financial and personal objectives. In such instances, acquisition attempts can initiate a bidding war that you do not have the resources to win. In these situations, you may be better off effecting a strategic plan through internal development, using those people, facilities, skills, and other resources resident in your existing business.

How to Fail at Strategic Acquisitions

If you want to assure failure in a strategic acquisition:

1. Try to fit an available company into your business strategy instead of letting the business strategy drive the acquisition process.
2. Pay too much in order to force an acquisition, even though the available company fits your strategic objective.
3. Find companies that fit your strategic objective but have unrelated businesses that also must be acquired.
4. Try to buy management expertise in an acquisition to cover up your own management deficiencies.
5. Pay a price that impairs your ability to support post-acquisition costs and to cover contingencies. There will always be unforeseen post-acquisition costs. You must have financial reserves.

SUMMARY

Strategic acquisitions will permit you to either improve your market battlefield position or exit the battlefield. Strategic acquisitions will help you react to maturing markets, or they will help you execute winning strategies by giving you tactical advantages.

In order to preserve the strategic opportunity, strategic acquisitions must be guided by the business manager who is responsible for the strategy and not by transaction-oriented "dealmakers," such as investment bankers, lawyers, accountants, or corporate staffers. The business manager must drive and control the strategic acquisition process to achieve its objectives. Faulty execution by outside dealmakers can cause a company to lose the strategic opportunity presented by an acquisition. If your primary strategic opportunity in an acquisition is surprise and the dealmakers drag out a transaction, you will lose this important element. If the competitive advantage acquired is in the skills of new employees and the dealmakers scare them away, you lose the strategic opportunity. If the competitive advantage is a low-cost manufacturing facility and you wind up with unforeseen environmental restoration costs due to post-transaction discoveries, you lose the competitive advantage.

The first step in the Strategic Acquisition Process is to develop a strategic plan. If the strategic plan can be most effectively facilitated by an acquisition or divestiture, the Strategic Acquisition Process will help you, the business manager, guide the acquisition to a successful conclusion through the SEARCH, SCREEN, CRITICAL EVALUATION, and INTEGRATION STEPS. The next seven chapters will take you through each step in the Acquisition Process from identifying suitable candidates to successful post-transaction integration. You will be shown how to control and direct the acquisition process to achieve your business's strategic objective.

Chapter Five

The Search Step in the Strategic Acquisition Process
Business Management Issues

How do you embark upon a strategic acquisition? Start with a Strategic Plan as described in Chapters 2 and 3; it will point the way to either a strategic acquisition or a divestiture or even to an entirely different approach to developing your business. For example, an acquisition may let you move from a HOLD strategy to a BUILD strategy in a high-return market. If your Strategic Plan points you toward a RETREAT strategy, on the other hand, a divestiture may be more appropriate. Changing the appropriate TYPE of strategy (Build, Hold, Harvest, Retreat, or Probe) follows when you MODIFY your COMPETITIVE POSITION in the Market Battlefield, ADJUST to MARKET MATURITY, and successfully EXECUTE your Strategic Battle Plan. Acquisitions can be used to:

1. MODIFY your COMPETITIVE POSITION (Add a competitive advantage or remove a competitive disadvantage)
2. ADJUST to MARKET MATURITY
3. EXECUTE the MARKET BATTLE

Your Strategic Plan will help you decide which of these three actions is necessary to facilitate your strategic initiative.

Whether your Strategic Plan points to divesting or acquiring, you must organize a team dedicated to making the acquisition process work. Then identify target companies as potential sellers or buyers and make initial contact to assess your people and financial compatibility. Business Management activity during the Search step begins with Strategic Plan direction and ends with a list of target companies. The process will include Strategic issues, People issues, and Operating Financial issues.

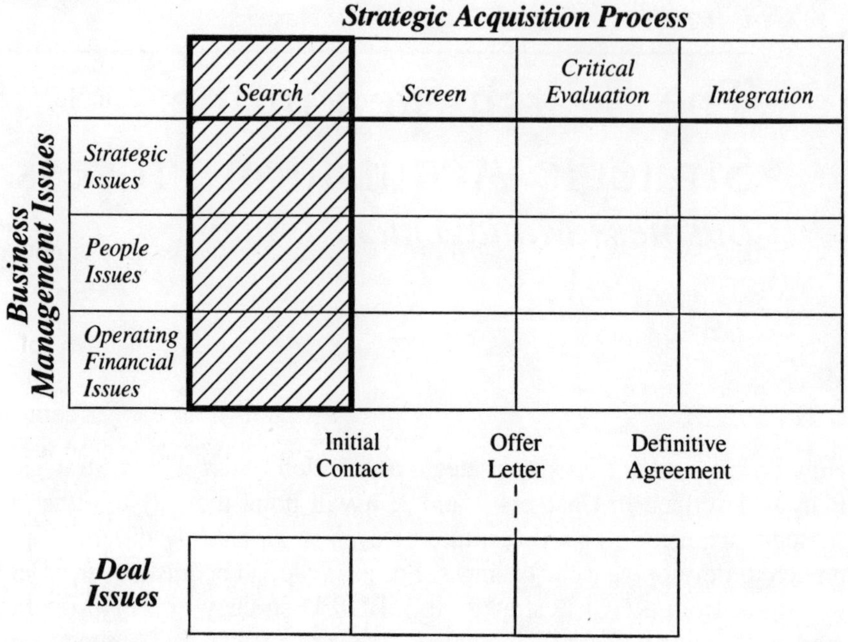
Strategic Acquisition Process
Search
Screen
Critical Evaluation
Integration
Business Management Issues
Strategic Issues
People Issues
Operating Financial Issues
Initial Contact
Offer Letter
Definitive Agreement
Deal Issues

WHAT ARE THE STRATEGIC ISSUES IN THE SEARCH STEP?

The first Strategic Issue is to develop your Strategic Plan and determine if an acquisition or a divestiture will help facilitate it. Chapters 2 and 3 show you how to develop a Strategic Plan (Market Battlefield Summary and Strategic Battle Plan). If you do not yet have such a Plan, reread Chapters 2 and 3 and Appendices A and B to develop one before proceeding. Can you use acquisitions to MODIFY your COMPETITIVE POSITION on the market battlefield, REACT to BATTLEFIELD MATURITY, or EXECUTE market battlefield INITIATIVES? Chapter 4 showed you how acquisitions can be used in each of these three scenarios. But, how do you find acquisition candidates (or buyers) to facilitate your strategic plan?

Finding Acquisition Candidates (or Buyers) to MODIFY Your COMPETITIVE POSITION

How do you find acquisition candidates (or buyers) that let you MODIFY your competitive position in your market and realize significant financial return for the effort through:

   a. Capitalizing on a clear competitive advantage?
   b. Repairing a competitive disadvantage?
   c. Reposturing your business to match market needs, for example, you have a performance product in a price market?
   d. Adjusting to changing competitor capabilities?
   e. Countering advances by new competitors?
   f. Exiting the market battlefield when changing your position is not feasible?

Each of these situations would lead you to look to different types of sellers (or buyers).

When searching for acquisitions to let you capitalize on a clear competitive advantage, you must look for facilitating candidates. These are companies that let you carry your competitive advantage to the market. Consider acquiring distributors when you need more market access. Look at acquiring suppliers if you need to get your proprietary product manufactured. Find competitors that can significantly benefit from the addition of your competitive advantage.

When you need to repair a competitive disadvantage, you must find businesses that directly compensate for that disadvantage. A supplier that will either reduce your costs or add a performance advantage may be feasible. A competitor that compensates for your competitive disadvantage may be a viable candidate.

You may be surprised by a competitor who introduces a new technology to your market, thus producing a significant change in capability. Perhaps they will shift to a completely new marketing strategy (like direct sales versus distributors). Or they may apply a much lower cost production capability. Through acquisition of a company with similar technology expertise, you can counter the competitor's initiative. The new marketing strategy may well be offset by your acquiring a marketing company. Acquiring a company with low-cost manufacturing capability will enable you to counter the competitor's lower cost initiative. To find companies with requisite technology expertise, you might read appropriate trade publications and the Thomas Register, as well as attend trade shows where this technology is presented. Companies successful with new marketing strategies can be found through marketing and sales agencies and their publications. These continually identify new marketing and selling techniques and the companies that use them. For low-cost manufacturing capability, look at price competitors in your own market, or you may elect to search for foreign producers. These are usually identifiable through government agencies, import-export companies, or local advertising media. You can use any of these approaches to adjust to changing competitor capabilities through acquisitions.

Similar tactics can be employed in the case of countering advances by new competitors, except that you may have the option of actually acquiring the new competitor.

Making a decision to EXIT the market battlefield leads you to look for divestiture candidates. The best strategic buyers are those competitors that can use a complementary capability of your business to enhance their own strategic position. The next best buyers are those suppliers or customers that can use your business's capabilities to enhance their competitive position.

To locate acquisition candidates (or buyers) to help you MODIFY your competitive position, you should look closely at your competitors, suppliers, and customers or distributors. You should be familiar with most of these businesses. When you are looking for supplementary capabilities outside your direct business, you must rely on trade periodicals, advertising material (Thomas Register), government agencies (Dept. of Commerce or equivalent), trade shows, or industry specialists to identify strategic acquisition candidates (or buyers).

Finding Acquisition Candidates to Help You REACT to MARKET MATURITY

How do you find acquisition candidates to help you REACT to MARKET MATURITY through:

a. Pursuit of new related growth markets?
b. Consolidation of a leadership position in a saturated market?
c. Acquisition of Market Alternatives to your existing products?
d. Exiting markets affected by Market Externalities, such as new government regulations?

When you discover New markets (in terms of Market Maturity) that have a need for the unique capabilities of your business and you want to enter those markets, you may be able to acquire an existing business already actively participating in that market. Identifying such businesses is as easy as identifying the competitors in the New market. Investigate who is advertising the New market's products or services and talk to customers. Be mindful, however, that identifying a suitable acquisition candidate is complicated by the lack of order typical of New markets. Companies that look like market leaders one month may be overwhelmed by competitors the next. A careful assessment of New market competition and customers' changing needs is critical to success in acquiring companies in New markets.

When your market is saturated and in the Mature, Decline, or Residual phase of Market maturity, acquisitions may be useful to consolidate your market position. In fact, expanding your market position in any other manner is very difficult as most customers and competitors have established positions in the Market Battlefield. Finding acquisition candidates is simply a matter of identifying the competitors. Success will hinge on selecting a complementary business that will not cause you to run afoul of antitrust regulations.

As you will recall, Market Alternatives are those products or services that are satisfying the same customer need as your products or services but are sufficiently different to reside in different markets. Passenger trains are a Market Alternative to passenger aircraft. When you perceive your market shrinking because customers are switching to Market Alternatives, acquisition of a business providing these alternative goods or services may be an effective strategy. Often you will be acquiring a business that is not related to your business except for common customers and that will have significant technical and people risks. Finding candidates is accomplished by talking to your customers and getting an evaluation of the market alternative companies that they endorse. Or you could use market research and advertising data to identify competitors in the markets served by the suppliers of Market Alternatives to your products.

Exiting markets affected by Market Externalities is critical to the survival of many businesses, such as suppliers of government services or equipment. A single piece of government legislation or a policy change can create or destroy market opportunities. Most often, competitors in this market will have accurately evaluated the Market Externality. If it is a negative externality and you are selling a business, existing competitors are poor prospective buyers as they will substantially discount their purchase offer. Buyers for businesses affected by negative externalities are usually limited to employee buyouts or financial acquirers (bottom fishermen). Investment bankers and business brokers are most useful in finding this type of buyer. If, on the other hand, the externality is a positive one, existing competitors or suppliers of Market Alternatives and New market entries may be interested buyers. Finding a buyer is approached in the same manner as described above for competitors and suppliers of Market Alternatives but finding businesses interested in entering New markets is usually left to the investment banker/business broker community.

Finding Acquisitions (or Buyers) that Will Help EXECUTE a STRATEGIC INITIATIVE

How do you find acquisitions that will help you EXECUTE a STRATEGIC INITIATIVE through:

a. Adding the necessary element of surprise to your strategic initiative?
b. Giving you an overwhelming competitive advantage?
c. Minimizing or eliminating a competitor's ability to react to your strategic initiative?
d. Allowing you to preserve your financial resources to pursue other strategic opportunities?

Acquisitions that add an element of surprise to your initiative may come from any of the above described sources. However, you must maintain strict confidence throughout the acquisition process. This eliminates acquisition of most competitors, as government regulations under the Hart-Scott-Rudino Act may require release of acquisition information.

Acquisitions that give you an overwhelming competitive advantage usually involve gaining unique competitive advantages in either performance or price. Competitors' advantages combined with your own competitive advantages seldom result in more than the sum of the two positions in the market battlefield (not overwhelming). Instead, suppliers and distributors you know through your day-to-day business activities may be the answer. Look for suppliers that will give you important cost savings or product (service) performance advantages or acquire distributors of your products that dominate their markets to achieve an overwhelming competitive advantage.

Finding potential acquisitions that minimize your competitors' ability to react to your strategic initiative means acquiring a scarce resource. Look for the only performance competitor in your market with a singular product offering. Look for the sole supplier of materials unique to your product or service. Look for the only distributor of your product in a given geographic area. Beware, your competitors may feel you have limited their ability to compete and initiate antitrust activity. These acquisition candidates can be found as described above but should be pursued only after you have evaluated the antitrust consequences of the acquisition.

Finding acquisitions that allow you to preserve your financial resources to pursue other strategic opportunities often involves acquiring competitors to maintain a minimum market share in order to remain a profitable business. Acquisitions of this type are often pursued in mature markets and are part of normal market consolidation. The alternative is to find a buyer for the business, usually a competitor that needs to acquire additional market share for profitability. Competitors are easily identified; finding the best fit is critical to the success of this type of acquisition.

An acquisition may be appropriate when the acquired company can help you change from a HOLD to a BUILD or from a HARVEST to a HOLD type of strategy. Divestiture may be appropriate when you can profit from a RETREAT type of strategy. Remember that the type of strategy you employ is a function of Market Position (Competitive Advantages and Disadvantages). Acquisitions can be used to MODIFY your market position. The type of strategy selected is also a function of Market Maturity. Acquisitions can help you REACT to Market Maturity. The success of a strategic initiative depends on how well you execute it, and an acquisition can be a decisive factor in successful execution of a strategic initiative. In all strategic initiatives the candidates for acquisition (or buyers) are close to your existing business. They are typically competitors, suppliers, distributors, customers, or suppliers of market alternatives. Occasionally you may be looking for a unique technology or related market opportunity, and professional acquisition specialists can assist you in locating suitable opportunities.

You now have a Strategic Plan and have identified suitable acquisition candidates that will help you execute that plan. But what are the People Issues that must be addressed at this step in the acquisition process?

WHAT ARE THE PEOPLE ISSUES
IN THE SEARCH STEP?

Who will make up your acquisition team? How much should you pay acquisition specialists and consultants? Who will lead the acquisition team? What skills are required on the acquisition team? Do I have enough management time available to dedicate to the acquisition process? What is the cost of deal specialists and operating support personnel? What kinds of skills must the acquired company management have to meet my requirements? These are the People Issues that must be addressed in the Search step of the Acquisition Process.

Who will make up the acquisition team? For strategic acquisitions to be successful, the team leader must be the senior business manager responsible for directing the strategic initiative. This should be the business manager, business owner, president, CEO, division manager, group executive, or project manager. The team leader is the operating "Champion" with a complete understanding of the business strategy and authority to execute the acquisition or curtail the activity. Most importantly, the team leader must have a clear understanding of the acquisition process in order to direct deal specialists in the transaction.

The complete acquisition team should include the following people:

1. A Team Leader "Champion" with a complete understanding of the business's strategic objectives and the acquisition process.

2. An Accountant who can translate accounting information from two different sources and methods into the same format, develop pro forma accounting information, and reveal accounting inconsistencies.

3. An Operations Manager who can understand fundamental requirements for successful competition in the market battlefield.

4. A Financial Analyst who can determine what financial returns are to be gained from the transaction and what additional critical financial objectives must be achieved.

5. A deal structure specialist (Investment Banker/Broker) who can develop the appropriate financial structure for the transaction.

6. A Certified Public Accountant (CPA) who can assure compliance with accounting rules and regulations.

7. A Tax Specialist who can assess tax consequences of the transaction.

8. An Environmental Specialist who can assess the environmental liability.

9. A Legal Specialist (lawyer) who can draft agreements and assure compliance with local, state, and federal laws.

10. A Human Resources Specialist who can evaluate compensation plans, benefits, and personnel development needs.

11. A Commercial Banker if additional bank debt is required.

Many of these skills may be found in a single individual, but all capabilities must be included in the acquisition team.

How much management time must be available to support acquisition activity? The senior operating management working on an acquisition must have 25% to 50% of their time available to complete the transaction and integrate the acquired company. Thus the acquiring management team must have their base business under control in order to free up the required time. When selling a business, the business managers must have adequate support to free up a similar amount of their time to support the divestiture activity. All senior management in a business that is being sold should be given a financial incentive to support a successful transaction and work the required extra hours. Too often transactions are left to the deal specialists because the operating managers are not available to make the business decisions. This will lead to acquisitions that don't accomplish the strategic objective or result in post-acquisition management surprises.

What is the cost of management diverted to acquisition activity and deal specialists called in to support the transaction? Management costs associated with doing an acquisition, along with all other transaction costs, are usually not a tax-deductible expense. The total time charged by management to the transaction should be costed with this tax impact in mind, along with an allowance for their travel and related costs at the site of the acquisition. Transaction specialists are usually compensated as follows:

1. For an investment banker or business broker, services are often based on a retainer charge applied against a success fee determined as follows: On smaller transactions, under $20 million in total financial consideration (price paid), the fee is typically established by the Lehman Formula: 5% of the first million, 4% of the second million, 3% of the third million, 2% of the fourth million and 1% of the remaining consideration. On larger transactions, over $20 million in total consideration, the fee is negotiated from ½% to 1½% of the price paid. Make certain that you have a fee agreement in writing with your investment banker or broker prior to engaging their services.

2. Accountants, lawyers, and other transaction specialists from outside your business are usually engaged on an hourly basis (except in very large

transactions). Have each of these specialists describe in writing what services they will perform and what they estimate their costs will be for those services. Then you have a cost basis for directing their activity. They must inform you during the acquisition process if they will exceed their estimated costs.

Total people costs for an acquisition can run from $100,000 to several million dollars and may not be tax deductible. These costs should be carefully managed against an acquisition process to minimize excess costs.

What kinds of skills must the acquired company personnel have to meet your business's requirements? Are college degrees required of senior management and in what specialties? Are specific technical skills required and in what areas of specialization? What trade or professional affiliations are required? In small companies you may find home-grown accountants, engineers, or management that cannot adapt to your business culture. You may find specific technical skills are required to meet the strategic business objectives. How do you retain these people? You may find trade and professional affiliations are necessary to maintain labor peace in the combined businesses after the acquisition. You should address labor requirements before initiating an acquisition. In today's business you are usually acquiring a team of people, not a factory, machine, or materials. You must carefully evaluate what minimum people requirements you place on an acquisition candidate prior to investing in a transaction.

WHAT ARE THE OPERATING FINANCIAL ISSUES IN THE SEARCH STEP?

The Operating Financial issues are those issues arising out of the day-to-day operations of the businesses. They have to do with financial controls, financial information, financial analysis, and presentation. If an acquisition candidate does not have adequate financial controls, you must invest to install those controls to have a reliable source of financial information after the acquisition. If you're expecting the acquisition to be self-sufficient, you must know what cash it can generate and what growth rate it will support. If you are analyzing financial information about acquisition candidates that is not in a form consistent with your current reporting system, you may make an erroneous management decision. You must also establish financial performance criteria that can be used to screen acquisition candidates. These are the Operating Financial Issues to be addressed in the Search Step of the Acquisition Process.

What cash flow expectations do you have for the transaction? What cash will be taken from existing operations to support the acquisition? Will this impose a cash problem on existing operations? If the acquisition is to be cash self-sufficient, what level of growth will the cash flow support? What are the cash flows required from a divestiture to compensate for lost operating cash flows generated prior to sale? You should set clear cash flow expectations for your acquisition or divestiture that will be the basis for structuring a transaction.

What are the minimum requirements for financial information from the seller at the Screen Step, the Critical Evaluation Step, and the Integration Step? Typical requirements are:

Screen Step: 1. Audited Financial Statements for the last two or three years.
2. One year of projected financial information.
Critical Evaluation Step:
1. Three to five years of audited financial information.
2. Access to all financial and accounting records.
Integration Step:
1. A cost accounting system. What type?
2. A computerized financial data collection system.

Don't wait until you have initiated an acquisition to find out that the quality of the financial information makes it impossible to analyze the business.

What operating performance criteria will be used to screen acquisition candidates? What return on operating capital is necessary to self-finance the growth of an acquisition? What operating financial ratios are considered critical to your selection process:

i. Inventory Turnover?
ii. Receivables Days Sales Outstanding?
iii. Profit on Sales?
iv. G&A, Marketing, R&D, to sales ratios?

Establish your operating performance criteria for an acquisition as a tool to screen candidates, knowing that substantial improvements are possible after the acquisition is completed.

Be prepared to restate financial information. If you are acquiring a company, you will need the information in a format consistent with your operating experience. This will let you analyze information and make the appropriate comparisons. For a divestiture, you want to restate financial information as follows:

    a. Restate the Profit and Loss Statement to remove any non-operating costs, such as corporate charges, interest expense, or accounting changes.

    b. Restate the Balance Sheet to reflect current value of assets and liabilities.

    c. Revise financial forecasts to reflect performance as a stand-alone entity or as part of the acquiring business.

    d. Prepare necessary supporting documents for acquirers' auditors to support financial statements and forecasts.

Keep in mind that most sellers are restating their financial information. Don't be misled. As an acquirer, you must restate these seller financials to your accounting standards.

SEARCH STEP SUMMARY

If you are an acquirer, at the end of the Search Step, you should have:

1. A Strategic Plan that establishes the strategic acquisition criteria.
2. An acquisition team able to devote adequate time to the acquisition process, focused on the strategic objective and strategic acquisition process, and knowledgeable about the confidentiality rules.
3. An established minimum skill criteria for the acquired management or available manpower to staff the acquisition.
4. An established minimum financial performance criteria.
5. A clear knowledge of available financial resources to be used for the acquisition.
6. A list of prospective sellers.

If you are selling a business, at the end of the Search Step you should have:

1. A strategic plan that leads to a RETREAT strategy or divestiture opportunity and points toward the most likely strategic buyers. -

2. A restated set of financial information to reflect the acquisition opportunity from a buyer's perspective.

3. A divestiture management team (same skills as an acquisition team) that will work with a buyer through a transition program and represent your business interests. Each member of this team must have a clear understanding of the confidentiality of the transaction.

4. A list of prospective buyers.

These are the Business Management Issues addressed during the Search Step in the Strategic Acquisition Process. The Deal Issues to be addressed next are associated with initiating a transaction.

The Search Step in the Strategic Acquisition Process
Deal Issues

Chapter 6 addresses the Deal Issues that you must work through in the Search Step. Deal Issues are those activities associated with initiating a transaction, structuring financing, reaching legal agreements, and complying with appropriate laws and regulations.

The following Acquisition Process Diagram shows the first Deal Issues following the Business Management Issues in the Search Step of the Acquisition Process.

Strategic Acquisition Process

		Search	Screen	Critical Evaluation	Integration
Business Management Issues	Strategic Issues				
	People Issues				
	Operating Financial Issues				

	Initial Contact	Offer Letter	Definitive Agreement
Deal Issues			

You have identified businesses that may be suitable acquisition candidates. How do you approach the owners? How do you set up a meeting? If you are successful in getting to a meeting, how do you approach the subject of acquisition value? These Deal Issues are addressed in this chapter, starting with establishing your understanding of valuation and ending with an approach you can use to meet with the prospective sellers.

PERSPECTIVES ON VALUE

Why should you care about perspectives on value (the quantitative methods and qualitative considerations used by sellers to set their acquisition prices)? You know the price that you can afford to pay based on your definition of acceptable financial returns. This price is predicated on meeting strategic business objectives and generating acceptable financial returns. If the seller wants a higher price, you can't do the deal. As Ross Perot says, "It's simple."

It's not that simple. Although you have arrived at your price using one or more theoretically sound valuation models, the final determination of price and the feasibility of a deal will hinge on the different, and often conflicting, value perspectives of buyers and sellers. It is not unusual for buyers and sellers to set widely varying initial valuations for the target company. There is an inherent conflict at the outset: the seller wants to maximize proceeds while the buyer wants to minimize cost.

For example, the CEO of Rapid Growth, Inc. decides that the strategic acquisition of Breakthrough Technology, Inc. will provide his company with a critical technology and a purchase price of $10 million will generate an acceptable rate of return. However, the founder of Breakthrough Technology is asking $15 million. Now what? Do you walk away or find room for discussion? First, step back and examine the seller's perspectives on value—how was the $15 million price tag determined. Perhaps the figure was produced by an investment banker's computer model and never tested by a firm offer. Or the seller's model may contain a more optimistic forecast of profits than you believe is realistic.

As you will see, the first requirement is to avoid becoming fixated on a specific dollar figure early in the process. Don't be too quick to take a seller's asking price at face value. By understanding the seller's perspectives on value, the strategic buyer may be able to bridge what, on the surface at least, is an insurmountable price gap. Since valuation is part art and part science, there is no single price that is absolute and no flawless valuation model. There should be room for negotiation.

You will encounter four principal types of sellers: retiring business owner, public company chief executive, corporate divestiture specialist, and financial owner of a private business. Before we describe these sellers and their varying perspectives on value, it is necessary to discuss definitions of value.

Definitions of Value

You can classify value in many different ways: market value, control value, fair value, asset value, intrinsic value, book value, investment value, and liquidation value. The relevant definition depends on the purpose of the valuation: acquire a company, settle an estate dispute with the IRS, decide when to sell a publicly traded common stock, set a price for an initial public offering (IPO), establish an Employee Stock Ownership Program (ESOP), or formulate a Chapter 11 reorganization plan. Those valuation definitions most relevant to a strategic buyer are control value, liquidation value, and intrinsic value.

Control value is the price at which a buyer and a seller are willing to exchange control of a business. In acquiring a publicly traded company, control value comes down to the size of the premium over the pre-merger stock price that will be required to induce shareholders to relinquish control. In the 1980s, control premiums for buyouts of publicly held companies typically ranged between 35 and 50%.

Liquidation value equals gross proceeds from the sale of a company's tangible and intangible assets, less payment of liabilities and selling expenses. Liquidation value provides a measure of maximum downside risk in the event the acquisition proves to be a mistake. It is the maximum downside risk because the business ceases to exist. Even when an acquisition does not generate the expected strategic benefits, reselling it as a going concern should generate more in proceeds than liquidating the business.

By understanding liquidation value and the conditions under which liquidation might become necessary, the strategic buyer will better anticipate potential problems. For example, does future growth of the target company depend on market acceptance of a new product that is the primary reason for acquisition interest? What is the value of the company if the product fails to produce forecasted revenues? Appendix F describes the calculation of liquidation value.

Intrinsic value is the theoretical price of a publicly traded security that offers an investor the appropriate financial return for assumed risk. A basic tenet of security analysis is that the market value of a publicly traded security fluctuates around intrinsic value. When market value is higher than intrinsic value, a publicly traded security is overvalued; if market value is below intrinsic value, the security is undervalued.

Prices of publicly traded securities are key variables in many valuation models and have a material influence on perspectives on value. Security analysts use four principal models to estimate the intrinsic value of a publicly traded security: (1) capitalization of earnings, (2) dividend discount models, (3) present value of cash flow, and (4) comparable firms.

The **capitalization of earnings model** requires a measure of earnings (usually net income after taxes) and an appropriate capitalization rate (interest rate). The reciprocal of the capitalization rate is the well-known price-earnings ratio (P-E) or multiple. For example, if the capitalization rate is 10%, the P-E or multiple is ten (1/.10). An investor who says a particular stock should sell at 20 times earnings is implicitly capitalizing earnings. Price-earnings ratios reflect investors' consensus forecast of earnings growth rates and volatility of earnings (risk). A company expected to grow at 25% per annum will sell at a higher price-earnings ratio than one expected to grow at 10% per annum.

The **dividend discount model** postulates that the intrinsic value of a publicly traded stock is equal to the present value of a stream of future dividends. This model requires an estimate of future dividends and selection of an appropriate discount rate (investors' required return for investing in a stock with a specific risk). For example, if a mature company is expected to pay a dividend of $1.00 per share in perpetuity and investors require a 10% return (discount rate) from investments of this risk class, then the intrinsic value is $10 per share ($1.00/.10). An investor will buy this stock when the market value is $10 or less per share. For companies expected to achieve dividend growth, present value (PV) is calculated by the following formula: $PV = D/r - g$ where D is the dividend in period one, r is the discount rate and g is the growth in dividends.

The **present value of cash flow model** will be familiar to business managers. It is similar to the technique used for capital equipment budgeting decisions. You forecast cash flow for a specific period, typically five to ten years, and estimate a residual asset value at the end of the forecast period. Cash flow and residual are discounted by the company's weighted average cost of capital (the rate of return that investors demand to supply capital to the company).

The **comparable firms method** uses actual prices for publicly traded securities. The target company is compared to similar companies in the served industry. Market value of equity and debt securities (market capitalization) for a comparable company is divided by selected financial variables, such as earnings before interest and taxes (EBIT), book value, and revenues. These valuation ratios are applied to the target company to obtain a comparable firms value. The validity and usefulness of this model depend on availability of similar publicly traded securities.

Each industry has a characteristic financial profile that becomes part of accepted valuation rule of thumb and influences sellers' perspectives on value. Acquisitions in the cable TV industry, for example, are based on prices per subscriber. Two companies with the same financial profiles but operating in different industries may sell at different valuations. For example, a retailer growing at 10% per annum may sell at a different valuation than a steel manufacturer growing at the same rate due to the greater cyclicity of steel industry earnings.

Individual firms within the same industry will not sell at uniform valuation ratios due to different operating and profitability characteristics. For example, there is usually a direct correlation between a company's profitability and its market share. The market leader, which can exercise greater control over product pricing, is likely to command a premium acquisition price. Similarly, a Performance competitor with a patented product will command a premium over a Price competitor with a me-too product.

The four intrinsic value models—capitalization of earnings, dividend discount, present value of cash flow, and comparable firms—underpin commonly used acquisition models. The business manager can expect that sellers' perspectives on value will be tied to these definitions.

Retiring Private Business Owner—Valuation Perspectives

The retiring owner of a private company typically founded or acquired a business that now enjoys a steady stream of income. The business may provide executive perks such as cars, country clubs, and frequent travel; family members are often on the payroll. The real estate used for the business will often be owned by another controlled entity. To minimize taxes, the corporation writes off expenses aggressively.

The retiring owner's perspectives on value include:

Adequate future income

Post-acquisition role

Personal tax planning—disposition of estate, timing of income, capital gains versus current income

Holding period influenced by age

Ability of buyer to finance the transaction

Other options for cashing out

A retiring owner may arrive at a selling price by first estimating the amount of retirement income needed. For example, the seller who needs $250,000 per annum of retirement income and plans to invest the proceeds from the sale of the business in tax-free municipal bonds yielding 5%, may ask $5 million for the business. If the seller can count on $250,000 per annum in income, he may not demand $5 million in cash at closing. There are innumerable income variations in practice, for example, the seller continues to own real estate and leases it to the buyer.

You can expect that tax planning will figure prominently in this seller's calculations. Thus, the gross selling price is not as important as net proceeds after taxes. Knowledge of the seller's tax situation can be used by the buyer's advisers to fashion a favorable structure that may not have been thought of by the seller.

Owners of private businesses often take back a note to finance part of the purchase price. In this instance, the buyer's financial condition will be carefully scrutinized. If there are competing bids, the buyer who presents the strongest ability to repay the obligation will be favored. It is not simply price. Assets of the firm can serve as collateral for financing the transaction. Assets that are not strategically important can be sold to finance part of the purchase price. A buyer wants to know the fair market value of assets, not historical cost figures on the balance sheet. Discrepancies between historical cost and fair market value will have a bearing on the tax consequences of purchase of asset transactions. Asset values are also important in estimating liquidation value.

The retiring owner's perspectives on value will be influenced by the portion of the purchase price in cash and the payout period for the non-cash portion. The age of the seller will be important in deciding on an acceptable payout period. An 82-year-old seller once told the authors he didn't buy any green bananas, which gave us insight into his acceptable payout period. And age will influence the seller's willingness to play a role in the management of the company after the deal closes. It is more than just a question of the selling price if the owner wants to walk away after the closing, while the buyer prefers that the owner stay on for several years to reduce the risks. The seller may be offered financial incentives during the transition period that are part of the purchase price.

The retiring business owner's perspectives on value will be influenced by his options to an outright merger. Can he obtain a higher price or better tax benefits by entering a strategic alliance, making a public offering, or selling the shares to employees in a transaction? These options are discussed in more detail in the Financial Owners' perspectives on value section below.

Armed with knowledge of the retiring owner's probable perspectives on value, the strategic acquirer will be prepared to discuss price in a broader context than simply putting a dollar figure on the table. Meetings with the seller will clarify the relative importance of these influences and help shape the final price. As with most complex business decisions, the "devil is in the details."

Public Company Executive—Perspectives on Value

Companies with publicly held common stock outstanding cover an extremely wide spectrum in terms of equity market capitalization (total common shares outstanding multiplied by the market price per share) and percentage of total shares outstanding held by insiders. Excluding inactively traded small companies held mainly by insiders, which are closer to private companies than public companies, executives of publicly held companies will share certain common perspectives on value shaped by the following considerations:

- Intrinsic value of the target company's common stock compared with current market price
- Current market valuations of competitors' stocks
- Prices paid for acquisitions of other companies in the same industry
- Post-acquisition titles and compensation of senior executives
- Valuation opinions of investment bankers and other experts
- Opinions of major shareholders
- Tax consequences to selling shareholders
- Value of buyer's securities in a share exchange

The strategic buyer of a publicly held company has to be prepared for material public disclosure due to securities regulations. A competitive bidding process is likely. To avoid potential legal liability, the seller's board of directors will typically consider more than a single bid for the company and hire an investment banker or valuation expert to render an opinion that the proposed terms are fair to selling shareholders ("fairness opinion").

While an auction process will help assure that shareholders of the target company receive the best available price, it presents problems for the strategic buyer when the seller attempts to trade one bidder off against another. In some situations, a strategic buyer can gain an advantage by being the first party to enter merger discussions with the target company, completing exhaustive due diligence, and making a preemptive bid. In other cases, when the board decides to sell the company and hires an investment banker to conduct an auction, this is not possible.

The challenge for the strategic buyer is to discover how executives of the public company are ranking the above perspectives on value. For example, a target company that is 50% or more owned by management wanting to continue to run the business will weigh the value of future compensation and the compatibility of the buyer's corporate culture against the amount to be received at closing, whereas another owner who wants to move on will have a different perspective. Minority shareholders may have yet another perspective.

Corporate Divestiture Specialist—Perspectives on Value

This seller may be divesting a business unit of either a public or private company. Common perspectives on value include the following:

No book loss on sale of assets

Operating results of the unit

Use of proceeds

Elimination of contingent liabilities

Options to selling the company

Impact of divestiture on seller's stock (public company)

For a public company, not incurring a writeoff of book value is often as important as expected proceeds from a divestiture. This seller may offer favorable terms that effectively dilute a price that is equal to book value when book value is more than you want to offer. For example, the seller may take back notes on favorable terms or reduce the amount of the note in case of a future writedown of obsolete inventory.

The person undertaking a divestiture will consider expected financial returns from use of proceeds compared with current operating profits of the business. Although your best bid for the business may not meet the seller's initial asking price, he will be interested if he expects to earn a higher return on proceeds than if the business remains unsold. Also, selling a company is a time-consuming process and there is no guarantee that a higher bid will be received.

For a business that is suffering heavy losses, eliminating the operating loss and removing contingent liabilities are major incentives. A public company may expect an immediate boost in the price of its stock from the sale of a money-losing division. Options to an outright sale include liquidation of the business, spinoff to shareholders, and sale of the company in a public offering. You should compare your price with the seller's proceeds from these options.

Financial Owners of Private Businesses— Perspectives on Value

Financial owners will be active sellers over the next few years due to the large number of leveraged buyouts in the 1980s. Buyout funds are usually structured as limited partnerships with a ten year life. When proceeds are distributed to the partners they prefer to receive cash rather than hard to sell securities in closely held companies.

Financial sellers' perspectives on value include the following:

Consideration to be received—cash or marketable securities

Feasibility of a public offering

Ending date of a limited partnership buyout fund

Feasibility of a management buyout

Feasibility of a company buyback of shares

There are four exit strategies available to financial owners of private companies who want to cash out: a merger, sale of the stock back to the company, sale to management, or an IPO. Terms and conditions of these exit strategies are usually specified in the acquisition documents. For example, management may have the right of first refusal if an acquisition bid is received.

The feasibility of an IPO depends on conditions in the stock market and whether the company is suitable for public ownership. There are periods like 1990 when the new issue market is dormant and only a few companies can find buyers at an acceptable price. At other times like 1993, there is great enthusiasm for IPOs, and investors will pay a higher price for the company stock than a strategic buyer will pay.

During hot new issue markets, equity capital can be raised on advantageous terms. Many companies that went private in leveraged buyouts have re-emerged as public companies in recent years, using proceeds from equity offerings to retire high-cost debt. Since underwriters place a limit on the number of shares that insiders can sell on the IPO, financial owners are only able to sell out later. Thus, one way for a strategic acquirer to negate the IPO option is to make a cash offer that gives the financial owner immediate liquidity and eliminates the risk of a post-IPO decline in the price of the stock.

Another way for the strategic acquirer to pre-empt an IPO by the financial owner is to enter a strategic alliance with the target company as a preliminary step to full acquisition. Financial owners may want to sell 100% of their equity in a company several years down the road, yet the company has a current need for equity capital. The strategic acquirer takes a partial equity interest with an option to purchase the rest of the company in the future. A strategic alliance can potentially strengthen your competitive position by providing access to resources that might be more expensive to develop internally.

A strategic alliance can help overcome a contentious issue in setting an acquisition price: different perspectives on future results. Despite the most thorough due diligence, a seller always knows more about the company than the buyer does. By taking a partial interest, a buyer can see how events unfold and learn more about the company. Purchase of the remaining interest will be based on actual future results. The parties agree in advance on the valuation model(s) to be used.

ACQUISITION VALUATION MODELS
FOR THE BUSINESS MANAGER

The business manager is best able to gauge the ultimate value of the target company—whether the acquisition will create a sustainable competitive advantage. This is the manager's unique perspective on value. The strategic buyer's perspectives on value also will be shaped by: (1) financial forecasts for the target company, (2) acceptable returns on investment, and (3) cost of the acquisition compared to internal development. Finally, the business manager will develop other perspectives unique to his strategic plan, such as management continuity, financing options, earnings per share growth, market perception and P-E impact, and goodwill.

We recommend that the strategic buyer adapt the intrinsic value models to acquisition pricing in two principal ways: (1) present value of cash flow, and (2) comparable acquisitions. Appendix F provides detailed instructions for use of the cash flow and comparable acquisitions models.

Although business managers may not perform the actual valuation calculations, they should have a working knowledge of the methodology. The business manager must approve the final price and be responsible for financial returns from the acquired company. Since these valuation techniques are also used by sellers, the business manager will gain a better understanding of their perspectives on value.

The *present value cash flow model* requires a forecast of the target company's cash flow for the next five years and a terminal value at the end of the forecast period. The target company financial data required for this model is developed during the Search, Screen, and Critical Evaluation Steps. Terminal value is calculated using the capitalization of cash flows and liquidation value models. The forecasted cash flows and terminal value are discounted by the acquirer's weighted cost of capital or a higher hurdle rate that adjusts for risk characteristics of the target company.

The main advantage of the discounted cash flow model is that it is linked to the projected performance of the acquired company. The financial forecast developed during the acquisition steps is the key determinant of acquisition value. Of course, the real value will only become known when we see how closely actual results track our financial forecast. And that is the weakness of the model—the uncertainty of cash flow forecasts and the possibility that actual results will fall wide of the mark. Another weakness is the sensitivity of the calculated acquisition value to differences in estimated terminal value.

The *comparable acquisitions model* requires two sets of data: (1) a control premium added to the comparable firms' intrinsic value, and (2) actual prices paid for mergers and acquisitions of similar companies in the target company's served markets. Market capitalization (total market value of a company's debt and equity securities) of comparable acquired companies is divided by the company's earnings before interest and taxes (EBIT), total revenues, and earnings before interest, taxes, and depreciation. Financial histories and balance sheets of the comparable companies are examined to explain differences in these valuation ratios.

The comparable acquisitions method uses total market capitalization in calculating financial ratios, because a buyer wants to know the total cost of acquiring a business. Though control may be obtained by acquiring the interests of the equity holders, the assumption of debt is also a real cost. Using total company value helps eliminate distortions in valuation ratios for comparable companies due to variations in debt-to-equity ratios.

The main advantage of the comparable firms methodology is that it is based on actual transactions and securities prices—not on uncertain forecasts of cash flow and terminal values. This method serves as a useful cross-check against the price calculated by the discounted cash flow model. For example, if the discounted cash flow model says we should pay $10 million for a target company at a time when comparable companies are selling for $15 million, we may want to re-examine our forecasts. In any event, because of widespread use of the comparable model, we must be prepared for the seller's perspective on value to be influenced by comparable transactions. The strategic buyer should decide whether the comparable firms are truly representative of the target company.

Time sensitivity is the main weakness of the comparable acquisitions method. Market conditions at the time an acquisition is valued may be markedly different from those when the comparable acquisitions were consummated. An analysis of stock prices for the period preceding the valuation of the target will reveal if there were unusual changes that require an adjustment in the comparable data. Another disadvantage of the comparable method is that it does not provide a direct calculation of internal rate of return.

PROFILED COMPANIES—PERSPECTIVES ON VALUE

The table on the next page shows the perspectives on value of the profiled companies. Transaction specialists (Investment Bankers, Brokers, Accountants and Financial Analysts) can help you develop valuation models. But as you can see, valuation is not an absolute science but rather a matter of perspective. You must enter the first meeting with a seller with an open

Company	Perspectives on Value
Bausch & Lomb	Concentration in health-care industry. Proprietary advantage of products.
EG&G	Earnings Per Share Impact. Sustainable 15% per annum earnings growth. Niche market leader. Technical excellence.
Loral	Broaden defense electronics capability. Earnings Per Share Impact. Ability to finance while maintaining targeted debt/equity ratio.
Perkin-Elmer	Post-divestiture valuation of core business. Investment banker's evaluation models. Divestiture proceeds versus book value.
Sysco	No dilution earnings per share. Continuity of target company management. Post acquisition costs.
Thermo Electron	Technology value. Return on net investment after three years. Who will run the acquired company? Opportunity for public offering of minority interest.

mind and attempt to determine the seller's perspective on value. What would satisfy their financial and personal objectives? But first you must meet prospective sellers.

INITIAL CONTACT

The objective of the initial contact is to obtain a face-to-face confidential meeting between buyer and seller.

How do you make initial contact with the target company?

a. Use a Dun & Bradstreet report, Ward's Directory, or other publicly available information to determine who owns the target business or has the most significant financial control position. If this information is not available, the CEO or president of the acquiring company should contact the senior operating officer or chairman of the target. Do not contact an employee or a director or you risk alienating the decision maker.

b. The most common approach is through a "waltz letter." This one-page letter (example in Appendix C) should introduce your company, explain that you have no reason to believe the target would consider buying or selling a business, but suggest that a confidential face-to-face meeting would be of interest to you should the target company ever want to contemplate a transaction in the future. Send the letter via overnight mail, mark it

PERSONAL AND CONFIDENTIAL, and follow up with a
telephone call to arrange for a confidential meeting.

Things to remember in making the initial contact with a buyer or seller:

1. Make contact at the highest level in the decision-making chain,
   that is, Chairman to Chairman, CEO to CEO.
2. Explain why you have a sincere strategic interest in a transaction.
3. Don't push too hard at the first contact; emphasize your desire
   for a confidential exploratory meeting.
4. Be prepared to sign a confidentiality agreement. It's best to prepare one to send along with your introductory letter or carry it to
   the first meeting.
5. Limit your first meeting to one or two members of your acquisition team.
6. If asked, be prepared to demonstrate a financial ability to acquire
   the target company. In a divestiture, be prepared to discuss valuation in the first meeting. However, do not fix the purchase price
   or terms and conditions until after the next step in the acquisition
   process, the Screen step.
7. Be prepared to describe what information you will need to make
   a decision, how you will get (or provide) that information and
   the steps in the acquisition process.
8. Keep your first contact (usually by telephone) focused on getting
   to a confidential face-to-face meeting to explore the possibilities
   of an acquisition.

Once you have made contact and scheduled the first meeting with the
prospective buyer or seller, you have completed the SEARCH Step in the
acquisition process. This Step can take one to four months. However, once
an acquisition or divestiture that will fulfill a strategic objective business
strategy is identified you may find the owners unwilling to talk about
acquisition or divestiture. Don't throw away the target business's information. Keep regular contact with the owners and show continuous interest. Many excellent strategic acquisitions and divestitures have occurred
after years of persistent courting. The end of the SEARCH step is the
beginning of the SCREEN step in the acquisition process.

Chapter Seven

The Screen Step in the Acquisition Process
Business Management Issues

Your business management objective in the Screen Step is to determine if the acquisition is feasible. Does the target acquisition meet the strategic objectives? Does the seller want to sell? Why? Do management and employees share common management values, ethics, and styles? Can confidentiality be maintained? Is the financial and accounting information available to permit you to evaluate the financial combination? If, during

Strategic Acquisition Process

	Search	Screen	Critical Evaluation	Integration
Strategic Issues				
People Issues				
Operating Financial Issues				

Business Management Issues

Initial Contact	Offer Letter	Definitive Agreement

Deal Issues			

the Screen Step, you decide the acquisition is feasible, you will signal your intention to negotiate a definitive agreement with a brief Letter of Intent (offer letter). If you decide the acquisition is not feasible, you will have spent a minimum amount of time and money in making your decision.

Why bother with a Screen Step? A successful Screen Step lets you explore a promising transaction while maintaining confidentiality and conserving both people and financial resources. Conducted at the highest levels in the buying and selling organizations with limited use of deal specialists and support personnel, the Screen Step usually involves several exploratory meetings to exchange a limited amount of information.

THE FIRST MEETING OF BUYER AND SELLER

The first meeting, arranged at the end of the Search Step, is the beginning of the Screen Step. This is a meeting of the decision makers on both the buyer and seller sides and lets each party assess the credibility of the other. Usually there is an exchange of public or nonproprietary information about each company. The real question in each party's mind at this meeting is: DO I TRUST AND RESPECT THESE PEOPLE? If trust and respect are not established at the first meeting, you will not be eager to proceed.

Typical negative responses to these first meetings are summarized by the following actual quotations:

1. "They don't even know their own business."
2. "They're just looking for a sucker to pay an outrageous price."
3. "They're bottom fishing for the lowest price."
4. "They would be laughed out of our boardroom."
5. "They don't care about me or my people; they only want a cheap quick deal."
6. "I wouldn't believe any information they gave me."
7. "They talk a big game, but I don't think they have the money to do a deal."
8. "I wouldn't spend another minute with those arrogant (expletives deleted)."

These are all SUBJECTIVE assessments of the individuals involved in the first meeting. They don't involve a financial appraisal; they represent an assessment of personal character and integrity.

What does this suggest you should or should not do at the first meeting?

1. Show respect for the other party and their company.

2. Show a willingness to share information about your way of doing business, including references.

3. Tell the other party why you are interested in an acquisition and what steps you envision for both companies to bring an acquisition to fruition as well as how much time it will take. (Use the acquisition process chart).

4. Share the history of your business and listen attentively to the other party's business and personal business history.

5. Discuss the importance of confidentiality and propose a simple agreement to facilitate an exchange of information. Agree what confidential information will be exchanged.

6. Talk about information that will need to be exchanged prior to negotiating a Letter of Intent (offer letter) at the end of the Screen Step.

7. Be realistic in your assessment of the effort involved to make a transaction occur. Don't promise what you can't deliver.

8. Involve only those people necessary to assess the character and willingness of the other party to do a deal. Don't bring along deal specialists with lists of questions.

A successful first meeting is terminated with an understanding that a confidentiality agreement and subsequent exchange of additional information will take place. Both parties must believe they are dealing realistically with the issues necessary to make an acceptable deal occur and that they are working with the appropriate decision maker.

If you decide not to proceed with a transaction after the first meeting, tell the other party immediately you have no interest in proceeding and terminate your discussions. Building false expectations on either the part of the buyer or seller will generate hard feelings that will make future business combinations impossible. Very often business situations change, making an unattractive acquisition today look perfect a few years later. Stay in contact with the prospect and be alert for positive changes, such as new products, new management or employees, or changing financial conditions that may make a future acquisition feasible.

FIRST ACQUISITION TEAM MEETING

Once you have a willing seller you should assemble your acquisition team during the Screen Step to describe the anticipated transaction and decide what specific information they will need to determine acquisition feasibility. First describe the acquisition candidate and what strategic objectives you hope to achieve by a business combination. Then hand out copies of the confidentiality agreement to all members of your team and explain the personal and legal commitments that have been made to maintain confidentiality. Establish a procedure with the seller by which all communication is coordinated through one individual. Establish with your team members a list of information needed to determine if the acquisition is feasible. This list usually includes, but is not limited to:

1. Recent financial statements (last two or three years)
2. Product literature
3. A summary of any open or pending litigation
4. A company ownership and debt structure summary
5. A management organization chart
6. A summary of employee benefits and perks
7. Market Battlefield data, such as competitors, etc.

Members of your team may at this point want to commence full scale due diligence investigations and may have prepared multi-page checklists. This will only consume time and money and frustrate the seller at this point. You must control the information request to focus on obtaining only that information necessary to determine *if an acquisition is feasible.* Extensive due diligence investigations will commence after you have signed a Letter of Intent (offer letter) at the end of the Screen Step.

CONFIDENTIAL COMMUNICATIONS

Too often negotiations are killed when there is a leak of confidential information. A salesman tells his distributor you are "taking over a competitor." An accountant calls the seller's accounting firm and requests information. A purchasing manager tells a supplier they will hold a purchase order until after the acquisition. These examples are actual situations where acquisition information has leaked and led to a termination of a transaction.

You must establish a fixed procedure for communicating information between buyer and seller. This may entail mailing all correspondence to a post office box or a home address. All correspondence should be marked "PERSONAL AND CONFIDENTIAL" and communicated through a single individual (communications coordinator) at both buyer and seller locations. No direct communication between acquisition team members should be permitted during the Screen Step without the approval of the communications coordinator.

SETTING THE SCREEN STEP SCHEDULE

Once the seller has received your list of requested information, telephone and establish a schedule for the balance of the Screen Step. This should include the following:

1. An estimate of when the seller can supply requested information and what information they are unable or unwilling to supply at this time.
2. An estimate of how long you will require to review the requested information and to formulate a tentative analysis of the business opportunity represented by the acquisition.
3. A schedule for a meeting to review your (the buyer) analysis of the business combination.
4. An estimate of how long it will take to draft an offer letter (Letter of Intent) based on the business analysis and information supplied to date.
5. A schedule for a meeting to review the offer letter and negotiate its contents.

Communicate this schedule to your acquisition team members and modify where required.

SECOND ACQUISITION TEAM MEETING

When you have received the information requested from the seller, distribute it to your acquisition team members and schedule a review meeting. At this meeting you should establish the following:

1. Is the information complete?
2. Is it adequate to develop a preliminary strategic plan and a financial plan for the combined companies?
3. What additional information is required?
4. Will an additional information gathering meeting be required?
5. How long will it take for each team member to conclude his/her preliminary analysis of the information and identify transaction risks?
6. How long will it take for the Team Leader (Champion) to develop the strategic plan and the resultant financial forecast of the future business combination and who will support that activity?
7. How long will it take the Accountants to translate the financial forecast into a consolidated Profit and Loss Statement, Balance Sheet, and Cash Flow Analysis on a Pretax/PreInterest basis?
8. Given the above, how long will it take the Financial Analyst to establish an offer price consistent with your company's financial return criteria?
9. How long will it take the Investment Bankers, Bankers, Financial Analyst, and Team Leader to develop deal financial structure alternatives consistent with your financial resources?
10. What Open Issues will be carried forward to be resolved during the Critical Evaluation Step?

Contact the seller and arrange transfer of additional information (if required), revise the Screen Step schedule (if required), and give the seller an overview of the transaction status.

SECOND MEETING WITH SELLER

The purpose of the second meeting with the seller is to review your perception of how the business will function after the transaction. Review the key assumptions in the strategic plan. Review your concept of post-acquisition staffing requirements and whether there will be a reduction of key personnel. Review your thoughts about competitor and customer reactions to the transactions. Review your concerns about transaction risks or Open Issues such as:

1. Antitrust issues that may arise out of the transaction.
2. Accounting issues that may arise out of the transaction.

3. Tax issues that may arise out of the transaction and how allocation of purchase price to specific assets can affect the taxable nature of the deal. If stock is acquired in a tax free (read as tax deferred) reorganization, transaction gains may be deferred until the shares of stock received as purchase consideration are sold.

4. Environmental issues that may arise out of the transaction. Many states require an environmental audit when a business is sold.

5. Legal, contractual issues that may arise out of the transaction. Some contracts with suppliers or customers may be difficult to transfer to a new company and may force the buyer to acquire the corporate entity to preserve their status.

6. Compensation, benefits, and employee perk issues that may arise out of the transaction.

The purpose in raising these issues is to get the seller to commit to work with you to resolve these issues and determine if there are any present barriers to a transaction. The seller should work on a transaction structure that appropriately allocates post-transaction risks.

With your deal specialist (Investment Banker, Broker, Lawyer or other expert) in attendance, talk to the seller about alternative deal structures and how they may affect the attractiveness of the transaction to both parties. Try to determine the seller's perspective on value and preferred deal structure without talking about specific purchase prices as you cannot establish transaction price separate from deal structure. Schedule a negotiating session with the seller where you will propose a transaction price and deal structure.

THIRD ACQUISITION TEAM MEETING

After disseminating the information obtained from your second meeting with the seller, schedule a third acquisition team meeting. The purpose of this meeting is to review team inputs for the offer letter. These inputs should include:

1. A commitment by the Champion that the strategic objectives of the acquisition can be met with the acquired company. This should include a first draft of the Market Battlefield Form and Strategic Battle Plan Form.

2. Open Issues that will affect deal structure or risk. Make a list of these Open Issues and determine if any are deal killers. Most of these issues should be resolved during the Critical Evaluation Step or negotiated in the final definitive agreement, not in the Letter of Intent.

3. Review revised forecasts and transaction structures and establish an offer price and deal structure.

The Business Management issues in the Screen Step (The Strategy Issues, People Issues, and Operating Financial Issues) have now been addressed along with some basic Deal Issues. A limited amount of information has been exchanged with a modest investment in time and money. You will have many unanswered questions (Open Issues) but most sellers will give you access to their employees, customers, and suppliers only if you negotiate an offer letter or Letter of Intent. You must, therefore, put your acquisition proposal in writing with only limited exposure to the seller's business. The Deal Issues portion of the Screen Step will show you how to develop an offer and negotiate the Letter of Intent.

Chapter Eight

The Screen Step in the Acquisition Process
Deal Issues

What type of transaction should you propose to the seller? How do you formulate a Letter of Intent? How do you handle Open Issues? What are the key factors in negotiating a Letter of Intent? These are the questions you must resolve during the Screen Step as deal or transaction issues.

Strategic Acquisition Process

		Search	Screen	Critical Evaluation	Integration
Business Management Issues	Strategic Issues				
	People Issues				
	Operating Financial Issues				

	Initial Contact	Offer Letter	Definitive Agreement

Deal Issues

WHAT TYPE OF TRANSACTION
SHOULD YOU PROPOSE TO THE SELLER?

Should you suggest an exchange of shares of stock in your business for shares of stock in the seller's business? Should you propose acquiring the seller's assets for cash? Should there be a contingent purchase agreement conditioned on the seller's meeting certain financial performance criteria after the transaction? As seen in Chapter 6, this is not just a matter of financial calculations, but a matter of perspective on value.

You should have determined the seller's perspective on value during your first meetings. You should have a good idea of the purchase price they require in order to consider sale of their business. But, what are their primary concerns in establishing their perspective on value: personal security, tax issues, asset value, earnings dilution, estate planning, values comparable to other transactions, or some other concern? What is their risk in selling their business versus a public stock offering, liquidation, employee stock purchase, or just harvesting the business? How does the seller's expectation compare to your ability and desire to proceed with a transaction? The proposed agreement must take into account not only the seller's asking price, but their personal business objective and risks as well. It must also take into account your (the buyer's) financial capacity and your chances of achieving your strategic business objective at less cost or with lower risk through a different acquisition, joint venture, or internal development.

To establish the price of a transaction, you use valuation models as established in Chapter 6 and Appendix F. You also have certain minimum operating financial criteria established in the Search Step (Chapter 5). These purchase price calculations do not take into account transaction risks, which are critical to structuring a transaction.

Figure 8–1, Deal Structure Risk Diagram, shows how transaction risk may vary as a function of deal structure and how it affects total purchase price (the sum of all financial consideration). THIS DIAGRAM IS AN EXAMPLE OF AN ACTUAL DIAGRAM USED IN A TRANSACTION. IT WILL CHANGE WITH EACH TRANSACTION AS A FUNCTION OF THE BUYER'S AND SELLER'S PERCEIVED RISK CHARACTERISTICS.

This diagram shows that the safest (least risky) action for a seller may be exchanging all equity interest (stock) in the business for a cash payment at closing. This gives the seller cash and most likely will relieve the seller of all past and future liability in the business. It shows that the safest

FIGURE 8–1
Deal Structure Risk Diagram

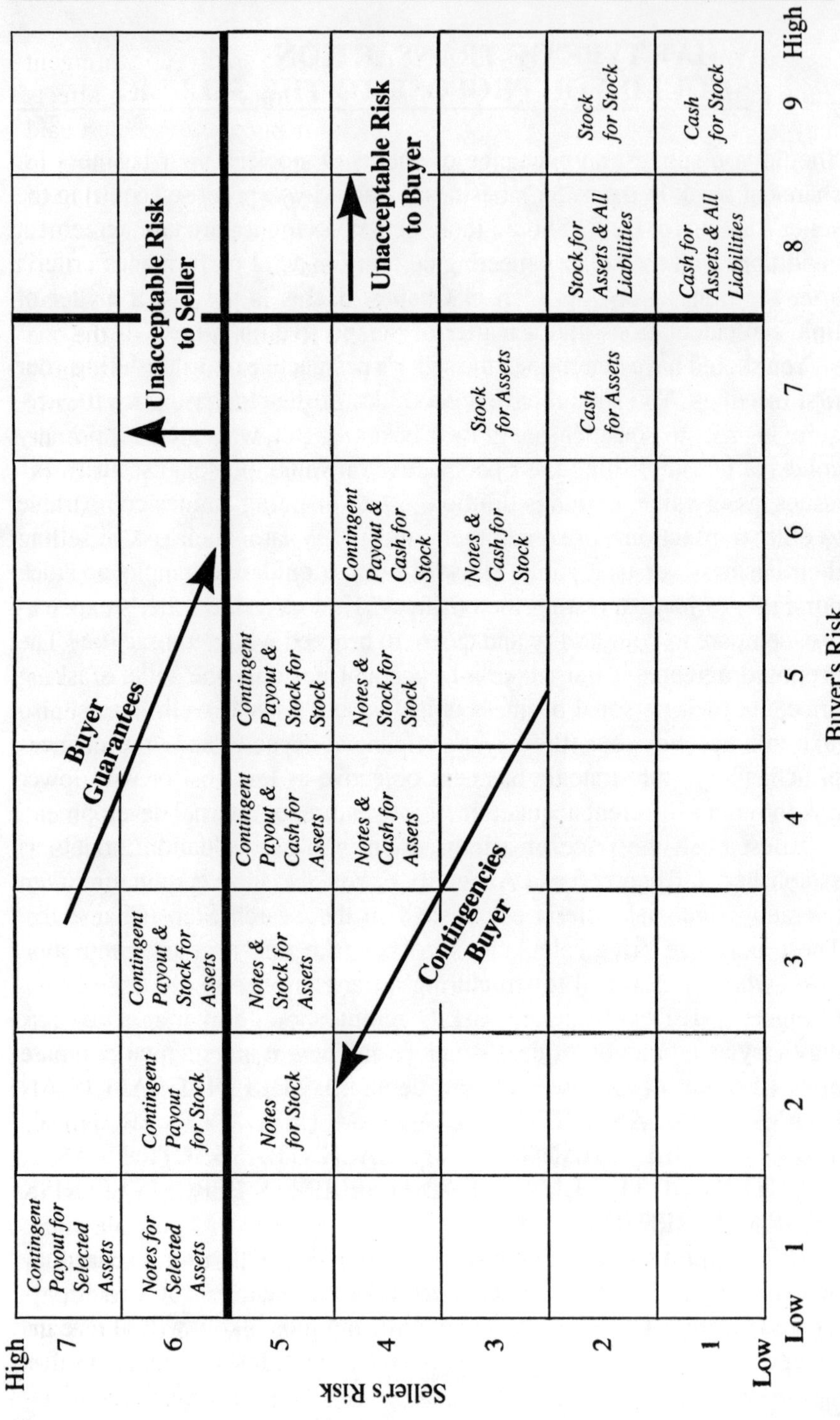

(least risky) deal for the buyer is to acquire specified assets for contingent future payments. This divergence in perceived transaction risk affects total purchase price consideration. A minimum purchase price is paid when the seller takes minimal transaction risk (usually corresponding to maximum buyer transaction risk). The maximum purchase price will have to be paid when the seller assumes maximum transaction risk (usually corresponding to minimum buyer transaction risk).

Your assessment of the seller's perspective on value will let you and your deal specialists construct a Deal Structure Risk Diagram like the one shown in Figure 8–1. With this diagram you can set your risk threshold and estimate that of the seller. The sample diagram in Figure 8–1 shows the buyer was unwilling to accept a transaction structure where he assumed all liability through either a purchase of equity (stock) or a stock for stock exchange or used cash or stock to purchase all assets and liabilities. The seller was unwilling to accept contingent payouts or notes for the purchase of selected assets or a contingent payout for stock. The seller also was unwilling to accept a contingent payout plus the buyer's stock for a purchase of assets. The seller would, however, accept notes (debt instruments) for stock if the notes were not too risky, a combination of notes and stock for assets, or a contingent payout and cash for assets or a contingent payout and stock for stock. Each of these latter deal structures appear of equal risk to the seller, but some will reduce the buyer's transaction risk if appropriately selected. As you can see from this Deal Structure Risk Diagram, understanding the seller's and your risk characteristics is essential to minimizing your deal structure risk.

Your deal structure risk is also a function of the guarantees you make to the seller and the contingencies you include in the transaction agreement. If you are offering the seller a note (or other debt instrument) that is subordinate to other financing, it may exceed the seller's risk threshold. If you are offering a note that is guaranteed by your business, secured with liquid assets and not subordinated, it is more likely to represent an acceptable risk to the seller. If your purchase offer is contingent on labor union approval, management contracts, and assuming no past liabilities, it will be less acceptable (more risky) to the seller. Your attorneys will encourage you to minimize your guarantees and put as many contingencies as possible in the deal structure, which will affect the seller's and your risk in the transaction. This will affect the price in most cases and may kill the deal if you don't understand the seller's perspective on value. What level of financial risk are you, the buyer, willing to take in the deal structure? The response to that question depends upon your confidence (or lack thereof) in the future of the strategic acquisition and the financing risk you are assuming. If you are a large business paying cash for an acquisition that represents less than 10% of your annual cash flow, you may be willing to assume considerable transaction risk. If you are financing an acquisition with a substantial amount of debt and will require cash flows and strategic success from the acquired business to service the debt, you are more risk averse in structuring a transaction. In that case, your confidence in future cash flows from the acquisition will determine your tolerance for transaction risk.

The type of transaction (deal structure) you propose to the seller is a function of:

1. Your calculated purchase price based on valuation model (per Chapter 6 and Appendix F).
2. Your calculated purchase price based on your ability to satisfy your investors and creditors and your operating financial objectives.
3. Your assessment of the seller's and your perspective on value and risk profile as shown in the Deal Structure Risk Diagram.
4. The confidence you have in your ability to forecast future financial performance of the strategic acquisition.
5. The level of financial risk you take in the transaction, that is, the more debt you assume or bring to the transaction, the greater your financial risk.

All of these factors enter into developing your Letter of Intent. That is why your acquisition team should include transaction specialists to help you create the most appropriate deal structure that also lets you achieve the business manager's Strategic Business Plan.

The Offer Letter (Letter of Intent)

The offer letter is intended to establish the basis for working toward a definitive purchase agreement. It is an agreement that both parties will *work diligently* toward a transaction and therefore it should not get too complicated (i.e., don't let the attorneys make it a definitive agreement). It should contain the following in a simple two or three page letter format:

1. A brief description of the deal structure proposed such as:
   a. XYZ company proposes to purchase all outstanding shares of stock in AAA Company.
   b. XYZ company proposes to purchase the following assets in AAA Company.

    c. XYZ company proposes the exchange of 1,234 shares of its common stock for each share of common stock in AAA company, providing the share price of XYZ shares is no greater than $7.50 per share and no less than $6.50 per share.

2. Closing of a final transaction subject to:
   a. Negotiating a satisfactory definitive agreement.
   b. Board of Directors and/or shareholder approval.
   c. Approval of requisite regulatory bodies, such as the SEC and Justice Department.
   d. Reaching agreement to transfer contracts, such as union contracts, supplier contracts, or customer contracts.
   e. Resolving significant Open Issues as identified by the acquisition team in preliminary evaluation of company information, such as environmental concerns, pending litigation, etc.
   f. An agreement on a target date to consummate the transaction with a definitive agreement and a closing date (when all legal papers are filed and approved and assets or stock are exchanged).
   g. Applicable statutory law, for example, State of New York or other state.
   h. Public announcement agreement, that is, parties will issue a joint public announcement in a form agreed to by both parties.
   i. Exclusivity agreement, that is, seller will not enter into negotiations with other parties during the negotiations with buyer.
   j. How transaction expenses are to be shared between buyer and seller.
   k. An agreement to provide necessary information to the buyer to evaluate the selling company.
   l. Signatures of both seller and buyer indicating agreement.

This letter is a legal agreement and should be drafted by your legal advisors. However, its purpose is to establish *only the agreement in principle* between the two parties, not to bind them to a definitive agreement. It does create an obligation to work diligently and openly toward a transaction exclusive of negotiations by the seller with third parties.

Negotiating the Letter of Intent

In preparation of the Letter of Intent you have established an offer price and a deal structure that make financial sense and let you accomplish your strategic objective with the proposed acquisition. You should also have a good estimate of the seller's expectations and know who will be negotiating for the seller. You are now going to sit down with the seller and his (her) representatives and negotiate a Letter of Intent.

Prioritize your Negotiating Objectives

First, you must be able to achieve your strategic objectives in the business combination. What are the key factors in achieving your strategic objectives? Often these factors will include capturing certain customers or transferring customer contracts. Sometimes they will encompass acquisition of proprietary processes or technologies. Occasionally acquisition of a key resource, such as a supplier of component parts, will be an important element. Negotiating a low price and favorable financial structure without accomplishing these strategic objectives would be senseless. Therefore, list your key factors in achieving your strategic objectives and keep them in the forefront of your thoughts as you enter negotiations.

Next you must prioritize the people issues important to implementing the strategic plan. Are you going to be able to retain the key people required to implement the business strategy? Will these key people be demotivated by the structure of the transaction? How will the post-transaction work environment be affected by the transaction? Remember, all companies have a formal and informal social and management system; if you upset the social and management equilibrium, you will have a different company. During the next phase of the transaction, every employee will hear rumors or know of the acquisition investigation. Their question, (what's in it for me?) must be answered by the way you structure the transaction. As you enter the negotiation, have a list of what you are offering to all of the affected people: the owners, the employees, and the seller's advisors.

Next, have a prioritized summary of your financial expectations from the transaction. For example:

1. Return on Invested Capital: 25%.
2. No dilution to earnings per share.
3. Transaction Loss, not to exceed $100,000.
4. Positive cash flow adequate to cover Debt service plus 50%.

Failing to achieve your financial goals from the transaction could indicate that the seller's price or deal structure is too costly or it could indicate a business strategy that yields inadequate future financial returns. As you enter into negotiations, have a clear understanding of your financial objectives and how your business strategy supports those financial objectives.

The Negotiating Meeting for the Letter of Intent

Now you are sitting across the table from the seller and his(her) representatives. Don't try to be clever. Think of this as a mutual educational process. Think of it as a process of meeting both parties' needs through an agreement or at least parting with a clear understanding of why one party's needs can't be met.

Clearly establish who the principal negotiator is for both the seller and the buyer. I usually will say "As I understand it, Joe will be representing the selling parties in this negotiation, so I will address my proposal to Joe." On one occasion I had negotiations with three nearly equal stockholders, which turned into a three-way shouting match among the sellers. If the sellers have not selected a principal negotiator, then ask them to make a selection prior to your meeting.

Address the seller's principal negotiator and explain your strategic objectives, your people objectives, and your financial objectives. Describe your proposed Letter of Intent and how you have crafted it to meet your business objectives and, hopefully, the seller's expectations. Make it clear that this is only a Letter of Intent and that there will be time for a detailed negotiation as part of the definitive agreement, but the large issues should be resolved with this letter. Make clear that some Open Issues need to be addressed during the CRITICAL EVALUATION Step and that you will need the seller's cooperation to address these issues. Take time to summarize the content of the Letter of Intent (as described earlier in this chapter) and suggest that the seller take time to read it. Offer to answer any questions the seller may have about content or structure.

Expect a concern or objection to certain aspects of the Letter of Intent. Listen attentively to the seller's concerns and list each one. Work to establish which issues are of primary importance to the seller. Restate your understanding of the issues to the seller and prioritize them as you perceive the seller prioritizes them. If necessary, ask for a private caucus with your advisors before you reply; this may require a telephone conference with specialists not present in the negotiating session.

Develop a modification to the Letter of Intent that will still let you achieve your primary strategic, people, and financial objectives and accommodate as many of the seller's concerns as possible. Mark up the agreement, (with legal counsel if possible) and re-enter negotiations.

Explain to the seller's principal negotiator your modified position and why you may not be able to accommodate all of their concerns. If these unresolved issues are sufficient to terminate the negotiations, then let them terminate with the caveat that you will continue to explore options that will address the seller's concerns. If these issues are to be resolved as part of negotiating a definitive agreement after the CRITICAL EVALU-ATION Step, you must assess the risk of never consummating the trans-action. If the unresolved issues are not material to the seller and they are willing to sign the Letter of Intent, clean typed copies should be prepared and signed by both parties, concluding the SCREEN Step in the Acquisi-tion Process and initiating the CRITICAL EVALUATION Step.

(NOTE: THERE ARE MANY STYLES AND APPROACHES TO NEGOTIATING DEALS AND EXCELLENT BOOKS AND SEMI-NARS THAT WILL REFINE YOUR SKILLS. THE AUTHORS HAVE FOUND THE ABOVE APPROACH EFFECTIVE.)

SUMMARY

Strategic Issues:

1. Develop your first estimate of The Market Battlefield Summary of the selling business combined with your business. (See Chapter 2.) Do you know the market competitors, market needs, driving force, externalities, and how the acquired business will fit on the Market Battlefield to accomplish your strategic objective?

2. Develop your revised estimate of the Strategic Battle Plan of the selling business combined with your business. Does the combi-nation provide a significant improvement to your business? What is the improvement to the forecasted sales profits, investment, and cash flow of your business that results from the acquisition?

3. Develop a list of Open Issues that must be resolved during the CRITICAL EVALUATION Step. There will probably be many Open Issues at this point as most of the information for your strategic analysis will be gathered in confidence with inputs from the seller.

4. Review the potential competitor reactions when the transaction is made public. Will they attempt legal or business actions to block the transaction?

People Issues:

1. Does owner (owners) want to sell? Why?
2. What are seller's financial and career objectives?
3. Establish acquisition team and identify key roles and principal negotiators for both acquisition team and seller's team. Establish a "Champion" within your organization who has adequate time to monitor the acquisition.
4. Establish how communications will occur between buyer and seller.
5. Evaluate selling management and determine if management capabilities and styles are adequate and compatible with your business.
6. Estimate effect of the transaction on incentive compensation and perks for the seller's employees.
7. Develop a list of Open People Issues to be resolved during the CRITICAL EVALUATION Step.

Financial Issues:

1. Obtain copies of the seller's historical financial statements, and have your accountants restate the information using accounting rules consistent with your business accounting practices. Use this restated information to forecast financial performance of the combined companies.
2. Are sellers willing to certify their financial information?
3. Are there additional costs of operations or lower costs of operations when the selling company is combined with your business?
4. Summarize open financial issues.

Deal Issues:

1. Establish a confidentiality agreement and confidential communications process.
2. Evaluate alternative deal structures and associated purchase prices, and develop a Deal Structure Risk Diagram
3. Negotiate a Letter of Intent
4. Draft and sign a Letter of Intent.
5. Reach agreement about details of a public announcement.

6. Establish a time schedule for completing a transaction.

7. Establish sources for financing the transaction.

8. Summarize Open Deal issues.

You are now ready to enter the **CRITICAL EVALUATION Step in the** acquisition process, verify business assumptions made in the **Screen Step,** resolve open issues, complete negotiation of a definitive agreement, **and** close the transaction.

Chapter Nine

The Critical Evaluation Step in the Acquisition Process
Business Management Issues

Your objective during the first part of the Critical Evaluation Step is to verify your business assumptions and assess operating risks in order to translate your findings into an Integration Plan and then into a definitive acquisition agreement. To verify your assumptions and assess risks you will need your marketing managers to critically evaluate the strategic

Strategic Acquisition Process

		Search	Screen	Critical Evaluation	Integration
Business Management Issues	*Strategic Issues*				
	People Issues				
	Operating Financial Issues				

	Initial Contact	Offer Letter	Definitive Agreement

Deal Issues			

plan, your human resources managers to look at people issues, and your accounting managers to examine operating financial issues.

In the meantime, you will have your "Champion" and business managers working to develop a plan to integrate the acquired business into your business after the acquisition agreement is signed. All of this activity will require a considerable commitment on the part of both your management and the seller's management. This phase, if not handled very carefully, can be so disruptive to a seller's business that it could affect the business's ability to maintain profitable operations. Therefore, you must organize and manage activities in such a way as to minimize business disruption and confusion over the two or three months required to complete the Critical Evaluation Step.

Organize Your Acquisition Team

How do you start? First assemble your acquisition team and review the Letter of Intent (offer letter) signed at the end of the Screen Step. Then review the Open Issues list developed at the same time. Establish a target date for closing the transaction (60 to 90 days hence). Ask each team member (including transaction specialists) to provide the following information describing his(her) activities during this step in the acquisition process.

1. Description of Activity
   (A brief description of what is to be done)
2. Seller Contact Required
   (Who will be required from the seller's team to support the activity)
3. Start Date/End Date
4. Estimated Employee Hours
   (An estimate of the number of hours your team members will invest to complete this activity)
5. Location of Activity
   (Where will activity occur? seller's offices, lawyers' offices, etc.)
6. Output from Activity
   (What is the expected output to the acquisition team?)

This information will help you develop a schedule for all acquisition activity and establish a target date by which the definitive acquisition agreement should be negotiated and the transaction signed and closed. Note that the date of signing a definitive acquisition agreement may not be the date of closing (transfer of assets and consideration).

Coordinate Schedule and Contact Procedures with the Seller

Contact the seller and review your proposed schedule. Establish a list of the seller's representatives (accountants, attorneys, business managers, etc.) and provide to the seller the names and telephone numbers of the members of your acquisition team. Reach agreement on procedures for communication and investigation by the acquisition teams. For example:

1. The seller will have one contact person to coordinate all visits and requests for information.
2. All information requests must be submitted in writing to the seller's contact person.
3. All visits to the seller's operations, customers, or suppliers will be scheduled through the seller's contact person.
4. Adequate office space will be made available on the seller's site to house acquisition team personnel.
5. On (seller's) site, acquisition team personnel will not disrupt operations by requesting information or enlisting support directly from personnel working for the seller.
6. No acquisition team member should engage in piecemeal negotiation of issues. All issues should be summarized for the principal negotiators to address in formal sessions.
7. Off (seller's) site meetings of lawyers and accountants will be scheduled through an identified contact person at the law firms or accounting firms with notification to the seller and buyer through the principal negotiator.

These suggested procedures may seem onerous to some of your acquisition team members but they are essential to an orderly Critical Evaluation process. Engineers and accountants roaming the seller's operation collecting information will disrupt daily business proceedings. Lawyers and accountants could conduct piecemeal negotiation of issues critical to the strategic success of an acquisition. Identical information may be requested by both accountants and lawyers and result in duplicate effort by the seller's team. Faithfully following procedures similar to those listed above and holding regular acquisition team meetings will help you manage a smooth acquisition process.

Public Announcement

The first item on your Critical Evaluation schedule should be the public announcement of the transaction. This may be either a general announcement to the press or a more limited announcement to selected groups. If your business or the seller's business is a public company (shares of stock traded on a public stock exchange) or a significant part of a public company, Securities and Exchange Commission (SEC) rules may require a full public announcement and press release. Your legal and accounting advisors will help make a decision on applicability of SEC rules. If neither business requires a full public announcement, then you and the seller must agree on how to inform your employees, customers, suppliers, creditors, and other affected parties.

It is virtually impossible to maintain strict confidence during the Critical Evaluation Step since so many employees and personnel outside the company must be involved in the process. You should formally notify all involved parties and employees and customers in order to control the type and quality of information disseminated. Otherwise the rumor mills will dominate the information transfer and employees, customers, and suppliers may be misinformed.

Agree with the seller on the information to be released and who is to receive it. Then, to minimize rumors, simultaneously announce the proposed transaction and answer questions from interested parties. Designate one person on your acquisition team to answer all questions from the press, other outside parties, or employees.

The Kick-Off Meeting

Your acquisition team combined with the seller's acquisition team may often include as many as twenty individuals. These people will be working together for two to three months and should be introduced to each other and to the schedule and procedures they are to follow. An all-hands kick-off meeting is the most effective way to communicate your acquisition schedule and procedures. It is also the time to listen to concerns of the team members. You will most likely hear:

1. The attorneys will complain about the limited amount of time available to complete necessary agreements. Usually this is a re-

sult of other client commitments, completing due diligence, or securing necessary government approval to complete a definitive agreement by the target date. If some specific delay is anticipated, discuss this issue at a separate meeting with the attorneys.

2. The accountants will complain about inadequate time to get a "clean cut-off" and prepare a set of financials to be used as a basis for the transaction. Usually this is handled by obtaining a set of financials a month or two prior to closing and then agreeing on how the transaction will be modified after the acquisition is completed to compensate for changes in the balance sheet of the company over the interim period.

3. The benefits and human resources people will complain about their inability to transfer benefits in the proposed time period. This is usually handled by the seller's carrying benefits (where possible) for an additional month or two after the transaction and the buyer's reimbursing for those expenses.

Take all concerns seriously, but don't let support personnel who are billing you by the hour or have other client commitments prolong the transaction unless there is a specific task that you agree must be accomplished before the transaction can be completed. Make sure your team of specialists has set aside adequate time to complete the transaction. A delay by one transaction specialist or your management will drive up costs as other specialists may continue to work and bill during the delay. The more months it takes to do a transaction, the higher the cost to your company and the more likelihood the deal will come apart. Experienced attorneys and accountants will give you a good estimate of the time and charges required to complete your contemplated transaction. Inexperienced people will not be able to make such an estimate. Use only experienced people as advisors.

The Due Diligence Process—Testing Your Assumptions

Due diligence is an expression you will hear repeatedly in the acquisition process. It refers to adequate investigation of the business you are acquiring to be sure that you understand the true nature of acquired assets and assumed liabilities. In the legal sense, due diligence is essential to minimize the possibility of a shareholder suit against incompetent management. It requires the seller to provide all requested information necessary for you to make a competent management decision. If the seller provides false information or fails to supply requested information, the seller may also be liable to the extent he(she) misrepresented the business to your acquisition team. Therefore, you should request information from the seller in writing and carefully date and log all information received in order to evaluate any misrepresentations. If it is apparent that the seller is not willing to share information or is intentionally misrepresenting the business, terminate the acquisition discussions early as it is impossible to make an accurate assessment of a business's value with a dishonest seller.

STRATEGY ASSESSMENT

Your decision to embark on this acquisition was based on the belief that there was a strategic business opportunity. Often, with the flurry of deal activity it is easy to lose sight of the underlying business strategy. What are the open strategy issues? How will customers react to the acquisition? How will key suppliers react to the acquisition? How are competitors reacting to the news of a pending acquisition? What is the competitive advantage of the business and how will you avoid losing it in the transaction? Has anything in the market changed that will impact your strategic reason for the acquisition? These are the issues that must be addressed outside of legal and accounting due diligence in order to assure a successful acquisition. Use your Strategic Plan as a guide to strategy due diligence. Go through the Market Battlefield and Battle Plan forms, verify the information, and assess the risks.

Start with product and service information. What fraction of sales comes from products unrelated to the products described in the strategic plan? Sometimes you will find that a large portion of a company's sales is in repair parts or service support for obsolete products. You may discover that most of the company's sales are in a completely different market than you anticipated. Does this change the strategic opportunity and should you continue with the transaction?

Look at the customers. Are they the type you anticipated? Sometimes you will find the seller is serving, for example, more military customers or foreign customers than you expected. Or perhaps the customers are geographically distributed in an unfavorable manner. Maybe they are all old business associates of the selling management. How does this impact the strategic opportunity?

Look at customer need and driving force behind purchase decisions. Sometimes you find customers purchasing because of favorable credit terms when you assumed they were purchasing due to a product performance advantage. Perhaps they are purchasing due to dealer discounts when you thought they were purchasing because of dealer proximity. How does this impact your strategic opportunity?

Look at Market Alternatives to the seller's products. Are there any alternatives to the product that could affect your strategic decision? Sometimes you find foreign market alternatives are a significant factor in the shape of the market battlefield. How would this affect your strategic opportunity?

Look at Externalities that impact on the seller's products. Local laws and regulations, such as environmental laws, may have a much different impact on the seller's business than you anticipated. How does this impact your strategic opportunity?

Look at competitors from the seller's perspective. Sometimes competitors do not participate in certain market segments or geographic regions. They may enter with different products or market strategies in different geographic markets. Do you perceive any changes in strategic opportunity as a result of evaluating the competitors of the selling company?

Look at the seller's Competitive Advantages. Sometimes they are substantially different than you first thought. Test the perceived competitive advantages by talking to selected customers (if possible). Are there differences that affect the strategic opportunity?

Look at the seller's Competitive Disadvantages. Can you still compensate for them as planned? Are there any disadvantages that you didn't anticipate? How do changes in Competitive Disadvantages affect your ability to implement the Market Battle in your strategic plan?

All of these Strategy Issues must be carefully evaluated as part of your assessment. Review and modify your Market Battlefield and Battle Plan forms. If your business strategy doesn't hang together in this assessment, don't proceed with the transaction. You can't make a good acquisition at a low price when the underlying strategy is flawed.

PEOPLE ASSESSMENT

You are going to find the seller's business has attracted different kinds of employees, has a different culture, and does things in a different way than your business. In nearly all business today, the most important asset is the skill of the people running and operating the business. This asset is not reflected on the seller's balance sheet, but failure to deal with People Issues in a transaction will make it impossible to achieve your strategic objectives. Because the seller's business has managers who operate in a different way from yours, don't assume they are wrong and your managers are right. If their work environment is casual and yours is strict, don't assume that imposing your environment on their workers will be successful. Too often, as a result of such methods, good businesses are acquired, new management is sent in to "fix" certain management problems, and the business immediately turns sour. You must face the people issues now, as part of the Critical Evaluation process, and not after you have acquired the business.

Organization Structure

You should get to know both formal and informal management at the seller's company. What is the formal organization structure? How do things actually get done? Determining the formal organization structure is straightforward; getting to know who really makes a business successful requires more effort. You must get to know the seller's management. Invite them to visit your business. Get to know them in an informal setting (lunch or dinner) where they can tell you how the business really works. Get copies of their resumes and ask about their backgrounds as you would any new senior management candidate. What motivates them in their current positions and can you provide similar opportunities? Once you and your management know the seller's management you can determine how effective they will be in your post-acquisition organization.

Skills Inventory

You should look at all key personnel in the selling organization to evaluate their skills inventory. This will let you determine if there are critical skills that cannot be replaced should an employee leave after the acquisition. If these abilities are not available in your business or in the job market, you may have to provide special compensation to retain people with critical skills. Often the selling management will identify their employees' critical skills and help you decide how to work with each employee.

Incentive Compensation and Perks

You cannot acquire a company and immediately remove the incentive compensation plan, the stock option plan, private offices, company cars, and baseball tickets without creating a major upheaval in employment.

Yet many acquirers do this each year and wonder why they can't retain management. If it is necessary to reduce incentive compensation or perks to the selling company's employees, make sure you can replace these employees without disrupting the business. If you can't maintain similar incentive compensation and perks, estimate the employee losses. If excessive, it may be a bad acquisition.

Make a list of incentive compensation and perks and decide what changes must be made. Offset stock options with new stock options or bonus programs. Where necessary, phase out incentive compensation programs over several years to minimize the financial hardship on employees. When you have decided on changes to employee incentive compensation and perks, meet with a representative group of affected employees and solicit their advice on how the changes will be received and how they may be improved. You must know before the acquisition how the employees will react to changes in incentive compensation and perks.

Career Planning

Many of the seller's employees have a notion where their career in the selling company is taking them. Now they find out their company is going to be sold. They have worked years to establish a relationship with their boss or the owner and now they find out he(she) is leaving and you are taking over. They want to know where they fit in the new organization and what career opportunities you can provide them. Or should they look for other employment? Spend time on career counseling. Talk to key employees about future job opportunities and what they will have to do to qualify for advancement. Several days of job counseling will help maintain stable employment after the acquisition and keep new employees focused on their job rather than on an external job search.

FINANCIAL ASSESSMENT

All accounting statements are not the same. In spite of Generally Accepted Accounting Principles (GAAP) and Certified Public Accountants, there are significant differences in the ways companies record accounting information. As the head of one acquisition audit team once told us, "I look at how much the seller's auditors weasel-word the accounting opinion to determine how tough a job I have." You must have your accounting managers or specialists translate the seller's information into financial statements using the same accounting rules your company uses in order to be able to compare and consolidate financial data. Although you may not have a strong accounting background, you should be asking the following questions when reviewing the seller's financial reports:

Profit and Loss Statement
Sales

1. Are there any contingent sales? (Sellers can use contingent sales to puff up performance prior to an acquisition.)
2. Are sales net of sales representative fees? (If not, sales revenue can be overstated—and selling expense understated—by the amount of the fee, 2% to 10%.)
3. Are sales stocked at distributors subject to a put back under the distributor agreement? (You don't want distributors returning overstocked items after the acquisition.)
4. Are sales net of discounts? (If not, sales revenue can be overstated and selling expense understated.)

Cost of Goods Sold

1. Are General and Administrative, Engineering, or Marketing expenses allocated to cost of goods sold? (This may overstate costs of goods sold and understate profit from operations.)
2. Are depreciation expenses on the same basis as in your business? (If you use straight line depreciation and the seller uses accelerated depreciation, the seller's profits may be understated in comparison to your profit calculation.)
3. Are employee benefits all in cost of goods sold? (Some businesses may put part of their employee benefits for direct labor into overhead. This may understate costs of goods sold and operating profit.)
4. Are inventories relieved on a first in first out (FIFO) or last in first out (LIFO) basis or some other basis? (Depending on inflation rates, the FIFO method may understate cost of goods sold.)
5. Are manufacturing equipment and leasehold changes expensed as incurred? (Private companies with aggressive tax planning may expense labor used to make manufacturing equipment or leasehold improvements, resulting in overstating costs of goods sold and a future tax adjustment.)

6. Are facilities and equipment leased or amortized at sustainable rates? (If leases are capital or operating leases, it may affect your accounting treatment.)

7. Are sales a result of Small Business or Minority-Owned Business preferences? Special profit margins may be permissible for small businesses doing government contracting that are not permissible for large businesses. Also certain costs are allowable for small businesses that are not allowable for large businesses. (If these costs become unallowable after the acquisition, cost of goods sold will increase.)

8. When are sales recorded? When shipped? When invoiced? When collectable under a contract? (If costs can be invoiced against progress milestones, the actual costs to complete a product may be overstated or understated.)

General & Administrative Expense (G&A)

1. Are all G&A costs captured, that is, have parent company services been accurately reflected in G&A expense? (When some G&A costs are paid at the parent company level, actual G&A costs may be understated.)

2. Are owner relatives or other unnecessary expenses part of G&A expense? (Private companies may have the owner's family members on the payroll or club dues or autos that would not be included after the acquisition.)

Marketing & Selling Expense

1. Are sales representative fees or distributor discounts reflected in Selling Expense? (If not shown in Selling Expense, it will be understated and show higher sales revenue.)

2. Are advertising and literature costs expensed as incurred? (When they are accrued, they may understate or overstate actual costs depending on the accuracy of the accrual method.)

3. Are sales commissions expensed as orders are booked or as product is shipped? (The timing of expensing of sales commissions may understate or overstate Marketing and Selling Expense.)

Research & Engineering Expense (R&E)

1. Are any research or engineering expenses capitalized and amortized against product lines? (Capitalized R&E expense may understate expenses unless appropriately amortized.)

2. What fraction of engineering expense should be in manufacturing cost of goods sold since it is in direct support of manufacturing? (When most Engineering expense is used in factory support, the actual investment in R&E may be overstated if not reflected as a manufacturing expense.)

Other Expense

1. What's in this account and how will it change? The "Other Expense" account is seldom comparable from company to company. (Get to understand every item in this account. This is where you may find surprises.)

Interest Expense

1. Does historic interest expense accurately reflect market rates? (If current debt, at a low interest rate, will be replaced with higher interest rate debt in the near future, interest expense may rise.)
2. Are bank fees or credit line costs in interest expense? (This may overstate interest expense.)

Tax Expense

1. Are tax loss carryforwards transferable? (If not, tax expense may be understated.)
2. Are regional tax incentives transferable? (If not, tax expense may be understated.)
3. When was the last IRS audit and what were the results? (Many adjustments to prior tax payments as a result of audits may give you concern about hidden tax liabilities on unaudited statements.)
4. Are historical tax rates changed when earnings are consolidated with your company? (A small company may have profits taxed at a lower rate, or higher rate if the parent has tax loss carryforwards, that will affect the tax rate of the consolidated businesses.)

BALANCE SHEET
Cash & Investments

1. Is cash reflected in U.S. dollars and are there potential currency exchange losses or gains? (If currency on deposit in foreign banks is not adjusted for current exchange rates, it may overstate or understate cash balances.)

2. What is market value of investments? (If investments are not adjusted to current market values, they may be overstated or understated.)

Accounts Receivable

1. Is the account net of bad debt reserves and how are bad debt calculations made? (If bad debt reserves are inadequate, then accounts receivable may be overstated.)
2. What accounts are disputed? (Disputed accounts may not only indicate quality of the receivables but may also tell you something about product quality problems.)
3. When is the account adjusted for returned goods? (If returned goods are not credited when returned or held for evaluation, Accounts Receivable may be overstated.)
4. How rapidly are invoices processed; 10, 20, 30 days? What are unbilled receivables? (If Accounts Receivable are not billed for 30 days, what is the level of Unbilled Receivables and can you change the billing process? This will affect the level of billed Receivables.)

Inventory

1. What is the basis for relieving inventory: FIFO, LIFO, other? (If high inflation rate affects purchased materials, older inventory will be reflected in the inventory account at a lower cost than newer purchases.)
2. How are Excess and Obsolete calculations made: 1, 2, or 3 years estimated usage? (If the seller keeps inventory on a balance sheet that exceeds your customary obsolescence policy, inventory may be overstated by your accounting standards.)
3. How much inventory is in products not introduced to the market? (New product inventory is high-risk inventory if product introductions fail.)
4. How often is inventory declared excess and subsequently used? (Aggressive inventory writedowns may understate inventory balances. For tax purposes, excess inventory must be systematically eliminated.)
5. Are all inventories held on-site and secured? (Inventory at subcontractors' facilities may not be secured or may have been scrapped, thus overstating inventory.)

6. How much inventory has recently been built to keep the factory floor loaded? (If inventory is built to keep the factory floor loaded instead of meeting customer demand, excess inventory thus created may be a sign of declining sales and excess manufacturing capacity. Don't be fooled by profits derived from building excess inventory.)

Accrued Expenses

When do accruals get expensed? The day after the acquisition? (If you do not have a schedule for expensing accruals, you may be surprised after the acquisition with sudden changes in profit.)

Fixed Assets

1. How are assets depreciated: over 3, 5, 15 years on an accelerated basis or straight line basis? (If fixed assets are depreciated on a more aggressive basis than your standard, you may understate fixed assets.)
2. Are assets depreciated on the same basis for tax and book purposes? (If there is a difference between tax and book depreciation methods, this may lead to accruals that will either understate or overstate actual fixed assets.)
3. Have assets recently been written up to market value as part of a prior transaction? (If so, they may be overstated. This is a trick some sellers use to inflate asset values.)
4. How do asset book values compare to fair market values? Should you get an appraisal? (If assets are well below fair market value, an appraisal may be necessary in order to minimize the tax consequences of certain types of transactions. It also will give you a better understanding of the replacement cost of the assets.)
5. Are all of the assets actually being used? (If assets are not being used in the day-to-day operation of the business, they may be subject to a write-off. This would indicate that assets are overstated.)

Accounts Payable

1. What are disputed accounts and why? (If accounts payable are disputed, it may be an indication of poor suppliers or just an excuse to stretch out payments. This may understate accounts payable or just make you aware of product problems.)
2. Are slow payments affecting deliveries from vendors? (Slow payments may have forced the seller to use lower quality

suppliers and may represent an opportunity to improve future payment terms and acquire better suppliers.)
3. Will vendors expect different payment terms after an acquisition? (Vendors may have demanded C.O.D. payments prior to the acquisition but will accept better payment terms after the acquisition or vice versa. This will either increase or decrease your accounts payable balances.)

Other Liabilities

1. Are they comparable to acquiring company? When are they payable? (This should be carefully investigated for unusual liabilities and adjusted to be consistent with your accounting standards and business practices.)
2. Are any liabilities to shareholders of selling company? (Often small private companies will make loans to shareholders. This may overstate company liabilities if these loans are to be paid off after the acquisition.)

Short-Term Debt

1. When is it due? (If secured by the seller, it may be due and payable at the time of the acquisition.)
2. Will you assume the liability or pay off with the transaction? (Some short-term debt may be assumable, but perhaps under different terms and conditions.)
3. What is market value? (If interest rates have risen, you may be able to discount the debt. If interest rates have fallen, you may have to pay a premium to get rid of the debt, depending on market conditions.)
4. How much is owed to owners? (If owed to owners, it may be at lower than market rates and difficult to replace. It could also be at above market rates, and you would want to replace it with lower-cost debt.)

Long-Term Debt

1. When is it due? (If not due at the time of acquisition, it may be a significant factor in financing the transaction.)
2. What is the market value? (If market interest rates are substantially different from the interest charged for long-term debt, it may be overstated or understated on the books of the selling business.)

3. Will you replace with more favorable debt at transaction? (If you replace it with more favorable debt, longer term or lower interest rate, it will affect the long-term debt on the balance sheet.)

4. Is it assumable? Are debt holders able to block a transaction? (If the debt is not assumable and it is secured by stock in the company or has anti-takeover terms, the debt holders may be able to block a transaction.)

5. Is it personally guaranteed by owners? Will you have to guarantee debt? (If the long-term debt is guaranteed by the owners, it may only be assumable if it carries a similar guarantee.)

Equity

1. Who are controlling shareholders? (If the controlling shareholders have not agreed on the equity value of the business, you may not be able to complete a transaction. For some types of transactions, as few as 10% of the stockholders may be able to block a transaction.)

2. Are controlling shareholders (owners) working together on the transaction? (If there are differing interests in selling the company, the owners may not work together to sell the business.)

3. Are there any dissident shareholders? (Even a few dissident shareholders may be able to delay or disrupt a transaction under some state laws.)

4. Are all warrants and options to purchase stock considered in calculations for shares outstanding? (The basis for calculating the equity should include a full dilution of equity by inclusion of all stock options and warrants.)

5. Will convertible debentures be converted at transaction? What happens to ownership? (Conversion of convertible debentures may affect the controlling interest and the debt equity ratio in a transaction.)

6. What are dissident shareholder statutory rights? (Dissident shareholder rights vary from state to state and may significantly affect the type of transaction.)

Expect to be surprised by your financial assessment of the seller's business. No two businesses account for their transactions in exactly the same way. Only after your accountants have restated the seller's financial information to match your accounting policies and procedures can you evaluate the financial opportunity of the acquisition and forecast the future of the business with precision.

INTEGRATION PLAN

What do we mean by an Integration Plan? You must identify those changes that must occur after the acquisition to prepare the acquired company to conform to your way of doing business and to accomplish the strategic objectives. These changes constitute your Integration Plan. The more carefully you plan for these changes the more likely you will be successful in their implementation.

What are the changes that constitute an Integration Plan? The following outline summarizes the types of actions required in an Integration Plan:

I. Strategic Plan Changes for Seller
   A. Change to a Strategic Plan that combines the capabilities of the seller's business with your business.
   B. When do you execute the new Strategic Plan Market Battle?
      1. When do you make your management aware of the changes?
      2. When do you make suppliers and employees aware of the changes?
      3. When do you make customers aware of the changes?
   C. What are the new strategic objectives of the combined businesses?
   D. What new facilities and equipment will be needed to implement the new business?

II. People Changes at Seller's Business
   A. To whom will senior management of seller's business report?
      1. Will Financial and Accounting personnel have a direct responsibility to your Financial staff?
      2. Will Research and Engineering be combined under one manager?
      3. Will Sales and Marketing be combined under one manager?
   B. Will seller's personnel be replaced by buyer personnel?
   C. Will personnel be relocated?
   D. What changes will occur in employee benefits?
   E. What changes will there be in the incentive compensation system and perks?
   F. What training programs will be implemented to facilitate the transaction?

III. Accounting & Financial Changes to Seller's Business
   A. When and how will banking be transferred to buyer's bank?
   B. When will the seller's accounting system be changed to your accounting system?

    C. How will funds be transferred to seller to handle payroll and
        accounts payable or will they be merged with your business?
    D. Will data processing be standardized?
    E. What contracts must be modified or transferred and when?
        (purchase orders, sales rep. agreements, leases, etc.).

With the above outline you should be able to identify what must be
accomplished in the post-acquisition integration step, who will be responsible for the changes, who must be involved in the changes, and when
each change will occur. This Integration Plan will permit you to organize
and control the next step in the acquisition process, the Integration Step.

SUMMARY

You should now have completed a careful critical evaluation of the seller's
business and assessed the risks associated with the transaction.

A revised strategic plan for the business, a list of open issues, and a
complete integration plan will highlight the business issues to be addressed in negotiation of a definitive agreement. You can now review the
proposed transaction and address the Deal Issues in the Critical Evaluation Step.

Chapter Ten

The Critical Evaluation Step in the Strategic Acquisition Process
Deal Issues

The Deal Issues addressed during the Critical Evaluation Step have to do with establishing the final transaction structure and writing and negotiating the final definitive agreement. It should bring together all of the business management issues and transaction issues should now be brought together into an agreement that lets you accomplish your strategic business objective.

Strategic Acquisition Process

		Search	Screen	Critical Evaluation	Integration
Business Management Issues	Strategic Issues				
	People Issues				
	Operating Financial Issues				

	Initial Contact	Offer Letter	Definitive Agreement
Deal Issues			/////

115

FINANCIAL STRUCTURE AND BUSINESS STRATEGY

How does financial structure affect your ability to accomplish your strategic business objectives? There are books available detailing alternative financing techniques used to accomplish an acquisition. Also, a considerable portion of Chapter 8 was devoted to structuring the transaction. The issue not adequately treated in many texts is the strategic business consequence of the financial structure. In general, competent investment bankers, financial advisors, accountants, and commercial bankers can help you determine various ways of financing the acquisition provided the forecasted earnings, cash flows, and asset base support the purchase price. Optimum financing can, on the other hand, drive away key employees, leave you with inadequate working capital to accomplish your strategic business objectives, or drive the acquired business into liquidation in order to service debt. You must be aware of the impact of specific financing alternatives on post-acquisition success and not focus on clever "financial engineering." The following summary outlines strategic business issues of concern to you when contemplating various deal structures:

1. Pooling of Interests Transaction: You issue shares of stock in exchange for securities in the seller's business. Typically common stock is exchanged for shares of common stock in the selling company. This is usually the case when the buyer has a publicly traded stock.
   Issues
   a. If the seller's managers receive shares of stock in the acquiring company, are they more loyal to post-transaction business?
   b. If the stock price declines after the transaction for reasons outside the seller's control, does this create a hostile management environment?
   c. If the stock is publicly traded, the competitors and employees of the selling company will know through public disclosure statements how much the sellers received.
   d. In a tax-free exchange (the seller pays taxes only when he (she) sells the new shares of stock) the seller will be induced to hold onto the shares of stock and help build the business's value.

2. Purchase of Selected Assets Transaction: You acquire selected assets and liabilities of the seller's business. This can give you effective control of the business without liability for past sins of

the seller's business. Your attorneys love this structure as they can write elaborate agreements to limit your liability.
Issues

a. Does dealing with the unpurchased assets and unassumed liabilities divert the acquired management's attention from the acquired business?

b. Were there any unacquired assets essential to the pre-acquisition success of the business?

3. Leveraged Buyout: Seller may take back a note for a large part of the purchase price, and the equity portion of the transaction is typically less than 20%. The seller's debt and other subordinate debt (subordinate to bank debt) is usually at a very high interest rate compared to bank debt.
Issues

a. Will servicing the debt force you to subordinate your strategic objectives to the lender's financial objectives?

b. Will employees leave for a position with a more financially secure company?

c. Will you have adequate working capital to implement your strategic plan?

These are three of the more common financial structures used in today's acquisition market. Your focus on financial structure must include an awareness of how each structure will inhibit or help you meet your post-acquisition business objectives, not just minimize your cost of financing.

THE DEFINITIVE ACQUISITION AGREEMENT

Who prepares the definitive acquisition agreement? How can it affect your business strategy? What are the essential ingredients of a good definitive acquisition agreement?

There are as many answers to these questions as there are attorneys drafting agreements. As the person responsible for success of the acquisition, we assume you are not an attorney and will not get into the technical detail of various types of acquisition agreements. You must rely on experienced legal counsel for detailed preparation of the acquisition agreement. You should, however, know some of the basic issues essential to a successful acquisition agreement.

First, you should know that the buyer usually prepares the acquisition agreement. Your legal counsel will draft an agreement that should be reviewed by your entire acquisition team. Expect your tax advisors to want to optimize the tax aspects of the agreement. Your accountants will want to obtain the most conservative accounting treatment for the transaction. And your attorneys may try to include exceptionally onerous language that could scare away the most willing seller. Expect your attorneys to try to protect you from all possible risks both real and imagined. Your role as the person responsible for operation of the business is to sort out these conflicting agendas and, with your legal counsel, develop an agreement that lets you accomplish your strategic business objectives. You will not be able to optimize all aspects of the agreement in your favor. You will have to tolerate reasonable business risk to develop a definitive acquisition agreement that the seller will accept. After you have reviewed the draft acquisition agreement with your entire acquisition team and your attorneys have redrafted it to include those changes you approve, send copies to the seller and schedule the negotiating session.

The following outline prepared by David Seidl and John R. Mentzer III of Miles & Stockbridge, Baltimore, MD, captures many of the essential ingredients of a definitive acquisition agreement.

The primary purpose of the acquisition agreement is to set forth the legal commitment of the parties to the agreement for the purchase and sale of the target company and the terms and conditions upon which the purchase and sale shall occur. In the ordinary case, the acquisition agreement merely sets forth the contractual commitment of the parties to proceed with purchase and sale of the acquisition candidate and does not transfer legal title, control or possession of the acquisition candidate from the seller to the buyer. These typically will transfer at the 'closing' of the transaction described in the acquisition agreement. At the closing, the seller typically will deliver to the buyer various documents to evidence the transfer of title, control and possession of the acquisition candidate, such as bills of sale, deeds, leases, assignments and other instruments. Until such time, the buyer has no legal claim to the acquisition candidate except for the obligations and rights set forth in the acquisition agreement.

Because the acquisition agreement generally sets forth the seller's and buyer's commitments to transfer legal title, control and possession of the acquisition candidate at some future time, the acquisition agreement generally has a title which reflects this concept and also generally describes the type of transaction in which title, control and possession of the acquisition candidate shall transfer from the seller to the buyer, such as, 'asset purchase agreement,' 'stock purchase agreement,' 'plan of reorganization,' 'plan of merger,' etc.

Notwithstanding the title of the acquisition agreement or the nature of the transaction described by the acquisition agreement, all acquisition agreements follow the same general format. The following is a general outline of that format.

The first part of the acquisition agreement will simply identify the parties to the agreement, set forth the date of the agreement, and, in most cases, contain several paragraphs describing the background for the acquisition as an introduction to the agreement. These introductory statements are included in order to enable an objective third party with no prior involvement with the negotiations that led to the acquisition agreement, such as a court, to understand the background for the agreement if called upon to interpret the substantive provisions of the agreement and to determine the parties' respective obligations and rights.

Typically, the next section of the acquisition agreement contains a listing of definitions used throughout the acquisition agreement. The definition section is included at the beginning in order to provide a handy reference for a reader of the acquisition agreement. Almost universally, all of the terms which are defined in the definition section will be used throughout the acquisition agreement in all capital letters or with their initial letters capitalized. This convention is used to signal to the reader that the capitalized term should be interpreted in light of the definition set forth in the definition section, and should not necessarily be interpreted in light of its dictionary definition.

The next section of the acquisition agreement generally sets forth the agreement of the parties to purchase and sell the acquisition candidate and the principal terms upon which the sale shall occur. For example, if the acquisition agreement relates to a transaction in which the buyer shall purchase certain assets of the acquisition candidate, this section will list the assets to be sold to the buyer as well as the assets which the buyer will not purchase. In an asset purchase, this section will also identify liabilities of the company that the buyer is willing to assume as well as those liabilities that the buyer will not assume. If the acquisition agreement relates to a stock purchase, this section will set forth the number of shares of stock of the acquisition candidate to be transferred and delivered at the closing to the buyer. If the acquisition relates to a merger or other reorganization, this section will set forth the terms of the merger, exchange of shares or other transfer of consideration by the parties to the agreement at the closing. This section of the acquisition agreement, in all cases, will also describe the 'purchase price' for the acquisition candidate. The purchase price may be a fixed dollar amount or a fixed number of shares of the acquiring company or other consideration or may be determined by a formula which will be set forth in this section. Typically, under a purchase price formula, the acquisition agreement provides for a sum certain to be transferred by the buyer at the closing with certain adjustments to be made after the closing. For example, the purchase price provisions may provide for a fixed amount to be transferred by wire based upon the estimated closing financial statements prepared for the seller and delivered to the buyer at the closing, with adjustments to be made to the purchase price based upon audited financial statements to be provided by the seller to the buyer following the closing which reflect the financial status of the seller as of the closing date. Sometimes if the buyer and seller are unable to reach an agreement as to the value of the acquisition candidate (for example because the seller believes that the potential earning power of the acquisition candidate is greater than that perceived by the buyer) the purchase price provisions may provide for a "earnout" formula under which the buyer agrees to pay a sum certain to the seller at the closing and to pay additional amounts to the seller if the acquisition candidate obtains certain operating results or benchmarks following the closing. These are but a few examples of the purchase price provisions you may see in an acquisition agreement; the actual provisions will depend upon the myriad ways in which the parties may structure the agreement. This section of the acquisition agreement also will include provisions relating to the escrow of any holdbacks of the purchase price by the buyer and the administration of these escrow funds.

The next part of the acquisition agreement typically contains 'representations and warranties' of the seller of the acquisition candidate. This section generally is the longest part of the acquisition agreement, and may be the most important from the buyer's perspective. The representations and warranties section enables the buyer to adhere to the old adage: 'get it in writing.' The representations and warranties section contains several paragraphs, prepared by counsel to the buyer, of factual matters relating to the history, condition, operations and status of the acquisition candidate and other parties to the acquisition agreement on the seller's side. Each of these paragraphs is designed to elicit disclosure of facts relating to these matters and generally reflects on those matters that were, or should have been, investigated in the due diligence examination of the acquisition candidate. For example, the representations and warranties will describe the legal status of the acquisition candidate and the authority of the acquisition candidate and other parties on the seller's side to enter into a performance of their obligations under the agreement, describe any consent or approvals necessary to consummate the transfer of legal title, control and possession to the buyer, identify material business issues relating to the acquisition candidate, such as the existence of pending or threatened litigations, any encumbrances on its property and assets, listings of its intellectual property, tangible and intangible assets and material contracts, employee benefit matters, employee and labor matters, listings of permits and licenses necessary to engage in this business, lists of applicable insurance coverage, environmental matters, quality of receivables and inventory, and any other matters deemed material to the buyer's decision to purchase the acquisition candidate. The representations and warranties are generally supplemented by various schedules to the agreement which contain listings and other information described in the representations and warranties section. The purpose of the representations and warranties section is to provide the buyer with a baseline for making his decision to purchase the acquisition candidate. Any important factual statement about the acquisition candidate which formed the basis of buyer's bargain should be included as a representation or warranty in this part of the acquisition agreement. Including representations and warranties in the agreement gives the buyer the ability to make any claim against the seller if, in fact, the representations and warranties made in the acquisition agreement are untrue.

The next section of the acquisition agreement generally contains representations and warranties of the buyer of the acquisition candidate. This representations and warranties section is not generally as extensive as the representations and warranties section relating to the seller, because the seller generally bears more risk with regard to factual matters related to the buyer than the buyer does with respect to factual matters regarding the seller. The buyer representations and warranties generally relate to its legal status and authority to execute the acquisition agreement and to perform obligations described in this document as well as disclosure of certain risks to its ability to perform its stated obligations. The buyer representations and warranties section may also include other representations and warranties depending on the nature of the transaction. For example, if the seller is financing a portion of the purchase price by allowing the buyer to pay in the form of a promissory note, the seller may ask for extensive representations and warranties as to the buyer's financial status and any collateral provided by the buyer to secure its obligations.

The next section of the acquisition agreement typically contains covenants and agreements of the parties to the agreement relating to certain activities to be undertaken during the period between the signing of the acquisition agreement and the 'closing.' For example, the seller generally will covenant and agree to continue to conduct its business in the ordinary course, to provide the buyer with access to its records in order to complete its due diligence, to obtain all necessary consents and approvals to the 'closing' and to otherwise cooperate with the buyer to ensure the orderly transfer of legal title, control and possession of the acquisition candidate. The buyer also, in the typical case, imposes other obligations on the seller during this time period depending upon the nature of the transaction and the risks perceived by the buyer. There will be a similar section which imposes covenants and agreements upon the buyer. There also may be a section which provides that the buyer and seller will take certain actions jointly.

The next section of the agreement generally sets forth certain conditions to the buyer's and seller's respective obligations to proceed with the purchase and sale of the acquisition candidate. Under the typical acquisition agreement, the occurrence of each of the conditions to each party's respective obligations is necessary before that party is obligated to proceed with the closing. The inclusion of these conditions in the agreement protects the buyer and the seller from the risk that certain events which are essential to make the transaction worthwhile will not occur. For example, the buyer may require a third party to provide financing to consummate the transaction. Accordingly, a condition to the buyer's obligation will be that it has secured adequate funding for the acquisition. Other typical conditions include the condition that the representations and warranties of the seller are true as of the closing date, that the seller has complied with all of the covenants and agreements described in the preceding sections of the agreement, that there has been no material adverse change in the business of the acquisition candidate, that the seller has obtained all necessary consents and approvals to the closing and that the buyer is otherwise satisfied with its due diligence review. The buyer may wish to include other conditions to its obligations depending upon the risks that it perceives in the transaction. The seller will also have various conditions to its obligations, such as that the representations and warranties of the buyer are true and that the buyer has complied with all covenants and agreements set forth in the acquisition agreement and obtained all consents and approvals necessary to consummate the transaction. As with the representations and warranties section, however, the conditions to the seller's obligations are generally less extensive than the buyer's conditions, because the seller generally does not bear as much risk in these types of transactions. The purpose of the conditions to the obligations of the parties is to enable the parties to back out of the transaction without liability to the other party if these events do not occur.

The next section of the acquisition agreement generally describes the closing of the transaction. This section establishes the date on which closing will occur, the place of closing, and generally contains a laundry list of documents, certificates and instruments to be delivered by the parties at the closing to effectuate the transfer of legal title, control and possession of the acquisition candidate from the seller to the buyer.

Following the section regarding the closing, the typical acquisition agreement generally contains various provisions which set forth the rights of the respective parties to the agreement to terminate the agreement and the effects of termination. Typically, termination provisions provide that the parties may, by mutual agreement, terminate the agreement. Termination provisions also provide that, in the event that any of the conditions to the respective obligations of the parties have not occurred, the agreement will be terminated.

Following the closing and termination provisions of the agreement, the acquisitions agreement typically includes various post-closing obligations of the parties. Most important among these types of provisions are the indemnification and non-competition obligations imposed upon the seller. From the buyer's perspective, these provisions may be the most important provisions in the document. The indemnification provisions set forth the legal obligation of the seller to compensate the buyer for any risks not assumed by the buyer. For example, the indemnification provisions will provide that the seller shall compensate if the representations and warranties are not true, and for other risks not assumed by the buyer such as product liability claims asserted against the buyer with respect to products produced by the acquisition candidate prior to the closing, the breach by the seller of the acquisition candidate's obligations of any contracts or agreements assigned to the buyer and for other risks negotiated by the parties. The non-competition provisions generally contain prohibitions against the seller competing against the buyer for a certain period following the closing and may be limited to certain geographical areas. These provisions may also prohibit the seller from soliciting business from its former customers and soliciting its former employees for certain periods. These provisions of the agreement are usually heavily negotiated and are frequently the subject of much contention, but the buyer may wish to stick to its guns with respect to the indemnification provisions in order to avoid acquiring the proverbial 'pig in a poke' and with respect to the non-competition provisions in order to avoid the possibility that the seller will use funds provided by the buyer to establish a competing enterprise and destroying any good will acquired by the buyer in the transaction.

The remaining provisions of the agreement generally are referred to as legal 'boilerplate' and set forth miscellaneous items necessary to make the acquisition a comprehensive document. Typically, the miscellaneous provisions will ensure that the acquisition agreement and its schedules and exhibits comprise the entire agreement among the parties and that there are no oral or other agreements between them, that the agreements shall be binding upon not only the parties to the agreement, but to their successors and assigns. Provisions describing the procedures for amendments and waivers of the provisions of the agreement, provisions describing the procedures for providing any notices to the other parties under the agreements, provisions that provide that each of the parties will take such further actions as may be necessary to 'clean up' or otherwise fully effectuate the transactions described in the agreement, provisions which identify the governing law under which the agreement shall be interpreted and other provisions which identify the forum in which any disputes arising under the agreement shall be resolved, or, in the alternative, that certain disputes or all disputes arising out of the agreement shall be determined by arbitrations. Although these provisions fall under the heading of miscellaneous and may be deemed to be boilerplate, you should not dismiss these provisions as unimportant, because many disputes have been resolved solely on the basis of these provisions.

You should keep in mind also that the foregoing is merely a summary of the typical provisions found in an acquisition agreement, and that your agreement may, and will, be tailored to address the particular concerns of the parties in your transaction as well as the terms of the transaction.

Although this outline is not intended to be comprehensive, you may want to use it to make sure all important issues are addressed in your definitive agreement. Remember, the reasonableness of this first draft agreement will set the tone for your negotiating session. An overly ambitious agreement will result in a lengthy detailed negotiation. A reasonable agreement that accomplishes your primary business objective will result in a more meaningful negotiation focusing on key business issues rather than legal nits.

It is customary for the sellers to meet with their legal advisors and mark up the acquisition draft you prepared, submitting these changes to you prior to your negotiating session. You will thus be aware of the seller's priorities in the negotiation and have time to prepare your own reasonable negotiating position.

Negotiating the Definitive Acquisition Agreement

You now have a draft definitive acquisition agreement with the seller's comments and concerns. You should have a list of "open issues" and concerns developed by your acquisition team. Now you must develop your negotiating strategy around your strategic acquisition objectives while addressing both the seller's and your team's open issues and concerns.

Your acquisition team members may have many different perspectives on the negotiating issues. They should each have a copy of the marked up acquisition agreement and should carefully review the seller's comments. You must spend enough time with each team member to understand his (her) perspective on every open issue and how they see the seller's position. Develop alternative solutions to each open issue and prioritize the issues into three categories:

1. Deal Killers
2. Serious Concerns
3. Deal Enhancers

Deal Killers are those issues that will terminate negotiations unless the seller works with you to find a practical solution. These may include transfer of key personnel, noncompete agreements, or indemnity against future environmental claims for past activities. Serious Concerns are those issues that would directly affect the quality of the transaction but which you may be able to accept. These may include seller guarantees on inventory and receivables quality, guarantees on patent protection, or warranty reserve guarantees. Deal Enhancers are those issues that would make the transaction more attractive to you. They could include more favorable tax treatment, longer noncompete agreements, or deferral of part of the purchase payment. You are now ready to enter into negotiations with the seller and his deal specifications.

The Negotiating Meeting for the Definitive Acquisition Agreement

You are now sitting across the table from the seller and his(her) representatives. Both you and the seller may be tired from the effort required to get to this negotiation. You have probably learned some things about the seller's business, which make it less desirable than you had hoped. The seller is no doubt tired of answering the questions posed by you and your acquisition team. He(She) is probably feeling some disruption in business operation and employee unrest inherent in the process. The seller may feel you have betrayed his trust and questioned his integrity by some of the things you have requested in the draft definitive agreement. You may feel the seller has been unreasonable in responding to your agreement. Some of your team members, as well as the seller's team members, are ready to show how tough they can be in a negotiation. Relax. This is where most acquisition negotiations begin.

First you must reestablish trust at the negotiating table. Make it clear that your objective is to reach a satisfactory agreement for both seller and buyer. Let the seller know you too are tired from the acquisition activity (if you're not, you've not been thorough) and you understand and appreciate the effort the seller and the support staff have put into the process. Explain how you would like to conduct the negotiation. Again, you must clearly establish who the principal negotiators are for both buyer and seller. Let the seller know you have reviewed his(her) comments on the draft acquisition agreement and you want to start the negotiations by better understanding the seller's concerns. Clearly explain your concerns to the seller.

Get the seller to tell you what issues are of most concern to them in the proposed definitive acquisition agreement. Listen carefully and try to categorize their issues into the three categories you have used: Deal Breakers, Serious Concerns, and Deal Enhancers. DO NOT BE LED BY YOUR ADVISORS INTO A PAGE-BY-PAGE REVIEW OF THE ACQUISITION AGREEMENT AT THIS TIME. This would result in a piecemeal negotiation without adequately prioritizing each party's issues. Summarize the seller's issues and explain your issues in order of priority. Some negotiators will leave known Deal Breakers until the last minutes of a negotiation with the hope that the other side will be more willing to capitulate once all other issues are resolved. This tactic has killed more transactions than it has won. It destroys trust between negotiators. The most effective negotiators list Deal Breaker issues for each side and start working on changes to the agreement that address these major issues. If you reach an impasse on these Deal Breaker issues, there is no sense in addressing the other issues. What are typical Deal Breaker issues and how are they most often resolved? For the seller they are usually centered around the amount and quality of consideration to be paid, the risk of personal or company guarantees, and limiting future liabilities.

Amount and Quality of Consideration to Be Paid Issues

If the amount of consideration to be paid has changed either in the mind of the seller or in your mind, deal with this issue first. The amount and type of consideration to be paid should have been established in the Letter of Intent. If you or the seller have found reason to change the purchase price or type of consideration to be paid (stock, cash, notes, etc.) you must renegotiate immediately.

The amount and quality of consideration paid issues are usually associated with the quality of securities (stock or debt securities) offered or with contingent payments. If you are offering shares of stock in exchange for the seller's business, the seller wants to know how soon those shares can be sold and at what price. If your stock price is highly volatile, the seller is at risk for any limitations imposed on marketing shares of stock paid for purchase of the business. If the shares have a limited market, sale of a large block of shares at one time can force the stock price down. There may be accounting, tax, or securities rules or regulations that limit the marketability of the shares.

Debt can have similar risks for the seller. If the seller takes back a note or debt security as consideration for purchase of the business, what is the liquidity of that debt? What is your ability to repay the note? What collateral is behind the note if you fail to repay it? If there is perceived risk on the part of the seller, your note or debt security will be discounted and the seller will either want further consideration or he(she) will demand additional security for the business.

Contingent purchase payments are common in today's acquisitions. The risk to the seller is that contingencies are controllable through actions taken by the buyer. If you propose additional payments to be made in future years based on achieving certain minimum sales volumes, who controls the sales force? If you propose additional payments based on achieving certain minimum earnings, who controls the accounting rules (depreciation rates, warranty reserves, inventory reserves, capitalization policy)?

How do you address these quality-of-consideration issues? First, provide the seller with all available information describing your business's history and your plans for future business. (Unfortunately, forecasts must be accompanied by the usual disclaimers.) Second, you should point out to the seller the risk of continuing to operate the business. It is not your intent to eliminate *all* business risk to the seller with the transaction. Finally, you may have to revise the transaction structure to improve the quality of the consideration given to the seller in exchange for the business.

Risk of Personal and Company Guarantees

For the seller, repeated requests for unconditional representations of the quality of the assets and liabilities to be sold may come as a shock. The seller will be asked to guarantee that all inventory is good and usable in the next year of operation, that the receivables are all collectable, that there are no unrecorded accounts payable or employee liabilities. Your attorney has put all of these representations in the agreement in order to get the seller to respond with assurance that you are acquiring what the financial statements say you are acquiring. All parties know that financial statements are only partially accurate.

Keeping in mind that the real value of the business is not in the accuracy of the accounting but in the success of your strategic initiative, you should be willing to negotiate some "basket" dollar amount below which you will not expect the seller to reimburse you for errors in his(her) financial representations. For example, if receivables are recorded at $1,200,000 (net of reserves), you may agree to pursue a claim against the seller or its company only if you find more than $60,000 uncollectible. If the seller is not willing to accept reasonable responsibility for financial representations made to you and your acquisition team, you must question the integrity of the seller and terminate the transaction.

Limiting Future Liabilities

Your draft acquisition agreement may ask the seller to assure you that there are no future contingent liabilities, such as claims for environmental pollution, workmen's compensation claims, or product liability claims. The seller's position usually centers around the notion that these are ongoing business risks. Your position may be that you will accept risks for future liabilities as long as they are not based on prior management decisions or oversights.

Usually these liabilities are limited to some fraction of the purchase price for a fixed number of years and then they fall to the buyer. You may want to assure that some liabilities remain the full responsibility of the seller. It is important to point out to the seller that he(she) is currently fully responsible for these liabilities. Again, a comprehensive discussion of these issues will usually reveal the liabilities of most concern to the seller. If they represent real risk, they must be dealt with in the acquisition agreement. If they are hypothetical risks imagined by the attorneys, develop hypothetical or imagined solutions. Often deals break apart when one or the other party is trying to protect against all possible risk. Both parties should be satisfied with risk comparable to that which they face in the normal course of business.

Page Flipping

Once you have dealt with the Deal Killers, the normal procedure is for the attorneys to lead you through an exercise where you take each page of the agreement sequentially and address the issues raised by both parties. Remember the Deal Killers are behind you and both you and the seller should be able to work out reasonable compromise agreements or trades on the remaining issues. You should, however, only tentatively agree to compromises on each issue raised in order to be able to trade a compromise on one issue against a firmer position on a subsequent issue. Expect to get compromises from the seller at least as valuable as what you are giving up. Once this phase of the negotiation is complete, the attorneys will schedule a signing and closing for the transaction.

SIGNING AN AGREEMENT AND
CLOSING THE TRANSACTION

Why are these events often separate? Signing the agreement is physically signing the definitive acquisition agreement that says what transaction will take place. Closing the transaction is when consideration is paid to the seller and control of the seller's business is assumed. You don't own the business until a closing is completed. Signing an agreement may occur up to ten days prior to closing. Frequently there are state or federal filings or approvals that must be obtained prior to closing the transaction. Often arrangements must be made to issue stock or transfer bank funds. Usually escrow accounts are established and securities or cash held until the closing event occurs. You should make every effort to have the closing occur as close to the signing of a definitive agreement as possible to reduce the possibility of control problems arising during the interim period.

Subsequent Events

Often you withhold a part—typically 10% or less of the purchase con- sideration—for a period of three to six months after closing. This amount will be used to adjust the purchase price to reflect changes to the seller's financial statement at the time of closing. Usually you receive a financial statement at closing that is 30 to 60 days old. After closing you audit the seller's financial statement as of the closing date and make a subsequent adjustment to the purchase price to reflect any changes in the balance sheet for the interim period.

Should you discover a misrepresentation was made by the seller, that portion of the purchase price withheld can be used to compensate for the misrepresentation. You must agree, as part of the definitive acquisition agreement, how subsequent adjustments to purchase price will be carried out and how the withheld consideration will be invested during the wait- ing period.

THE DEAL IS DONE BUT
THE ACQUISITION IS NOT OVER

You have completed the acquisition agreement and closed the transaction but the acquisition is not over until you have completed the next step in the acquisition process, the Integration Step. If you have kept your stra- tegic objective in the forefront of your thinking as you worked through the acquisition process, you should be well postured for the Integration Step. You should not have compromised your strategic objective to make the deal happen. You should not have alienated the seller's management or other employees to expedite the transaction. You should have a detailed integration plan in your hands and be ready to implement it. Whether the investment you have made in the acquisition will meet your strategic business objectives is now a function of how well you carry out the Integration Step.

Chapter Eleven

The Integration Step

Your objective in the Integration Step is to manage a smooth transition in ownership and direct the necessary changes in the acquired business to effect the strategic plan and conform to your way of doing business without destroying the advantages gained in the acquisition. What changes are you going to make to the business's strategy, its management, its financial controls? Mismanagement of these post-deal changes is one of the most common reasons many acquisitions fail. The deal specialists are gone. Now it's up to you and your staff to successfully merge two business entities.

Strategic Acquisition Process

		Search	Screen	Critical Evaluation	Integration
Business Management Issues	Strategic Issues				
	People Issues				
	Operating Financial Issues				

	Initial Contact	Offer Letter	Definitive Agreement
Deal Issues			

As part of the Critical Evaluation Step, you developed an integration plan. Now you must execute that plan. Who will be involved in managing the integration plan? How do you get the acquired company management to buy in to the changes? How do you gain control over the financial operations of the acquired company? How do you manage common suppliers and customers? First, let's consider what you should *not* do in the integration step.

"I'm from Corporate Headquarters and I'm here to Help!" The management of the acquired company will either panic or roll over to the whim of your corporate staff, which claims to be helping them improve the way they run their business. You must understand which changes are necessary and which are for the convenience of your corporate staff. Don't let overly zealous corporate staff push around the management of the acquired company. Force your staff to plan all changes and manage the transition through you and the person running the acquired company.

You can assume that the acquired company management have full-time jobs managing the day-to-day activities. They don't have time to change all of their procedures to conform to your procedures without additional personnel. You must manage the changes to fit the available personnel.

"We'll have your company straightened around in a few weeks." Don't denigrate employees of the acquired company. They will sit back and revel in your failure. Bring those employees into the decision process as part of your team.

"It will take us a few months to find out who the good people are in your business." You should have spent enough time in the Critical Evaluation Process to know whether you have problem employees in the acquired business. Make employee changes early and all at once. Threatening layoffs only alienates employees and costs you their support.

"We'll control all cash. Just ask us for funds when you need them." Don't relegate the seller's management team to begging for funds to operate their business. Include them in the financial planning and budgeting processes so they know what financial goals they have and how much is available to help them reach their goals.

"We're planning to move many of your employees to a new location in the next few years." Most people don't want to move. You will only create an incentive for employees to look for employment elsewhere. Don't announce your intention to relocate employees until you are ready to talk about the details, including the costs and benefits, of a relocation plan.

"It's only a matter of time before we replace your distributors." It will be a much shorter time than you think if you let this information reach the sales force and distributors. Sales forces are not known for their ability to keep confidences. The distributors will find other products to represent if they believe they will lose a product line.

These are only a few examples of what you should not do in the Integration Step. They all contain several fundamental types of mistakes:

1. Don't let your management presume they have absolute control over the acquired company's management and staff.
2. Don't create a mysterious decision-making process that excludes the acquired company's management.
3. Don't speculate about changes without having a well-defined implementation plan.
4. Don't overload the acquired company's management with change for the sake of change.
5. Don't impose matrix management on the acquired company until lines of management control are clearly established.

Manage the acquired company's employees with the same respect you do your own employees. Don't strip them of their authority or question their ability and integrity and expect them to continue to support the business.

ESTABLISHING MANAGEMENT GROUND RULES AND BUILDING COMMITMENT

How do you encourage your management team to know and respect the acquired company's management team? How do you get the acquired company's management team to commit to your strategic objectives for the acquisition? Holding a series of brief meetings at the office will not permit you to get to know the individual personalities of the acquired company's management. If you only interface with the senior operating officer of the acquired company, then the management team will not learn your corporate culture and the personalities of your management. The best approach to initiating the Integration Process is to hold a three-to-five-day meeting of the combined management teams to review and refine the Integration Plan and agree on the reporting structure and ground rules. Combine formal meetings, working sessions, and informal gatherings to both build rapport between the managers and promote commitment to the common business strategy. Often this meeting can be accomplished over a long weekend to minimize disruption to the business's operation. It should focus on the new Strategic Plan, the People Changes, and the Accounting and Financial Changes to the acquired business.

INTRODUCING THE NEW STRATEGIC PLAN FOR THE ACQUIRED BUSINESS

How does the acquired business fit into the overall strategy for the combined businesses? You must establish the market battlefield strategy, goals, and objectives and show how the acquisition facilitates your business strategy. Start by reviewing the Market Battlefield Summary and explain how you perceive the competitors, market alternatives, and external market forces. Then introduce the specific battle plan you will implement through a review of the Strategic Battle Plan Summary. Solicit improvements to your strategic plan and involve the acquired management. There are capabilities within the acquired company that were not considered when you developed the overall strategy. Involving the acquired company management in both a review and improvement of your strategy for the combined businesses will not only show them how the acquisition fits but also bring them into the strategic decision-making business.

How will management of the acquired business work with you to execute the Strategic Battle Plan? Develop a detailed market battle execution plan for implementing the combined company strategy. Ask the questions:

1. Are we realistic in the investment required to execute the market battle?
2. Are we realistic in the time required to carry out the market battle initiative?
3. Are we realistic in the objectives we hope to achieve from the market battle?

Modify the Strategic Plan to reflect inputs from the combined management team and immediately provide copies to all parties. Include a detailed execution milestone chart. You will not achieve success in execution of your strategic initiative unless the management team has bought into that action. This understanding and commitment to a common set of goals and objectives will give perspective to People Changes and Administrative Accounting and Financial Changes you must make.

PEOPLE CHANGES TO
THE ACQUIRED BUSINESS

To whom will senior management of the acquired business report? What personnel will be reassigned from your business to the acquired company? Will people from the acquired company be relocated? What changes will be made to employee benefits? What changes will be made to incentive compensation and perks? What training programs will be offered? These are all issues that must be resolved and formalized at the outset of an acquisition. If People Changes are implemented in a piecemeal fashion, employees of the acquired company will focus on their personal security issues and not meet their business goals and objectives.

Define the formal organization structure. Start with the person designated as the chief executive officer (President or Division Manager) of the acquired company. Establish your commitment to the authority of this individual and define his role in your organization. Define the organization under this CEO, their roles and responsibilities, both to the CEO and to your functional organization. For example, will the senior accounting and financial manager of the acquired company report to your organization on financial control and accounting issues?; will the Research and Engineering Manager of the acquired company report to the Research and Engineering Manager of your organization on technical matters?; who in your organization may directly interface with the acquired company management and who must work through the CEO? You may decide to either combine or eliminate some functions at the acquired company and provide those services through your organization. What organizations will be combined or eliminated? These issues must be resolved now, in a manner that lets management accomplish their strategic objectives and establish an implementation plan.

Tell the management team which of your personnel you are transferring to the acquired company and explain their responsibilities, both to you and to the acquired company's management team. Most often the acquiring company uses its own accounting manager to make certain that financial reporting at the acquired company is consistent with your financial reporting system. One of the most common errors in post-acquisition decision making is misinterpretation of financial information that is presented in a different format than the acquiring company is used to working with. You may decide to introduce new support personnel where the acquired company is weak in their staffing. Make it clear that they are not "spies" from the acquiring company but will report through its formal reporting system. Decide what changes must be made and implement them on a time schedule the entire management team is aware of.

When you decide to relocate people, you must offer them adequate incentive or they will find other local employment. Most employees and their families resist relocation since it usually involves many hidden personal costs such as loss of friends, organization ties, and familiar surroundings. Some employees will refuse to move regardless of the financial incentive you offer and this reluctance will be intensified if they don't trust in their future with the business. Establish a detailed relocation policy that is flexible enough to let you compensate personnel for all reasonable costs associated with the move and which provides a clear job opportunity and continued employment. Many grand strategies for relocating personnel have failed when the spouse said "No!" Be prepared for resistance to relocation.

When you change employee benefits you must provide a comprehensive package describing those changes. First review your proposed changes with the acquired company's management and solicit their support. Then meet with all employees of the acquired company and review the benefit changes and show how they will be implemented. (Note that some union or employee agreements may prohibit changes to employee benefits). Again, the most common error in changing benefits is failure to act in a deliberate manner in announcing changes. Modifying benefits a little each year will lead to employee distrust and a "Here we go again!" attitude.

You have established a new set of goals and objectives for the acquired company. What changes are you making to the incentive compensation plan? What happens to managers who had stock options prior to the acquisition? Review your incentive compensation and stock incentive plans with the acquired company's management and implement the new programs immediately.

Training programs are the fastest way to give comfort to the acquired company's employees. They want to know how your company operates and how they can support its growth. Start by educating all employees at the acquired business about your company ethic, vision, and mission. Supporting job related self-improvement training in computers, writing skills, or technical and trade skills is the best way to let employees know that you care about their personal development and you are committed to investing in their future. Establish training and personal development programs immediately to demonstrate your commitment to the employees of the acquired company.

All personnel changes are fraught with uncertainty. If the acquired company employees do not feel you are effectively and decisively managing these changes, you may lose the greatest asset in the acquired business—the commitment of its people.

ACCOUNTING AND FINANCIAL CHANGES TO THE ACQUIRED BUSINESS

The previous owners of the company exercised accounting and financial control over the business. If they left the company after the acquisition, this control probably left with them. If they have stayed with the business after receiving substantial payment for their ownership interest, their motivation may have dramatically changed. The accounting and financial control of the business now rests with you and your representatives.

You must immediately gain control over the banking and cash management of the acquired company to make certain access is limited to those persons designated by you as responsible. You also must get monthly financial reports produced in a form that you can use for management decision making. Then you must establish limits on financial authority to be certain unauthorized individuals are not making commitments to purchase goods and services, change compensation, or lower product prices.

Gaining Control Over the Cash Management System

The day the acquisition is completed you should have control over all cash receipts and disbursements by the acquired business. A new checking (or lock box) account should be established and all receipts deposited into this account. Access to this account should be limited to those persons you designate as responsible. A separate cash disbursements checking account should be established for payroll and accounts payable. Typically, the financial management of the acquired company requests a weekly transfer of funds to the disbursement account (the checking accounts for payroll and accounts payable) with appropriate justification, such as payroll, vendor payments (by name and invoice number). You, or your designee, collect all receipts and transfer funds to the cash disbursement account as requested, giving you effective control over cash management of the acquired business.

Conforming the Accounting Information

Unfortunately, when we look at a set of financial information we look at it in a comparative way. We similarly examine financial ratios like return on sales, return on investment, gross profit to sales, G&A expense to sales, and marketing expense to sales. As shown in Chapter 7, there are many ways of accounting for a business's activities, which can make a comparative financial analysis difficult unless the same accounting rules are used for the acquired company as is used by the acquirer.

For example, the acquired company may include distributor commissions in selling expense while you may record sales net of distributor commissions. When you look at a comparative ratio of selling expense to sales, the acquired company will indicate a much higher expense ratio than will your business. This could lead to a management decision to cut selling expense when the only difference is in the accounting treatment.

Accountants call this restating of financial information "conforming" the accounting statements. As pointed out in Chapter 9, you should have made the final acquisition financial decisions based on a set of financial information conformed to your way of reporting. Now you must conform each month's financial information to your accounting methods and reporting format in order to evaluate the progress of the acquisition.

This is initially accomplished by making conforming adjustments each month to the acquired business's financial statements. However, your accounting personnel should develop a parallel system that will generate financial information in the appropriate format. Once the new system is operating in parallel (and not until then), the acquired company's accounting system can be replaced. Nothing is more traumatic than shutting down an operating accounting system and having its replacement not operate or provide erroneous information.

Limiting Financial Authority

We have seen situations where managers of acquired businesses have issued purchase orders for millions of dollars worth of goods and services without appropriate approval from the new ownership. There have been post-acquisition cases where the acquired company management has committed to service contracts with multimillion dollar environmental risks in order to get the benefit of an incentive compensation plan. Although owners and managers may have been prudent in their financial commitments prior to the acquisition, they often view the acquirer as a "deep pockets" source of funding for their business's future after the acquisition. The good judgment demonstrated prior to the acquisition may or may not linger. You must immediately establish the lines of financial authority. This is typically done through a budgeting process and a signatory level requirement.

The budgeting process varies from company to company but usually involves identifying revenue sources and expenses for the upcoming twelve months, along with a forecast of balance sheet changes that will be required to meet the business's requirements. Once you have agreed to this budget, you monitor the acquired company's progress monthly against the forecast. If there are changes or trends indicating that the budget is inaccurate, you revise it or find management that can operate to a budget. The operating management of the acquired company is responsible to operate within the budget guidelines.

In addition to budget controls you can implement signature level controls such as:

1. All checks over $5,000 must be signed by the senior financial officer and the chief operating officer of the acquired business.
2. All checks over $25,000 must be co-signed by a member of your staff.
3. All sales contracts over $1,000,000 or with potential liabilities over this level will require signature by you or your designated manager.
4. All compensation to senior management (define by job function or name) must be approved by you.

The purpose of these changes is not to diminish the authority of the acquired business management, but to set limits on how much trouble they can get you into without your prior knowledge.

In many ways you become the banker for the acquired business. This must be done in a way that does not alienate the acquired company's management. Set reasonable limits on their financial authority and truly involve them in the budgeting process and most managers can operate effectively with accounting and financial controls as described above.

The following summarizes the Accounting and Financial Changes you must make to the acquired business:

1. Gaining control over the cash management system
   a. Set up checking accounts you control for all cash receipts and disbursements.
   b. Wire transfer funds to the acquired company's disbursement accounts on a weekly basis as needed.

2. Conforming the accounting information
   a. Have your accounting personnel restate (conform) the monthly financial data from the acquired business to match your accounting and financial reporting procedures.
   b. Have your financial and accounting personnel set up a financial reporting system at the acquired company that lets them generate financial information conforming to your accounting standards.
3. Limiting Financial Authority
   a. Establish an operating budget for the acquired business.
   b. Measure monthly success against the operating budget.
   c. Replace management that cannot meet the operating budget.
   d. Limit management authority to sign checks, approve purchase orders and approve sales proposals to specified dollar levels.

SUMMARY

Some successful acquirers say the Integration Step is never done. For a strategic acquisition we say it is completed when you have successfully achieved your strategic business objective.

The strategic basis for your acquisition is the reason you started this acquisition process. If you have followed the guidelines of this text, you should achieve your strategic objectives. But no text can tell you how to motivate and inspire the people in the acquired company to work with you to achieve your business objective.

The people issues are often the most important factor in the success or failure of an acquisition. If you are not sensitive to the individual and collective needs of the employees in the acquired company, your acquisition will be likely to fail even if you gain absolute financial and operating control during the Integration Step.

Financial control is essential for you to measure and direct the activities of the acquired company toward your strategic objective. Too often past acquisition decision making is clouded by financial reports that misrepresent (on a comparative basis) the success or failure of an acquired company. This may lead you to misjudge your strategic success and the integrity of the acquired management team.

A well-thought-out strategic acquisition is focused on specific strategic objectives, implemented with a clear understanding of people issues, and controlled by appropriate accounting and financial measures. It is a way to build your business in the markets you know and serve.

Chapter Twelve

Lessons Learned by Strategic Acquirers
Concluding Thoughts

You now know how to prepare a Market Battlefield Summary, develop a Strategic Battle Plan, complete the Search, Screen, Critical Evaluation, and Integration Steps, and deal with sellers' Perspectives on Value. The companies profiled in this chapter have successfully implemented strategic acquisition programs, which incorporate many of the principles advocated in this book. The authors have worked closely with their managements and have first-hand knowledge of their strategic acquisition programs.

The profiled companies have used strategic acquisitions (divestitures) to achieve one or more of the following strategic objectives:

1. **BUILD** market share,
2. **EXECUTE** entry into new geographical markets,
3. **PROBE** new markets by acquiring technologies,
4. **MODIFY** competitive position to strengthen core activities,
5. **REACT** to Market Battlefield Maturity by investing excess cash flow in new industries, and
6. **RETREAT** from market battlefields where an overwhelming disadvantage exists.

Bausch & Lomb's acquisitions in the health-care industry have accounted for one-half of its strong sales growth since 1982. **EG&G's** strategic acquisitions actively involve operating managers in a program that redeploys the company's excess cash flow from defense activities to commercial markets. **Loral Corporation** has acquired critical technologies to build $4 billion of sales in the mature defense electronics market. **Perkin-Elmer's** strategic plan required a major restructuring involving multiple divestitures so that the company could focus on its core analytical instrument business. **Sysco Corporation** shows how horizontal acquisitions can help a company enter new markets and gain market share in a fragmented growing industry. **Thermo Electron's** rapid growth has been driven by acquisitions and an innovative spin-off strategy, which has helped finance its development on favorable terms. Through a series of product line acquisitions, the company's chief division, **Thermo Instrument,** which is Thermo Electron's largest subsidiary with public shareholders, has established itself as the third largest company in the analytical instrument industry. **Tracor,** in sharp contrast to the successes of the other profiled companies, ended in bankruptcy due to excessive debt incurred in the LBO of a defense electronics company.

The bottom line measure of the effectiveness of a strategic acquisitions program is creation of shareholder value. For shareholders of a publicly held company, this is the total return on holding a common stock—dividends plus capital appreciation. For the owners of a private company, total return is equal to distributions to the owners plus proceeds received from the sale of an ownership interest.

Over the last ten years (1983 to 1993), shareholders of the profiled companies have earned an average annual return of 16%. Shareholders of four companies earned a higher rate of return than the 15% return for the Standard & Poor's 500 Index (a benchmark for average returns earned by equity investors).

In the table below, returns for individual companies are tabulated:

Company	Stock Price 12/31/83	Stock Price 12/31/93	Total Return*
Bausch & Lomb	$12.50	$51.25	17.5%
EG&G	16.25	18.38	3.2
Loral	12.38	37.75	13.5
Perkin-Elmer	24.63	38.50	11.7
Sysco	4.56	29.25	21.3
Thermo Electron	10.00	42.00	20.5
Thermo Instrument	3.56	34.88	36.1

*Compound annual total return; Perkin-Elmer for the five-year period 1988 to 1993. Thermo Instrument return calculated from IPO in 1986.

BAUSCH & LOMB DERIVES 50% OF GROWTH FROM STRATEGIC ACQUISITIONS

Bausch & Lomb's dynamic growth has been driven by a strategic plan that seeks acquisitions of health-care companies that are market leaders in Value and Performance Markets. Total sales increased to $1.87 billion in 1993 from $433 million in 1982 when its new strategic plan was formulated. The company's 1995 sales goal is $2.5 billion. Daniel Gill, the driving force behind the company's growth, became CEO in 1981. From 1983 to 1993 acquisitions accounted for about 50% of the company's growth. The company's sales growth is even more impressive than the reported numbers indicate because in the 1981 to 1987 period, businesses representing 50% of the 1980 sales were divested, resulting in $45 million in after-tax charges to earnings. Bausch & Lomb's divestitures illustrate an important point about strategic acquisitions: What you sell is often as important, if not more important, than what you buy. The company RETREATED from Mature or Declining markets.

Bausch & Lomb focuses on the global market share of a target company; 85% of total sales are from products in which they are a *world* leader. The company's international division, which was established in 1984, accounted for 45% of total revenues in 1993. The company's strategic goals are translated into an overall objective of consistent 15% per annum growth in earnings. From 1983 to 1993 earnings per share grew at 14% per annum. Shareholders have been the beneficiaries. A shareholder who bought $1,000 worth of stock in 1982 would have seen the value of his(her) holding rise to $5,700 in 1992, a 19% compound annual rate of return (19.6% including dividends).

Bausch & Lomb officially launched its "new ventures program" in 1983. The label "new ventures" signifies that the process is not limited to acquisitions but also encompasses licensing agreements, joint ventures, R&D partnerships, and minority equity investments. The company had completed only one small acquisition in the three years prior to 1983. There was no deal flow, little external growth orientation, and minimal merger and acquisition expertise.

According to Diane Harris, the company's Vice-President of Corporate Development, the new ventures program involved four major areas of action:

1. A strategic planning process was put in place, which included acquisitions. In order to gain the enthusiastic support of the organization,

it was necessary for the CEO (Champion) to lead the process by articulating his vision for the company, have the courage to make the tough acquisition decisions, and be actively involved.

2. Establishing a network of merger and acquisition intermediaries resulted in much greater deal flow (Search Step). In the recent past, Bausch & Lomb has usually been presented 1,000 acquisition opportunities per annum, of which 75% originate from M&A intermediaries. Management will look at 200 of the 1,000 deals, visit/negotiate (Screen Step) with 50–75 target companies, and close 20–30 transactions (Critical Evaluation and Integration Steps).

3. The company set up an in-house capability to manage the following steps: deal search, analysis, due diligence, valuation analysis, and deal structuring and negotiation. Due diligence is separated into financial, legal, and business components. The company has developed a valuation model and software that is based on deal-market multiples (Comparables Valuation Model) and discounted cash flow (Discounted Cash Flow Model).

4. The company developed the internal mindset that external strategies had a vital role to play in the company's growth. The corporate development office conducts a training program for operating managers. In the initial years, the central office for Corporate Development managed most of the external growth strategy. More recently, decision making has been decentralized so that division managers actively participate in the process.

These initiatives have generated 190 new venture transactions in the last nine years. Management has learned a number of important lessons, including:

1. The importance of an "operating champion" who is personally committed to the success of each new venture;
2. The need to be comprehensive in its due diligence;
3. The need to reject opportunities where target company management doesn't plan to continue with the business, or does not share a common vision with Bausch & Lomb.

EG&G—INTEGRATION OF STRATEGIC PLANNING AND ACQUISITIONS

EG&G has used strategic planning and financial control systems to manage the company's diversified activities for more than 20 years. The company's excess cash flow in the Mature defense professional services market has been deployed to acquire companies in Growth markets. EG&G's acquisition criteria include the following Perspectives on Value: (1) operations confined to a single well-defined market (Value and Performance markets); (2) Build market share; (3) sales growth of at least 15% per annum (New and Growth stage markets); (4) technological barriers to entry (Performance Market); and (5) use of pooling of interests accounting.

John Kucharski, who was appointed chief executive officer of the company in 1987 and chairman of the board in 1988, has redirected the company's acquisition program. One of his Perspectives on Value is an objective to make a larger acquisition, defined as a company with annual sales of more than $150 million. In the past the emphasis was wholly on small commercial technology companies competing in niche markets. Other changes include a willingness to dilute earnings for one year and to consider turnaround situations.

EG&G's total revenues of $2.7 billion for 1993 were divided into the following industry segments: Technical Services (1993 sales of $636 million), Department of Energy Support ($1,378 million), Instruments ($237 million), Mechanical Components ($245 million), and Optoelectronics ($201 million). The company's diversified activities are organized and controlled by business elements (profit centers); there are approximately 150 business elements. These units compete in small niche markets with annual revenues averaging $30–35 million per annum. Approximately two-thirds of the company's commercial revenues are derived from markets in which they hold the largest market share, with another 20–25% of revenues coming from markets where EG&G holds the number two position. A significant number of these markets have been entered through acquisitions.

It is this combination of diversified niche markets and leading market shares that underpins the company's above-average profitability (return on equity has averaged 21% for the past five years). Management has found a direct correlation between market share and return on investment.

The company consistently generates cash in excess of requirements for working capital, additions to fixed assets, and dividend payments. There is almost no need for investment in plant and equipment on the government side of the business, because contracts primarily involve management services at government-owned facilities and work on research and development programs.

Commercial products are produced mainly in assembly plants, which typically do not require large investments in fixed assets per dollar of sales. Excess cash flow has been used to enter new markets through acquisitions.

The company's diversified portfolio of products and services makes it somewhat difficult for investors to place an appropriate valuation on the company. Recent valuations of the stock have been constrained by negative investor sentiment toward companies with a heavy reliance on defense contracts. However, we expect that over the long term, shareholders will be well rewarded by the company's continued above-average profitability coupled with an increase in the relative profit contribution from commercial businesses stemming from its strategic acquisition program.

LORAL—STRATEGIC ACQUISITIONS IN A DECLINING INDUSTRY

Loral's strong growth trend began in 1972 when Bernard Schwartz, Chairman and Chief Executive Officer, took control of a nondescript electronics company with annual sales of $27 million. Sales for the March 1994 fiscal year were $4.0 billion. Historically, Loral pursued a three-pronged strategy: (1) focus on defense electronics, which represents an increasing percentage of total defense spending; (2) an aggressive acquisition strategy to broaden and strengthen proprietary defense electronics technology; and (3) expand international sales. Recently, the company added a fourth strategic objective: conversion of proprietary defense technologies into commercial applications.

Growth can be achieved in New and Growth Markets without acquisitions, but in Mature or Declining Markets a company's very survival as an independent entity may depend on acquisitions. The strategic plan must either identify acquisition opportunities or develop a HARVEST or RETREAT strategy, otherwise it will become a victim of price cutting as competitors seek to expand market share. Loral reacted to Battlefield Maturity caused by a Market Externality (collapse of the Soviet Union) by making acquisitions (taking advantage of competitors who wanted to RETREAT from defense businesses).

Loral's growth has been all the more remarkable because it has been achieved during a period of declining defense spending. Department of Defense outlays declined in real terms between 1985 and 1993 while Loral's sales expanded from $500 million to $4.0 billion. The company has taken advantage of the shrinking defense budget to purchase on favorable terms businesses from large companies that no longer have a strategic interest in the defense industry. In early 1994, Loral completed the largest acquisition in its history: the $1.5 billion purchase of the Federal Systems Division of IBM.

From an operational standpoint, each new division joining the company becomes a partner. Because these are not financial transactions, emphasis is placed on operational issues: management continuity, product synergy, marketing and technological cooperation. Divisional entrepreneurialism is basic to Loral's culture. "Loral is a family with shared values and common objectives," says CEO Schwartz. "While we are accountable to each other for our individual commitments, we also share a collective success."

Loral has found that acquisitions are the best way to BUILD positions in new sectors of the defense electronics market rather than pursue internal growth. Established companies have important advantages: the original company on a defense program enjoys an edge in bidding on the follow-on, upgrade contracts; R&D contracts favorably position a company to win production contracts; access to highly sensitive intelligence information is restricted; and foreign competitors for the most part have limited access to the U.S. Department of Defense market.

Loral has divested those parts of the acquired businesses that did not fit its long-term focus on defense electronics. Loral has realized important benefits from this strategy. Its negotiating position improves because the seller solves his problem in a single transaction. Examples of this technique include the following Loral transactions:

1. In March 1987 Loral purchased Goodyear's Aerospace division for $580 million in cash. A wheel & brake operation that did not fit Loral's strategic focus on defense electronics was sold for $460 million in April 1989. Thus Loral purchased the remaining defense electronics business with annual sales of about $370 million for $120 million.

2. In October 1990 Loral acquired Ford Aerospace (FAC) for a net price of $419 million after selling the BDM division of FAC and a 49% interest in FAC's commercial satellite business to Aerospatiale, Alcatel, and Alenia. In a complex transaction of this type, outside assistance is required. In the case of FAC, Loral established a holding company, which was 48.5% owned by an investment banking firm. In June 1992 Loral acquired the investment banking firm's equity interest in exchange for 6,150,000 shares of its common stock.

3. In August 1992 Loral purchased LTV Corp.'s missile and aircraft division for $475 million. The company teamed with Northrop Corp. and the Carlyle Group (a financial buyer) to top Martin Marietta's bid of $440

million. Loral retained LTV's missile business at a cost of $244 million, and the co-bidders kept other parts of the acquired businesses.

Between 1983 and 1993, Loral's sales from continuing operations grew at a 27% compound annual growth rate, and earnings per share increased 15% per annum. An erosion of price/earnings ratios accorded defense electronics stocks relative to other stocks offset part of the earnings gain. Loral common stock at the end of 1993 sold at 14 times earnings while the market P-E was 21. Loral common stock sold at an average P-E of 15 during the 1980–85 Reagan defense buildup, which was equal to or higher than the market multiple. Nevertheless, Loral shareholders over the last ten years still earned a 13.5% total annual return including dividends.

TRACOR—A BUSTED LBO

Tracor, Inc. is an example of a failed acquisition that was undertaken primarily for financial reasons, not achievement of a clearly defined strategic objective. This leveraged buyout of a defense electronics company which was undermined by excessive debt and a drop in defense spending, ended in bankruptcy. The principals who formed Westmark Systems, Inc. in 1986 as a vehicle for acquiring defense electronics companies had investment banking backgrounds. Their vision of opportunities in the consolidating defense industry was based on a financial, not operating, perspective.

In 1987, Westmark completed a tender offer for 87% of the then publicly traded shares of Tracor, Inc. The $837 million tender offer was financed by $710 million of debt and $127 million of equity. The crushing debt burden pushed the company into Chapter 11 bankruptcy in early 1991.

In December 1991 Tracor emerged from Chapter 11. Creditors who held $526 million of debt (a portion of the original $710 million of debt was repaid earlier and ownership of a former subsidiary, Littlefuse, Inc., was spun off to the creditors) received $60 million of long-term debt, 9,021,542 shares of Tracor common stock, and warrants to purchase 2,820,000 shares of stock. Westmark Systems, which had invested $127 million of equity in the LBO, received 978,458 shares of Class A common stock and warrants to purchase a total of 10,704,000 shares of common stock. Based on a year-end 1993 price of $9 per share for Tracor common stock, the former creditors' stock and warrants were worth approximately $117 million, and Westmark's common stock and warrant holdings were worth about $60 million. Thus, total debt and equity investments which cost $653 million were valued at $177 million at year-end 1993.

Why did Tracor enter bankruptcy while the other profiled companies have prospered? First, the principals who put together the Tracor LBO were deal specialists. The CEO recruited to run the business, Admiral Bobby Inman, had an impressive military background and experience as Director of the Central Intelligence Agency, but he did not have experience running private businesses for profit. Second, financial projections showing the company's capacity to service acquisition debt proved highly optimistic, which was typical of LBOs during this period. Admiral Inman has been quoted as stating, "Everyone in Congress knows that I know nothing about finance." The financing structure can have a major impact on post-acquisition success. A business manager cannot claim ignorance if the deal sours. Although the profiled companies have used debt to finance strategic acquisitions, they have maintained conservative debt-to-equity ratios.

With its debt burden reduced, Tracor has experienced nine straight quarters of increased profits since emerging from bankruptcy, and has completed a successful acquisition.

PERKIN-ELMER—STRATEGIC RESTRUCTURING AND DIVESTITURES

In the mid-1980s Perkin-Elmer management recognized that the company's disparate portfolio of technology businesses was unlikely to produce maximum returns for shareholders. After completing a strategic analysis of each business unit, management initiated a radical restructuring of operations in 1989–90 when the company was still profitable and had a balance sheet that could absorb the costs of restructuring. The motivation for the restructuring was succinctly explained by Horace McDonell, former chairman of the company and chief architect of the restructuring program, "Throughout most of the 1980s, the company's performance has been inconsistent and, for the most part, inadequate. It has been characterized by low return on equity, poor stock performance, and inadequate predictability and control."

Prior to the announcement of the restructuring plan on April 21, 1989, the company's principal operating divisions included analytical instruments, semiconductor production equipment, a West German avionics company, surface coating materials, and an optics division selling principally to the U.S. Department of Defense and NASA. A minicomputer division had been sold earlier. The company targeted its semiconductor equipment, West German avionics, and government optics businesses for sale.

Criteria used to decide which business units to divest included: sales and profit histories and forecasts for each unit; market share and competitive position; management strength; and compatibility with the core analytical instrument business. With the advice and assistance of its investment banker, the company developed a computer valuation model to estimate probable selling prices. Valuation model inputs included sales, assets, earnings per share, and price/earnings multiples for comparable companies.

The semiconductor equipment business (electron beam equipment and optical lithography machines) proved the most difficult to sell, reflecting the risks associated with the highly cyclical capital goods market, the need for large ongoing research and development expenditures, and a loss of market share to Japanese competitors. The semiconductor equipment sale was further complicated because a sale to a Japanese company would probably have been blocked by the U.S. Government due to national security considerations.

The divestiture of the semiconductor equipment division is a good example of the wisdom of seeking strategic buyers for hard-to-sell assets. A consortium of buyers with strategic interests in the semiconductor industry purchased the division. Silicon Valley Group, Inc., a manufacturer of semiconductor production equipment, was the lead buyer. IBM, an important Perkin-Elmer semiconductor production equipment customer with a vested interest in the next generation of technology, provided Silicon Valley Group with a firm backlog of business and purchased a minority equity stake in the newly formed company. Perkin-Elmer retained a minority equity interest in the operation and ownership of a manufacturing plant, which was leased to the buyer.

Operating managers of the divested businesses were offered incentives and severance guarantees so they would play a constructive role in the sales process. In two divestitures, operating managers and employees became part of the buying groups. Business managers may undermine a divestiture if they are not given incentives to support the process. The uncertainty created by a divestiture announcement can cause employee morale and division performance to suffer. To overcome this potential problem, a buyer must also support key employees of the target company by providing information on post-acquisition plans. Otherwise, there is a risk that there will be an insidious deterioration of the business that will prove costly after the closing.

Perkin-Elmer received a total of $345 million in cash from the divestitures, took back $27 million in notes and securities, and retained minority equity interests valued at $14.6 million in three of the divested units. The company incurred cash restructuring expenses of approximately $80 million. In fiscal 1990, the company used $248 million of the cash proceeds to purchase 10.1 million shares of its own common stock at $24.50 per share through a Dutch auction, reducing total shares outstanding by 23%.

Following the divestitures, Perkin-Elmer's core businesses were analytical instruments and surface enhancement coating systems and materials. In order to improve the profitability of the analytical instrument business, the company made a $53 million provision in fiscal 1991 for restructuring costs. In February 1993 Perkin-Elmer exchanged 10.1 million of its common shares in a merger with Applied Biosystems, a supplier of systems and instruments used in life sciences research. In July 1993 management announced the planned divestiture of its material sciences business. One of the principal markets for material sciences is the aircraft engine market, which has been adversely impacted by the deteriorating profitability of the airline industry (Market Externality).

In 1991–92 the company's analytical instrument and materials technology businesses have been hurt by the U.S. recession, so it is too early to predict financial returns for the remaining businesses. For fiscal 1993, Perkin-Elmer reported total revenues of $1.0 billion and net income of $24 million. Over a complete business cycle the remaining operations should produce returns significantly higher than those that would have been earned by the historical businesses.

In time Perkin-Elmer shareholders should be well rewarded. Even at this juncture (late 1993) the stock is selling at 50% above its price prior to the divestiture announcement in April 1989. The question of what would have happened to shareholder values in the absence of restructuring is somewhat subjective, but we feel that downturns in the defense and semiconductor industries would have hurt the company. In a communication with the authors concerning the results of the program, Horace McDonell stated "Disaster had we not done it!"

In terms of magnitude and complexity, the Perkin-Elmer restructuring was a major strategic exercise and is a good example of the key principles of divestitures:

1. Strategic plans and valuations for each of a company's business units must be prepared before final acquisition and divestiture decisions are made.

2. Capital should be concentrated in those businesses where a competitive advantage seems sustainable.

3. Low-return businesses should be sold and proceeds invested in higher-return businesses or returned to shareholders in dividends or stock repurchases.

4. A strategic buyer will often pay the highest price for businesses to be divested because of the buyer's opportunities to enhance competitive positions.

5. Managers of units to be divested must be actively involved in the selling process.

6. Acquisitions and divestitures are a continuous process (Applied Biosystems and Material Sciences are examples).

SYSCO CORPORATION—ACQUISITIONS TO ENTER NEW MARKETS

Sysco is an outstanding example of the benefits that can be derived from a disciplined and highly focused strategic acquisition program. The Sysco management team led by John Baugh, founder, and John Woodhouse, Chairman, has concentrated the company's acquisition program in the foodservice industry (Price and Value Market).

Sysco Corporation has found that a fragmented industry offers fertile ground for a company to use acquisitions to achieve significant market share gains (BUILD) and dynamic growth. In 1969 the institutional food-service distribution industry was highly fragmented when John Baugh convinced nine regional food wholesalers to merge their operations. He recognized that customers would increasingly place their orders with multi-line, one-stop distributors rather than with distributors selling narrow product lines. Multi-line distributors would also benefit from economies of scale by operating large warehouses, an increase in the average dollar value of each delivery stop, volume purchasing, and the use of private label merchandise. Considering the increase in the percentage of dollars spent on food away from home as a percentage of total food outlays, Mr. Baugh anticipated that Sysco would enjoy an advantage in implementing its strategy in a growth industry.

The principal strategic objective of Sysco's acquisition program is to gain access to new geographical markets (Modify Competitive Position). In each geographical market there are well established distributors with experienced sales representatives and strong customer relationships. The company has found that it is faster and less expensive to enter a new market by buying an established distributor than building a position from scratch. The majority of its entries into new markets have been via acquisitions. Occasionally, it will use an established base, which is within driving range of a new market, for example, its entry into San Diego from Los Angeles.

After acquiring a distributor, Sysco typically closes the existing warehouse and builds a much larger facility that can support a broader product line and effectively serve customers within a radius of approximately 250 miles. The acquired operation is substantially upgraded by introducing Sysco's product line knowledge and expertise, computer systems, and planning disciplines. These changes substantially improve the productivity of the acquired distributor's sales force. The results can be dramatic. For example, a distributor acquired in 1982 with annual sales of $9 million is now doing $250 million in annual volume.

Since its founding in 1969, when annual sales totaled $115 million, Sysco's sales climbed to $10 billion in 1993. During the same period, the company acquired 53 distributors in new markets, and these distributors in turn made 20 purchases of product line assets. Since 1980, the company has paid $886 million for acquired companies, of which the 1988 purchase of CFS Continental accounted for $700 million.

After identifying the new markets it would like to enter, Sysco management directly contacts the major distributors in that market, which are typically family-owned private companies. Most of the company's acquisitions have resulted from this search technique. In many cases, management has maintained a dialogue with a target company for a number of years before an acquisition is consummated (Search and Screen Steps). Sysco did employ an investment banker in the CFS Continental transaction because there was a rival bid. Sysco needed access to experience and expertise in contested takeovers, which it did not possess internally.

Top Sysco management handles acquisition negotiations and structuring of financial terms. Sysco operating managers are generally consulted for their opinions when the target company's marketing territory overlaps the manager's territory. Once an acquisition is completed, operating managers will be responsible for implementing the Sysco systems at the acquired company.

Management's Perspectives on Value include a cardinal pricing rule: the price must not dilute the earnings of existing shareholders. It is believed that a dilution of earnings would result in a lower stock price. A purchase for cash must show a return in the first year at least equal to what the company would otherwise have earned on its idle cash. In addition to the price to be paid for the acquisition, a key qualitative consideration is whether existing management has the desire and capability to expand the business at a rapid pace. This requires that existing management of the acquired distributor stays in place.

The problems that the company has experienced in its acquisition program have primarily involved a longer-than-anticipated period to integrate Sysco's systems with those of the acquired company. They have acquired only one company that was later closed down. In that case, the primary problem was the inability of existing management to adapt to the Sysco system; a secondary problem was Sysco's failure to understand the sales potential of the served market.

For the past 20 years, Sysco's sales have increased at an average annual rate of 17.6%. Acquisitions contributed approximately one-third of total sales growth. In calculating the contributions of acquisitions, an acquired distributor's sales for the 12 months prior to acquisition are used to measure the sales impact. Subsequent growth is considered internal growth. During this same period the company estimates that food product inflation averaged 2.2% per annum.

Sysco's net income has kept pace with sales growth, increasing at a compound annual rate of 17.6% over the past 20 years while earnings per share expanded at a 17.9% annual rate. The company's shareholders have been the beneficiaries. Over the past ten years the average price of the stock has increased at a compound annual rate of 18.7%.

THERMO ELECTRON—A DYNAMIC GROWTH STORY

Thermo Electron Corporation, a diversified technology company, was founded in 1956 by George Hatsopoulos, a professor of thermodynamics at MIT. The company's dynamic growth rests on three building blocks: strategic planning, acquisitions, and a decentralized management structure. Strategic planning gives the company the flexibility to respond to shifting customer needs and enter New markets. An innovative element in Thermo's decentralized management structure is the "spin off" of equity interests in subsidiaries through public offerings.

The company reported total revenues of $1.25 billion for 1993, which broke down as follows: Analytical Instruments, $517 million; Alternative-energy Systems, $243 million; Process Equipment, $168 million; Services, $122 million; Biomedical Products, $128 million; and Advanced Technologies, $76 million. Thermo Electron's sales in 1981 totalled $231 million.

In its early years, the company was engaged primarily in research and development, exploring commercial applications of thermodynamics research with an emphasis on ways to improve the energy efficiency of energy intensive process industries. When the strategic decision was made to convert from an R&D firm to an operating company, management chose the acquisition route to achieve its goal. The company's first acquisition occurred in 1968 when it acquired the Holcroft Corporation, a manufacturer of high-temperature furnaces used for heat treating metals. Since 1968 the company and its majority-owned subsidiaries have acquired a total of 75 companies. Over the last ten years, acquisitions have accounted for one-third of the company's total growth.

Of the acquisitions completed to date, the majority have resulted from deals brought to the company by investment bankers and other third parties. The remaining 20% resulted from company-initiated contacts with target companies. Thermo's experience is typical of active strategic buyers: It is important to establish a network of intermediaries to promote maximum deal flow (Search Step).

Management seeks a first-year financial return on the price of an acquisition at least equal to what would have been earned on cash in the bank. Within 3 to 5 years the goal is a 30% to 40% pretax return on the total acquisition investment (cash and securities paid, plus debt assumed, plus additional net cash investments in the acquired business). Financial due diligence is the responsibility of the subsidiary controller who will oversee the financial performance of the acquired company.

Thermo Electron generally expects management of the acquired company to continue to manage the business. The company does not have excess management resources that can be transferred to acquired companies. The operating managers who will have oversight responsibility for the acquired company assist corporate staff to evaluate acquisition opportunities. The two or three acquisitions that developed serious problems lacked management depth at the time of acquisition.

Thermo Electron has created an innovative solution to the challenge of managing diverse operating divisions and providing capital for internal growth and acquisitions. Since 1983 it has pursued a strategy of "spinning out" minority equity interests in various subsidiaries to outside investors.

At year end 1993, there were nine publicly held majority-owned subsidiaries, all traded on the American Stock Exchange. Proceeds from the sale of newly issued shares go to the subsidiaries; the parent does not sell any of its stock. The publicly held subsidiaries typically issue convertible debentures in the United States and Europe to meet subsequent financing needs.

There are now nine Thermo Electron subsidiaries with outside shareholders:

Name of Subsidiary	Thermo Electron's Ownership Percentage
Thermedics	52%
Thermo Instrument	81
Thermo Process	72
Thermo Power	52
ThermoTrex	55
Thermo Cardiosystems(1)	57
Thermo Voltek(1)	67
Thermo Fibertek	80
Thermo Remediation(2)	67

(1) Subsidiaries of Thermedics.

(2) Subsidiary of Thermo Process Systems

Public offerings of minority interests have produced the following benefits: (1) business managers and employees of the subsidiaries develop a closer identification with the strategic goals of the subsidiary; (2) the chief executive officer gains recognition as the head of a public company; (3) subsidiaries become self-financing; and (4) the valuation of the parent company's common stock is higher than that typically accorded a conglomerate with wholly-owned subsidiaries. With market prices available for subsidiaries, investors are better able to value the company's individual businesses.

Thermo Electron completed its initial public offering in 1967. Shareholders have benefitted from the company's acquisition program and spin-off strategy because consolidated growth is a great deal faster than it would have been otherwise. In turn, the above-average growth in earnings per share has been reflected in a premium P-E ratio for the parent company. The market value of Thermo Electron common stock at year-end

1993 was $2.0 billion. From 1983 to 1993 Thermo Electron shareholders saw the value of a share of common stock increase by a compound annual rate of 21%.

THERMO INSTRUMENT—FOCUSED INDUSTRY ACQUISITIONS FUEL GROWTH

Thermo Instrument Systems, which is Thermo Electron's largest and most profitable publicly held subsidiary, has BUILT a leading position in the analytical instrument industry through a series of acquisitions. The objective of its acquisition program is to add product technologies and niche businesses in order to realize the economies of scale of a broad analytical instrument product line. The strategic aspects of the company's acquisition program are best understood by examining the competitive characteristics of the analytical instrument industry. A company with a multi-instrument product line benefits from economies of scale. Its sales force can offer customers solutions for multiple problems, increasing sales per employee. The costs of research and development can be spread over a larger sales base.

There are significant barriers to entry into established niche analytical instrument markets (Performance Markets), which make acquisitions a better growth strategy than internal development. Fragmented niche markets are usually not large enough to support more than a few competitors. Changes in technology tend to be evolutionary and feature product enhancements and greater ease of use. Thus, it is difficult for a new competitor to displace an established supplier with a technological breakthrough. The analytical chemists and other professionals who make the purchase decisions are a conservative group and give preference to known vendors. Purchase decisions are primarily based on the performance characteristics of the instrument and the reputation of the supplier. Thus, a Price strategy is usually not effective. An installed instrument base produces significant recurring maintenance and consumable revenues, giving the entrenched vendor a competitive cost advantage. Finally, it is costly to build the direct sales and maintenance organizations that are necessary in this industry.

Thermo Instrument has made the following major acquisitions:

1. The 1986 acquisition of the Jarrel/Ash division of Allied Signal, which at the time of acquisition was doing about $30 million in sales. The principal Jarrel/Ash products are atomic absorption (AA) and atomic emission (AE) spectrophotometer.

2. The June, 1989 purchase of the liquid chromatography (LC) division of Milton Roy for $22 million in cash. Liquid chromatography sales were in the area of $25 million per annum.

3. The May 1990 acquisition of Finnigan Corporation for $110 million in cash. The aggregate cost exceeded the estimated fair value of the acquired assets by approximately $90 million, which is being amortized over 40 years. Finnigan Corporation, a world leader in the production and marketing of highly sophisticated mass spectrometers, reported total revenues of $131 million for 1988. Foreign sales were $71 million. The Finnigan acquisition added new product lines and improved access to customers in the medical industry.

4. The August 1992 purchase of Nicolet Instrument Corporation at a cost of approximately $168 million by means of a tender offer. Thermo Instrument gained entry into a new market sector: Fourier transform infrared (FT-IR) spectroscopy. For the fiscal year ending March 29, 1992, Nicolet reported total operating revenues of $139 million, a loss from continuing operations of $6.3 million, and shareholders' equity of $60.3 million. In early 1993 Thermo Instrument sold Nicolet's biomedical instruments business to Thermo Electron for $75 million, including the assumption of debt. Biomedical instrument sales were about $55 million per annum.

5. The February 1993 purchase of Spectra-Physics Analytical, Inc., a manufacturer of liquid chromatography and capillary electrophoresis instruments, for approximately $69 million in cash. The business, which was previously a unit of Spectra-Physics AB of Stockholm, had 1992 revenues of approximately $68 million.

6. The March 1994 acquisition of several instrument businesses from Baker Hughes for $87 million in cash. The acquired businesses had combined sales of $129 million in 1993.

Thermo Instrument's Perspectives on Value emphasize the potential improvement in profitability of the acquired product lines. Most of the acquisitions listed showed below-average profitability prior to acquisition. Thermo Instrument's CEO, Arvin Smith, has a demonstrated ability to increase the profitability of acquired companies.

Thermo Instrument completed its initial public offering in 1986 at a price of $3.56 per share (adjusted for subsequent stock splits). The company's revenues climbed more than tenfold from $52 million in 1986 to $584 million in 1993. At year end 1993 the stock was selling at $35 per share, producing compound annual gains of 36% for its shareholders since the IPO in 1986.

CONCLUDING THOUGHTS

The companies profiled in this chapter show that strategic acquisitions will help grow businesses and create shareholder value. EG&G, Loral, Sysco, Thermo Electron, and Thermo Instrument have all built much larger companies through strategic acquisitions than would have been possible relying only on internal growth. Perkin-Elmer has used strategic divestitures to focus on core businesses where it has competitive advantages on the market battlefield. Tracor demonstrates the risks of "financial engineering" and a lack of a strategic purpose.

These strategic acquirers did not learn their lessons overnight. A serious long-term commitment is required, led by the company's CEO and backed by business managers (Champions). This book will bring you up to speed faster and result in fewer missteps than if you plunge into the complex deal business without a reliable guide.

You are now ready to *Grow and Enhance the Value of Your Business Through Strategic Acquisitions:*

- **Visualize the Market Battlefield.**
- **Develop a Strategic Battle Plan.**
- **Use acquisitions (divestitures) to facilitate a strategic plan.**
- **Follow the Strategic Acquisition Process Steps: Search, Screen, Critical Evaluation, and Integration.**

The resulting growth and enhanced value of your business will be well worth the effort!

Introduction to Appendices

The Appendices comprise an integrated methodology. Forms and detailed instructions are provided for each Appendix (shown in bold type). The Appendices are shown in the sequence that would normally be followed in the acquisition process. First, the **Market Battlefield Summary** forms the basis for the **Strategic Battle Plan,** which in turn leads to the development of a strategic initiative and the selection of a target company. Next, a **Profit & Loss (P&L) Forecast** and a **Forecasted Investment Plan** are prepared for the target company. These Plans provide the target company financial data required for the **Valuation Models: Comparables and Discounted Cash Flow.**

The first iteration of this process results in a decision on the strategic and financial desirability of the target company which, if positive, leads to negotiation of a Letter of Intent. All forms are then revised during the Critical Evaluation Step, which ends with a Definitive Agreement. The final iteration is during the Integration Step when all forms except the Valuation Models are revised. Although the Profit and Loss (P&L) Forecast and Forecasted Investment Plan are used to forecast the financial performance of the target company, they are also a useful management tool for measuring the financial performance of the acquiring company and as a benchmark for comparative financial analyses of target companies.

As will be explained in the detailed instructions for each form, forecasts for the target company incorporate any changes planned in operations of the target company. For example, headquarters expenses for the target company may be eliminated but there may still be an allocation of corporate overhead from the acquiring company.

Appendix A

Market Battlefield Summary

The Market Battlefield Summary form lets you translate the Market Battlefield model into a working description of your market to provide the conceptual basis for a business strategy. It is divided into nine distinct sections of information required to describe the market battlefield:

1. Product or Service
2. Customers
3. Customer Need and Shape of Battlefield
4. Market Alternatives
5. Externalities
6. Market Saturation
7. Competitors
8. Market Size (History and Projections)
9. Market Maturity

Focus your efforts on succinctly describing each section; review the information entered with your marketing and industry specialists to improve its accuracy. Over time you should continuously collect more and better information to update this form to account for changing market conditions. The quality (accuracy and timeliness) of the information entered in this form will make the difference between winning and losing market battle plans. But, what specific information should be entered in each of the nine sections?

Section 1—Product or Service (offered)

A succinct description of the product or service offered. This description will define the scope of your market battlefield. If too broad, you will not be able to focus on the appropriate set of customers, their needs, and competitors. If too narrow, you will miss customer opportunities and competitor actions. It should include the products and services you currently provide and those to be added over the five-year forecast period. For example, if you owned a domestic airline:

1. Air passenger transportation service—too broad?
2. Scheduled air transportation passenger service—too broad?
3. Scheduled, coach class air transportation passenger service—too broad?
4. Regularly scheduled, coach class air transportation passenger service—too broad?
5. Regularly scheduled, coach class air transportation passenger service with average price of $0.15 per passenger mile—too broad?
6. Regularly scheduled, jet (turbine), coach class air passenger transportation service with an average price in excess of $0.15 per passenger mile—too broad?
7. Regularly scheduled, jet (turbine) coach class air passenger transportation service with average price in excess of $0.15 per passenger mile with full cabin meal service—too narrow?

How do you know when your product or service description is too broad or too narrow? First, does the description accurately describe your existing products or services. That is, does it exclude a significant portion of your existing products or services? If so, it may be too narrow. Does it include products or services that you do not supply or plan to supply? Then it may be too broad.

Think about your competitors—those taking customers from you or from whom you are taking customers. Does your product or service description include or exclude products or services used by competitors to take away business? Are these products "market alternatives" or just variations in the products and services offered in your market? If you're a niche, performance, or price competitor, you may tend to define your product or service too narrowly, concentrating on your niche and other related niche competitors.

Your description of products and services will define "market alternatives," those products or services that satisfy the same customer needs in a different way. For example, if we choose description #6 of a domestic airlines market:

"Regularly scheduled, jet (turbine), coach class air passenger service with an average price in excess of $0.50 per passenger mile,"

market alternatives would then include:

1. Unscheduled air passenger service
2. Non-jet (piston propeller) air passenger service
3. Discount air passenger service (under $0.15 per passenger mile)
4. Rail service
5. Bus service
6. First class passenger service

These and other passenger transportation services must then be monitored as a "market alternative." The market alternatives will not be analyzed as critically as products or services in your own market. The risk of too narrow a definition of products or services is exclusion of direct competition from your Market Battlefield Summary.

If we choose description #1 of a domestic airlines market:

"Air passenger transportation service,"

market alternatives would then include non-air passenger transportation services: bus, train, automobile, etc. You would have to monitor a much larger set of competitors to maintain your awareness of competitive actions, that is, all air passenger services including charter services, unscheduled air services, corporate air services, small piston propeller services, etc. As you can see, your market battlefield would become unmanageably large with many competitors that would have very little effect on your competitive strategy.

Defining your product or service offering will always be a matter of judgment. It is not that easy. You must go through the process of looking at your market in the broadest sense (description #1 in the example) and in the narrowest sense (description #7 in the example). Then look at the intermediate descriptions in order to choose the most appropriate one for your markets. Spend time to develop the intermediate descriptions. Ask yourself:

1. Are my day-to-day competitors' products or services included in the description along with mine?
2. Can I manage the competitor data?
3. Am I inadvertently including products or services that I don't supply and never intend to supply?

4. If I change the described product or service offering, what customers and competitors will react?

You must use your judgment in describing the appropriate scope of your product or service offering, which in turn will define the size and character of your market battlefield. You should plan to continually re-evaluate this description and refine it until it most closely correlates your market battlefield to the competitive actions you experience (or will experience) in your operation of the business.

Defining your customers too narrowly will result in missed market opportunities and competitor actions. In the airline example, "Transcontinental first-class air travelers" was the only market served by MGM Grand Airlines. They concentrated on serving the unique needs of first-class air travelers between New York and Los Angeles. Unfortunately, the large domestic air carriers offered low cost first-class upgrades to frequent travelers. The economic downturn in the late 1980s also made air travelers more conservative in their spending for transportation.

Although MGM Grand Airlines was able to focus (and do a great job) on the unique needs of the first-class transcontinental air traveler, it built its business strategy around such a small set of customers that the slightest competitive action (discount upgrades) and economic change forced it out of business.

You must look at your customers in the broadest and narrowest sense. Define the sets of customers in between the broadest and narrowest definition and select the appropriate definition for your market. As with the product definition, the scope of your customer definition will determine the size and character of your market battlefield.

Section 2—Customers (served)

A succinct description of the customers served by your market. This description will limit the scope of your market battlefield to that set of customers served by you and your direct competitors including those that will be served during the five-year forecast period. For example, if you were an airline, you may describe your customers as:

1. Air travelers
2. Domestic (U.S.A.) air travelers
3. East Coast U.S. air travelers

4. East Coast U.S. business air travelers

5. Transcontinental first-class air travelers

If you define your set of customers too broadly, you may not be able to satisfy their specific needs. If you define them too narrowly, you will miss market opportunities and competitive activities.

Defining your customers too broadly will require you to satisfy the most diverse set of customer needs. In the airline example above, description #1, "air travelers," requires you to address the needs of all air travelers. If you are American Airlines or United Airlines, this definition may be appropriate. However, even these airlines segment their market battlefields into customer sets having specific needs to better identify and satisfy those needs.

Section 3—Customer Needs

Think about why the customers you have described in Section 2 will be motivated to purchase products or services offered in Section 1 of this Market Battlefield Form.

The generally accepted theory of customer motivation was postulated by Abraham H. Maslow and is based on the following premises:[1]

1. A person will have many needs.
2. These needs will vary in importance and, therefore, can be ranked in hierarchy.
3. The person will seek to satisfy the most important need first.
4. When the person succeeds in satisfying an important need, it ceases being a motivator for the time being.
5. The person will then turn his or her attention to the next most important need.

According to Maslow, individual needs can be ranked in order of importance from (most important) physiological needs, safety needs, social needs, esteem needs, and self-actualization needs.

For individuals these are defined as:

1. *Physiological Needs*—the fundamentals of survival, including hunger and thirst.

---

[1] Abraham H. Maslow, *Motivation and Personality* (New York: Harper & Row, 1954).

2. *Safety Needs*—concern over physical survival, ordinary prudence, which might be overlooked in striving to satisfy hunger or thirst.
3. *Belongingness and Love Needs*—striving to be accepted by one's family and others close to them.
4. *Esteem and Status Needs*—striving to achieve a high relative standing, including prestige, mastery, and reputation.
5. *Self-Actualization Needs*—A desire to develop personal value systems that lead to self-realization.

For business we may rank needs in order of importance (most important first) from operations needs, regulatory and safety needs, customer acceptance needs, and status needs.

For business these can be defined as:

1. Operations Needs—the fundamental needs of raw materials, trained workers, utilities necessary to manufacture goods or provide services.
2. Regulatory and Safety Needs—the basic need to comply with rules, regulations, and reporting requirements imposed on business by acts of law or governing bodies.
3. Customer Acceptance—The need to be accepted by customers as a well defined supplier of goods and services, such as managing company image through advertising, product presentation, etc.
4. Status Needs—the desire to be the biggest or best supplier of products and services.

What is the need hierarchy for your business? Develop your own rank order for your customers.

When you think about your individual customer needs, they should fall into one of the individual customer need categories. The customers pursuing needs at the top of this list will tend to be more consistent through economic downturns as they will always require the basics of food, water, and shelter. Customers motivated to satisfy needs lower on the list will tend to be more cyclical as they will forego self-actualization needs to satisfy more basic needs.

For example, customer needs for air transportation may be:

1. Commuting weekly to job location.
2. Regular business travel to meet job requirements.

3. Regular business travel to meet job requirements while maintaining contact with the office and working on job-related tasks.

4. Occasional job-related travel.

5. Regular personal travel to meet family.

6. Vacation travel.

As you can see, the air traveler at the top of the list is driven to travel by a very basic need to earn a living, where the air traveler at the bottom of the list is satisfying a discretionary need. What type of need is driving your customer? Is there a segment of your market that is driven by basic needs and a segment driven by more discretionary needs?

Next consider the needs of your customers (where appropriate) to establish the driving force behind their needs.

Is the customer in our example commuting to job locations via air travel to satisfy a government contract? Is the vacation travel to satisfy family needs? What is the driving force behind the customer needs? The above air transportation example may be rewritten to say:

1. Commuting weekly to job locations. Required under provisions of federal government DOE contracts.

2. Regular business travel to meet job requirements to coordinate federal transportation policy.

3. Regular business travel to meet job requirements to coordinate sales meetings while maintaining key account status.

4. Occasional job-related travel to review status of NASA government contracts.

5. Vacation travel to satisfy family entertainment needs.

These examples may seem too specific—but when you consider what drives a customer's needs, you have better insight into future market changes. For example, what impact does a reduction in DOE government spending have on example #1? What effect do increased divorce rates have on example #5? If you're selling widgets to a defense contractor, you had better know what contracts are driving their purchase requirements in order to properly assess their needs. If you are supplying metal to a machine shop that sells to the General Motors Saturn automobile plant, you had better understand the needs of the Saturn plant as they will drive your customer needs.

The customers' needs define the shape of the market battlefield as described in Chapter 2. If customers' needs are driven primarily by obtaining the lowest possible cost product, the market is described as a Price market. If the customers' needs are driven primarily by obtaining the best product performance, the market is described as a Performance market. If there is an equal number of customers desiring price or performance, the market is described as a Value market. Identify the overall needs of customers in your market by checking the appropriate Shape of Battlefield box (Price, Value, Performance) on the Market Battlefield Form.

When you define customers' needs, you must describe the motivating factors behind the customer's purchase decision. Satisfying these needs will be the focus of your business strategy.

Section 4—Market Alternatives

Market alternatives are those products or services that will satisfy your customer needs but are not defined in the "Products and Services" section of the Market Battlefield Form. They directly affect market maturity and therefore the growth (or decline) of your markets. For example, with a passenger automobile, market alternatives may be:

1. Pick-up trucks (+)
2. Rail transportation (+)
3. Air transportation (+)
4. Bus transportation (−)
5. Motorcycles (−)
6. Aircraft, private (−)

In listing market alternatives you should also indicate the growth trend in the market alternative with a (+) for growth and a (−) for decline. Also rank market alternatives in order of those having the most impact on your market size. As in the above example you can see the pick-up truck market is growing (indicated by [+] sign) and is having the most impact on the passenger automobile market. Private aircraft has the least impact on the passenger automotive market and is a declining market. You must first identify market alternatives to your products and services. Then you must continuously evaluate market alternatives in order to understand market maturation and predict the future of your market battlefield.

Section 5—Externalities

Externalities are those forces outside your market that cause the total market to rise or fall. For the scheduled air transportation passenger carrier, externalities are things like:

1. Federal government deregulation of air fares.
2. Local landing fee increases.
3. Oil price increases due to Middle East wars.
4. Federal government mandated aircraft overhauls.

These are forces unrelated to customer or competitor actions that will affect the size or shape of the market.

Think about pending legislation, national disasters, materials shortages, or other events that are beyond your control that will affect the future of your market. These are externalities that must be identified to predict the future of your market battlefield.

Section 6—Saturation

Saturation is the percentage of customers in your market who have already acquired the products or services offered and have satisfied their need for that product for the forecast period (usually five years). Once purchased, if a product or service satisfies their need for the forecast period, the assumption is that the customer will not buy another product.

Not all markets saturate over a five-year forecast period. Many markets do not saturate as they offer consumable (not reusable) products such as food, paper towels, or gasoline. Some markets, such as new housing construction, telephones, environmental clean-up services and aircraft, do saturate over the five-year forecast period. Unless made obsolete with new product offerings, sales into saturating markets will decline.

You will need to understand market saturation in order to predict the future of your markets.

Section 7—Competition

Competitors are identified and analyzed in Section 7 of the Market Battlefield Summary Form. Each competitor should be listed and ranked according to size, with their strengths and weaknesses, recent sales history (this year and last year), and changes in sales revenue noted as both dollars

and percentages. Their strategic initiative is summarized as indicated by
their market behavior. This information forms the basis for selecting and
ranking target competitors for your future strategic initiatives.

How do you get this information?

1. Hire a Market Research firm.
2. Talk to industry specialists.
3. Continuously interview key industry managers.
4. Attend trade and professional sessions and ask questions.
5. Count cars in parking lots.
6. Talk to suppliers.
7. Talk to media consultants and ad space salespeople.
8. Talk to your own sales personnel.
9. Ask distributors who carry competing products.

Few U.S.-based companies do a good job of masking their sales and
marketing positions and strategies. Initially your competitive data may
just be estimated but over time you should sharpen this data to precisely
characterize your competitors.

Start by identifying your competitors. Ask your customers, your sales
force, your sales representatives, or distributors. You will often be surprised
to find new or different competitors. Talk to this same group about their
strengths and weaknesses. Your competitors' customers will tell you their
strengths and weaknesses. You can hire someone to survey customers or
do it yourself. Often your sales force will have a less objective perspective
on customer strengths and weaknesses. The customers' perception is what
counts, particularly as the strengths and weaknesses relate to specific customer needs.

Specific sales data is usually the most difficult information to obtain.
Trade associations may publish this information and salespeople at trade
shows are often proud to reveal their accomplishments (sales volume).
Ex-distributors, ex-sales representatives, and ex-employees frequently
know the sales volume of their former businesses. Over time you can develop a good information network to analyze the sales of your competitors.

The type of strategic initiative (Build, Hold, Harvest, Retreat)[2] is
usually guarded internal information but there are external indicators.

---

[2] Note: See page 25 for a detailed description of types of strategic initiatives.

1. What kind of people are your competitors hiring? Engineers to develop new products, salespeople to promote old products?
2. What does their advertising feature? Volume discounts or performance features?
3. How are they paying their bills? Obtain a Dun & Bradstreet report (your bank will often supply it to you) and look at their credit history.
4. Have inquiries been made about the possible sale of their business?
5. How are competitors reacting to competitive bids? Are they sacrificing profits to stay alive?

All of this information will let you speculate about the strategic initiative of your competitors. Remember, at best, most strategic initiative data on competitors is incomplete. However, it will aid in defining how competitors may react to your strategic initiative.

The selection of the target priority is completed as part of developing your Strategic Battle Plan. Leave blank at this time.

Section 8—Market Size

The market size is characterized by sales revenue dollars (best estimated in constant, uninflated dollars). There are two distinctly different sets of data to be developed in characterizing market size. Historical data is developed using industry information, often available through trade associations, market surveys, or market research reports. If you have to develop this information yourself, it will require lengthy interviews with individuals who have been in the business and know its history.

Forecasted market size is more a function of how you believe the market will grow (or shrink) in the next five years based on trends, market alternatives, externalities, and saturation, along with changing customer needs and market history.

We have found the most effective technique for forecasting the future growth (or decline) of your markets is called bracketing. First look at all of those factors that will tend to increase the size of the overall market and estimate their effect on market growth. Forecast the best case growth in future market sales volume based on these positive factors. Second, look at all of those factors that will tend to decrease the size of the overall market and estimate their effect on market growth. Forecast the worst case market sales volume. Reality is somewhere between the best case and worst case forecasts. You have "bracketed" the forecast. The amount of spread in the forecasts is your measure of market uncertainty.

If the best case forecast is only 10% higher than the worst case forecast, your estimate of future market sales should be relatively accurate. If your best case forecast is 100% higher than your worst case forecast, you have a high degree of market uncertainty. In this case your best estimate of future market size will be speculative at best. But you still must estimate the future of your markets in order to develop your future business strategy. Remember, history is just the starting point for market forecasts and must be modified by those forces affecting market maturity to estimate the future.

Section 9—Market Maturity

This category describes the current phase of market maturity, either New, Growth, Mature, Decline, or Residual, as described in Chapter 3. You should indicate the phase of market maturity consistent with the history of the market and your forecast of changes in overall market size in Section 8 of this form.

Market Battlefield Summary

1. Products or Services	2. Customers	
3. Customer Needs		Shape of Battlefield ☐ Price ☐ Performance ☐ Value
4. Market Alternatives	5. Externalities	6. Saturation (%)

7. Competition		Strategic Initiative	Strengths	Weaknesses	Sales This Year $ / Last Year $	Change $ / %
	Target Priority	#				
1.						
2.						
3.						
4.						
5.						
6.						
Total of _____ Others						

8. Market Size (Sales $)								9. Market Maturity
– 5 Yr	– 4 Yr	– 3 Yr	– 2 Yr	Last Yr	This Yr	Next Yr	Yr 2	Yr 3	Yr 4	Yr 5

Form A

_____ Date _____ Subunit _____ Strategic Business Unit _____ Company

The Strategic Battle Plan (Form B)

You have now completed the Market Battlefield Summary, permitting you to reflect on the overall market position of your business and to identify available opportunities (or lack thereof). The Strategic Battle Plan form (page 180) helps you translate these market opportunities into a design of action for your business. It lets you convert your competitive position (Advantages and Disadvantages) (Strengths and Weaknesses) into the most appropriate strategic initiative. It helps you estimate competitive reaction to your initiative and the effect of future market growth (maturity). It aids you in translating your strategic objective into a strategic initiative and then a tactical plan of action. It shows how to measure strategic success by achieving maximum possible return on your invested capital over the long term (five years) with acceptable levels of business risk.

How do you start? By asking questions about your current market battlefield position, how it may change in the future, and whether or not you can alter your position. What are the market opportunities (Opportunity Questions)? How will they change over time (Timing Questions)? What can you do to alter your position (Resource Questions)? The answers to these questions will lead to a definitive Strategic Battle Plan.

Market Opportunity Questions

1. Do I have a significant competitive advantage? Against one or many competitors?
2. Can I develop or acquire a significant competitive advantage? Against one or many competitors?
3. Is there an opportunity to combine with competitors to upset market equilibrium (given antitrust limitations)?

4. Is there a weak competitor, such as a large competitor spread too thin or a poor niche competitor?

5. Are customers loyal to suppliers or are they primarily transient customers? What percentage of my customers are first-time buyers versus repeat buyers?

6. Is market maturity forcing out competitors? What void are they leaving?

7. Is there a dominant competitor? Who manages the market? Will they aggressively pursue market opportunities and defend weaknesses?

8. Is market demand shifting away from competitor offerings (Performance Market shifting to a Price Market, for example)?

9. Has any competitor lost its strategic focus? A good niche competitor leaving its niche position to pursue a broader offering?

10. Can I overcome a significant strategic disadvantage (competitive weakness)?

11. Can I posture my product or service to more closely match the market's needs? Why are competitors finding receptive customers?

12. Should I counter new competitors or exit the market?

13. Are there new market growth opportunities in this market (i.e., is it a growing or declining market)?

14. Do market alternatives represent a better strategic opportunity?

15. Do market externalities threaten my market position or the market as a whole?

16. Is there a supplier of critical parts or services I could capture to produce a competitive advantage?

17. Are there distributors that can be acquired to produce a competitive advantage?

Resource Questions

1. What rates of return on invested capital are achievable in this market? Some markets characteristically yield very low returns on invested capital.

2. Do I have adequate (any) financial capacity to pursue a strategic initiative? How much?

3. Do I have management resources to dedicate to a strategic initiative? Who and how much time?

4. Do competitors have financial resources to defend against a strategic initiative? Which ones? How much?

5. Do competitors have the management resources (or can they acquire them) to defend against a strategic initiative?

6. Do dominant market competitors have adequate resources to take out marginal competitors with price wars? Are they currently running financial losses to attract customers?

7. Can I afford to project an overwhelming competitive advantage and inhibit competitor reaction?

8. Can I limit the resources available to competitors to retaliate against a strategic initiative?

9. Do I have adequate reserves beyond that required for the strategic initiative?

Timing Questions

1. How fast can competitors react to a strategic initiative?

2. Are market changes causing opportunities to grow or decline?

3. What is the current stage of market maturity? How fast is it changing?

4. Can I complete a strategic initiative in time to capture a market opportunity?

5. How quickly might market alternatives, externalities, or saturation force a change in my strategic initiative?

6. Can I surprise competitors and gain a market position before they can react to my strategic initiative?

7. How long will my competitive advantages last before being neutralized by competitors?

8. How long will my competitive disadvantages last before I can correct them?

DEVELOPING THE STRATEGIC BATTLE PLAN

First, select your target competitor or competitors—those competitors against whom you will focus your strategic initiatives. Then complete Sections 10 and 11 of the Strategic Battle Plan form as follows:

Strategic Battle Plan

10. Competitive Strengths (vs. Target Competitors)	11. Competitive Weaknesses (vs. Target Competitors)	12. Strategic Initiative	(T)ype	Now	Future	
Company A	Company A					Build
						Hold
Company B	Company B					Harvest
						Retreat
Company C	Company C					Probe

13. Objectives

14. Strategic Plan

15. Tactical Plan

16.	History						Future			
	− 5 Yr	− 4 Yr	− 3 Yr	− 2 Yr	Last Yr	17. This Yr	Next Yr	Yr 2	Yr 3	Yr 4	Yr 5
Market Size $										
Market Share %										
Sales $										
OP/Sales %										
ROI										

Form B

_____   _____   _____   _____
Date   Subunit   Strategic Business Unit   Company

180

Section 10—Competitive Strengths (vs. Target Competitor[s])

Identify your competitive strengths (advantages) against your targeted competitors. List these competitive strengths versus each target competitor in order of their ability to attract customers. This means that customers must recognize these strengths in order for them to be of value in developing your strategic plan. For example:

Competitive Strengths vs. Competitor X

1. 3% lower price
2. 50% more sales outlets
3. More dedicated sales organization
4. Immediate product availability

Once you have listed these competitive strengths against Competitor X, you must test their value. For #1 (3% lower price), is this significant to your targeted customers? In some markets it may be, in others not. For #2 (50% more sales outlets), does this mean 50% more availability of product to your target customers? Are these outlets convenient to your targeted customers? For #3 (more dedicated sales organization), this is not a competitive strength. The competitive strength would be what this more dedicated sales organization does that is recognized by the customer, for example, 10% more frequent customer contact, more prompt resolution of customer problems, etc. For #4 (immediate product availability), in some markets this is a real advantage. In others, availability within several weeks is acceptable. What does immediate product availability mean to your customers?

Remember to consider the type of market you are addressing. A Performance Market is looking for improved products or services; a Price Market is looking for the lowest price. Then look at the market segment you are targeting. There may be a price-driven segment of a Performance Market or vice versa. In all cases the effectiveness of your competitive strengths (advantages) is a function of how well they address your target competitors' customer needs.

Next consider the significance of your competitive strengths. To be significant enough to gain market share, a strength must upset market equilibrium. This means it must change customer behavior. A 3% price advantage may be real and may address customer needs but it may be inadequate to change customer loyalty. It may take a 10% price advantage to take loyal customers from targeted competitors. Significant competitive advantages upset market equilibrium and change customer behavior. Are your competitive strengths significant enough in the mind of the customer?

How defendable are your competitive strengths? In many cases a performance or price advantage is only a transient advantage. We have all seen price advantages in air travel destroyed within weeks. Can competitors react to your current strengths? How fast can they neutralize these strengths? List your competitive strengths and include an estimate of the life of these strengths, such as:

Competitive Strengths vs. Competitor X

1. 3% lower price (1 year)
2. 50% more sales outlets (3 years)
3. Immediate product availability (6 months)

This gives a more complete assessment of the value of your competitive strengths over the life of your strategic plan. It highlights the obvious: You cannot build a five-year strategic plan around a short-term competitive advantage.

Section 11—Competitive Weaknesses (vs. Target Competitor[s])

Identify your competitive weaknesses (disadvantages) versus your targeted competitors. List these weaknesses against each target in order of maximum exposure to your business, that is, the most significant weakness first. As with competitive strengths, weaknesses (or disadvantages) must be evaluated as perceived by your customers. For example:

1. 10% higher price (1 year)
2. 30% fewer sales outlets (3 years)
3. 30-day delivery (2 months)
4. Fewer product features (be specific where possible) (1 year)

As with competitive strengths, identify (in parentheses) the anticipated life of the competitive disadvantage.

Once listed, you must test the significance of these weaknesses. For #1 (10% higher price, 1 year), is this significant to your customers and to the targeted competitor's customers? Are there offsetting performance advantages? For #2 (30% fewer sales outlets, 3 years) is the existence of more outlets critical to reaching your customers and targeted competitor's customers or have you limited your outlets intentionally to focus on your specific market segment? For item #3 (30-day delivery, 2 months), is this a temporary delay caused by supplier problems or a large order, or does it represent a flaw in the way you operate your business? For item #4 (fewer product features, 1 year), are you losing customers to suppliers who have these features or are your targeted competitors adding these features? It is possible to add too many product features and drive away your customers with complexity and high prices.

Each of these disadvantages must be considered in developing your strategic position on the market battlefield relative to your targeted competitors. It is often not possible to fix all of your competitive weaknesses. In countering a (high) price weakness, you may lose performance advantages that are the basis for your existing market position. (You may also eliminate profits). In fixing a performance weakness, you may price your product higher than your customers are willing to pay. Recognizing your product or service weakness does not mean you must correct it. It means that it should be considered as a factor in developing your strategic initiative. If it blocks your initiative, then it should be addressed as part of the Strategic Battle Plan.

Section 12—Type of Strategic Initiative

There are five types of strategic initiatives: BUILD, HOLD, HARVEST, RETREAT and PROBE. Section 12 lets you indicate your current (NOW) type of strategic initiative and how you may change it (FUTURE) when you implement your Strategic Battle Plan. Chapter 2 develops the theory of selecting the appropriate strategy, which can be summarized as follows:

BUILD—To invest in a strategic initiative to BUILD market share. This strategy is most appropriate when you have a significant competitive advantage, no significant competitive disadvantages, competitors unwilling or unable to defend their customers, and an acceptable financial return on your investment. It is an acceptable strategy, in some instances, where competitors will defend their position but will not be able to block your initiative. To be successful you must either already have the opportunity (strengths and weaknesses) or develop it. You must have the resources to carry forward the BUILD initiative and time that initiative to match the market opportunity. To many businesspeople, BUILDING their market share is the only acceptable strategic initiative. The Strategic Battle Plan that leads to a successful

BUILD strategy is one that points to a significant competitive advantage and no significant competitive disadvantages in a segment of the market where competitors are unwilling or unable to deter your initiative. Otherwise, a less aggressive strategic initiative will let you preserve your resources for another growth opportunity. You can BUILD market share in all phases of market maturity. However, in New markets, you are usually forced to BUILD market share in order to survive. But, don't let your desire to BUILD your business be like Gettysburg to General Lee. Wait until you have gained competitive high ground, then seize the initiative.

HOLD—To invest only in strategic initiatives that help retain and defend market share (position). This doesn't mean you sit still. HOLD-ING your market position requires continuous investment, although usually at a lower rate than when building market share. It is the most appropriate strategy under the following situations:

1. Significant competitive advantage, no significant competitive disadvantage, competitors unwilling or unable to defend market share but return on investment is too low to justify a BUILD strategy.

2. Significant competitive advantage, no significant competitive disadvantage, competitors willing to defend their position and block a BUILD initiative where returns on investment are high.

3. Significant competitive advantage, no significant competitive disadvantage, competitors willing to defend market position but not aggressively with low returns on investment.

4. No significant competitive advantage, no significant competitive disadvantage, competitors unwilling or unable to defend market position and high return on invested capital.

5. Same as 4, but low return on invested capital where very little investment is required to HOLD market position.

6. No significant competitive advantage, no competitive disadvantage, competitors willing to defend market positions, and high return on investment opportunities.

7. Significant competitive advantage, a competitive disadvantage competitors will not attack, and potential returns on investment are high.

8. Significant competitive advantage, a competitive disadvantage competitors will not attack, and low potential returns on investment but little additional investment is required to HOLD market position.

9. Significant competitive advantage, a competitive disadvantage competitors will not attack, but returns on investments to defend market position are high enough to warrant a defense.

HOLDING market share is the appropriate strategic initiative in most phases of market maturity (except New, as explained previously). In a Growth market phase, it may take all of your available resources just to hold market share. In a Mature market, holding market share may present an opportunity to maximize your financial returns from investments during New and Growth phases of market maturity. In Decline and Residual phases of market maturity, returns on investment may be too low to justify strategies more aggressive than a HOLD strategy but adequate to maintain your market position. Holding a leadership position or a niche position in a market throughout the market maturation process can be a winning strategic initiative producing the best possible returns on invested capital.

HARVEST—To withdraw from a market battlefield making no additional investment or gradually reducing investment. This means you make an orderly, usually slow exit from the market, trying to withdraw as much of your investment capital as possible for redeployment into other markets. This is the most appropriate strategy in the following situations:

1. Significant competitive advantage, no significant competitive disadvantage; competitors will defend their competitive position and financial returns are too low to justify staying in the market.

2. No significant competitive advantage, no significant competitive disadvantage, competitors will not defend their market position but financial returns are too low to justify staying in the market.

3. No significant competitive advantage, no competitive disadvantage; competitors will aggressively defend their position, limiting you to an unacceptably small market share even though financial returns may be acceptably high.

4. No significant competitive advantage, no significant competitive disadvantage; competitors will aggressively defend their market position and financial returns on investment are unacceptably low.

5. Significant competitive advantage, a significant competitive disadvantage; competitors will not attack your market position but return on invested capital is too low to justify staying in the market.

6. Significant competitive advantage, a significant competitive disadvantage; competitors who will attack your competitive position so aggressively that even high returns on investment are not adequate to defend your market position.

7. Significant competitive advantage, a significant competitive disadvantage; competitors who will attack your competitive position and low potential returns on investment.

8. No significant competitive advantage, a significant competitive disadvantage, competitors who will not attack your competitive position and high potential returns that will let you extract your invested capital.

9. No significant competitive advantage, a competitive disadvantage, and competitors who will attack your market position but not too aggressively to permit extraction of your investment where there is high potential return on investment.

When appropriately applied, a HARVEST strategy can be a cash generating strategy to feed better business opportunities.

Harvesting market position is most common in more mature market phases such as the Decline and Residual phases. Often potential returns on invested capital are low in more mature markets and drive the HARVEST decision. However, any time you are faced with conditions described in the preceding nine situations, the HARVEST type strategic initiative may be most appropriate.

RETREAT—To exit the market battlefield as fast as possible while attempting to minimize losses.

Retreating from the market battlefield is a strategic initiative executed when facing insurmountable competition. To be successful, you should execute a RETREAT strategy with the same level of effort you put into a BUILD strategy while preserving your resources for other markets. It is the most appropriate strategy under the following situations:

1. No significant competitive advantage, a significant competitive disadvantage, competitors who are not attacking, but an unacceptably low return on investment.

2. No significant competitive advantage, a significant competitive disadvantage, competitors attacking where returns on investment are high but inadequate to defend your position.

3. No significant competitive advantage, a significant competitive disadvantage, competitors attacking where potential returns on investment are low.

In these three situations, the RETREAT strategy is clearly most appropriate, but you may be forced to rapidly exit the market battlefield at any time.

Whenever you face overwhelming competition that will destroy your market position, a RETREAT strategy may be appropriate. In a New or Growth market you may lose a critical resource and not find a replacement. In a Mature market, you may find a competitor willing to sacrifice all profits to drive you from the battlefield. In a Declining or Residual market you may find your customers' needs rapidly shifting from your specialized product offering to a low-cost alternative. The RETREAT strategy should be used at any phase of market maturity where you must exit the market and there is no chance of harvesting additional cash flow in the process. Where preserving your resources is of primary importance, a RETREAT strategy should be executed. Remember, waiting too long to retreat is a great temptation and very costly.

PROBE—To make a small investment to explore market battlefield strategic opportunities, limiting resources, and time invested. This strategy lets you test a perceived competitive advantage or disadvantage in a targeted market or market segment to determine customer acceptance. It can also be used to determine competitors' ability or willingness to defend their positions or attack new market entries.

Financial resources and time spent executing a PROBE strategy should be limited and considered expendable as most PROBE initiatives will not identify strategic market opportunities. It is a way to test a perceived market opportunity with the risk of acceptable losses.

STRATEGIC INITIATIVE SUMMARY

You should now be able to select the most appropriate type of strategic initiative based on your analysis of target competitors, your position on the Market Battlefield, the potential financial returns, and your ability to commit resources. There are two columns in Section 12 of the Strategic Battle Plan Form, one marked NOW and one marked FUTURE. This gives you an opportunity to indicate how your FUTURE strategy may change from the initiative you are currently executing. For example, you may be executing a HOLD strategy while planning for a change in market position that will permit a BUILD strategy. Or you may be in a HARVEST strategy but planning a RETREAT strategy in the future. You may be executing a PROBE strategy, which should lead to a BUILD strategy. Check the appropriate box (NOW) for the type of strategy you are currently executing. Then check the appropriate box (FUTURE) indicating the type of strategy you are planning. The focus of your Strategic Battle Plan will be the FUTURE strategy; the current (NOW) strategy is an indicator of past strategic initiatives.

Section 13—Objectives

Define your strategic OBJECTIVES in terms of measurable strategic position to be obtained:

1. Increase market share from 5% to 10% over two years while holding 10% gross profit margin, investing no more than $1 million (for a BUILD strategy).

2. Increase sales to Price segment of market from $1 million to $3 million over three years, investing no more than $1 million while maintaining profit margins (for a BUILD strategy).

3. Hold market share while increasing return on invested capital from 15% to 25% over two years (for a HOLD strategy).

4. Determine if sales of $500,000 per annum are obtainable in new market segment with a minimum return on invested capital of 25% in one year (for a PROBE strategy).

5. Exit market over three years while harvesting $1.5 million in positive cash flow (for a HARVEST strategy).

6. Exit market within six months with net losses not to exceed $200,000 (for a RETREAT strategy).

Each of these objectives is measurable in both a financial and strategic sense and relate to the type of strategy you selected. They set clear objectives to be used as a basis for your strategic and tactical plan.

Section 14—The Strategic Plan

The strategic plan should succinctly state your strategic position, how you will change it, what competitors you will target (or that are targeting you) to achieve the strategic objectives and how competitors will react. For example:

1. If you were setting item #1 (above) as your strategic objective, your strategic plan may read:
   BUILD market share by acquiring Company X to obtain a significant performance advantage of _____ over target Competitors

A, B, and C. Overcome sales and distribution weakness by increased investment in sales and distribution organization to counter reaction anticipated by competitors A and B. Competitor C is unable to react.

2. If you were setting item #2 as your strategic objective, your strategic plan may read:
BUILD market share by acquiring Company Z to obtain a significant advantage in the Price segment of the market. Maintain low overhead cost advantage of Company Z to defend against Competitors A and B.

3. If you were setting item #3 as your strategic objective, your strategic plan may read:
HOLD market share by investing in competitive advantage _____ to maintain position relative to target competitors A and B. Acquire Supplier Y to lower overall manufacturing costs to achieve target returns on invested capital. Competitors A and B should not react, providing competitive advantage can be maintained.

4. If you were setting item #4 as your strategic objective, your strategic plan may read:
PROBE the high performance segment of the market battlefield by acquiring distribution rights to high performance product X for one year. Determine how Competitors A, B and C will react.

5. If you were setting item #5 as your strategic objective, your strategic plan may read:
HARVESTING existing segment as investment to overcome competitive disadvantage _____ would be excessive given current low-profit margins in market. Withdraw cash by selling excess inventory and equipment while looking for a strategic buyer. Hold positive cash flow by reducing expenses as sales volume decreases and emphasizing remaining competitive advantages to selected customers.

6. If you were setting item #6 as your strategic objective, your strategic plan may read:
RETREAT from market as performance advantage _____ was lost to Competitor A and Competitors B and C are attacking competitive disadvantage _____. Low market returns do not warrant defensive investment. Search for strategic acquirer who can use remaining competitive advantages to complement existing business. Minimize losses by emphasizing price advantage associated with inventory liquidation.

Each of the above strategic plans tells how your market position competitive advantage or disadvantage will be affected by executing a specific type of strategy. It also addresses how specific targeted competitors are likely to react to your strategic initiative or are driving your strategic initiative. Remember, business strategy is "the science or art of meeting your competitors on the battlefield under advantageous conditions." Its corollary is: "When you can't achieve an advantage, exit the battlefield, preserving your resources." The strategic plan addresses the issue of strategic advantages and disadvantages and how you will change these vis-à-vis target competitors. The tactical plan details the actions you will take to implement your Strategic Plan.

Section 15—The Tactical Plan

The tactical plan is a detailed description of what actions you will take to achieve the strategic plan and the strategic plan objectives. Where the strategic plan talks about changes in your strategic position, the tactical plan details how you will make these changes. For example:

1. Implementing objective and strategic plan #1 above, your tactical plan may read:
   a. Acquire Company X assets for $750,000 in cash and notes (6%) by April 23, 1994.
   b. Invest additional $150,000 in advertising (magazine) targeted at performance market segment over three years.
   c. Invest an additional $100,000 in expanding distribution system and training sales force in sale of performance products.
2. For objective and strategic plan #2 above, your tactical plan may read:
   a. Acquire low-price Competitor Z for $800,000 in common stock in a pooling of interests transaction by September 19, 1994.
   b. Add Competitor Z products to current distribution where Z does not have coverage and invest up to $100,000 in retraining sales force.
3. Executing objective and strategic plan #3 above, your tactical plan may read:
   a. Acquire Supplier Y assets for $1.5 million cash by August 15, 1994, with transaction costs not to exceed $150,000.
   b. Shut down high-cost in-house manufacture of supplied parts by October 15, 1994, and obtain parts from Supplier Y at 50% lower cost.

4. For objective and strategic plan #4 above, your tactical plan may read:
   a. Acquire distributor rights for high performance Product X by June 1, 1994, at cost of $30,000.
   b. Develop a product introduction marketing plan by April 10, 1994, advertising and training plan by May 15, 1994, and a market test plan by June 1, 1994.
   c. Set up prototype manufacturing plant and build 100,000 of Product X by December 1, 1994, at cost not to exceed $30,000.
   d. Introduce product to selected market segments by December 1, 1994.
   e. Measure market response against test market plan by March 3, 1995.

5. Looking at objective and strategic plan #5, your tactical plan may read:
   a. Engage appraiser to value business by April 20, 1994.
   b. If value is in excess of $1.5 million, engage broker or investment banker to seek prospective buyers.
   c. If not sold by October 1995, commence sale of assets and liquidation inventory to recover $1.5 million investment.

6. Your tactical plan for objective and strategic plan #6 may read:
   a. Revise sales and marketing plan to discount product for liquidation of inventory over next six months.
   b. Sell off equipment as it becomes available and reduce staff as warranted.
   c. Immediately advertise facilities for sale through local real estate broker.
   d. Contact competitors who may be able to acquire product designs and tooling to complement their existing product lines.

Section 16—History of Strategic Business Unit

Market Size Total dollar sales into market in constant dollars (inflation removed) where possible, pull data from Market Battlefield Summary.

Market Share % = Sales $/Market size $

Sales $ Your total sales into market over past five years in constant dollars where possible.

OP/Sales % Divide the historic operating profit $ (net profit before tax and interest) by the corresponding sales $.

ROI   Return on Investment is the historic operating profit
                 $ divided by the net dollar investment in the
                 business.

Section 17—Future (Forecast) of Strategic Business Unit

Market Size $ Total dollar sales forecasted into market in constant
                  dollars where possible. Pull data from Market
                  Battlefield Summary.

Market Share   Forecasted sale $/Forecasted market size $

Sales $ Your forecasted sales as a direct result of your
                  strategic initiative.

OP/Sales %   Divide the forecasted operating profit from the Profit
                  & Loss Forecast Form by the corresponding forecasted
                  sales $ resulting from your strategic initiative.

ROI   Return on investment is the forecasted operating profit
                  $ divided by the net dollars invested in the business.
                  Investment increased by additional amounts invested to
                  accomplish your strategic plan or decreased by
                  amounts withdrawn from business over the forecast
                  period.

NOTE: You may have other measures replacing OP/Sales or ROI
       measures to indicate success of your strategy. However, you
       should use pretax and pre-interest measures to avoid addition
       of strategic factors to your data such as, interest rate fluctua-
       tions, tax rate fluctuations, etc.

SUMMARY

With the Market Battlefield Summary and Strategic Battle Plan, you
should be able to identify acquisition opportunities that are driven by strategic decisions. Review Chapter 4 to see how acquisitions can facilitate a
strategic plan.

Waltz Letter Example

(LETTERHEAD STATIONERY)

March 9, 1994

Mr.(Ms.) _____
Title
XYZ Corporation
108 Elm Street
Waverly, New York 14892

Dear Mr.(Ms.) _____:

    I am _____ at ABC Corporation and have admired your company's ability to _____. We manufacture/or provide services to the _____ industry and feel your products (or services) would complement our products (or services) by _____.

    Although you probably have not considered a joint venture or acquisition by a business like ours, I would like to meet with you to tell you more about our business and explore the possibility of a future transaction.

    I can assure you that our meeting will be in strict confidence and only to explore a joint business arrangement.

    I will call you in the next few days to discuss the possibility of a meeting.

Sincerely,

(Name/Title)

Appendix D

Profit and Loss (P&L) Forecast

The Profit and Loss (P&L) Forecast for the target company uses historical financial data, as reported, as a base from which to forecast annual operating results for the next five years. The target company P&L Forecast will reflect the financial contribution the acquired business will make to the combined company even if it is fully integrated into the operations of the acquirer. For example, the acquirer's strategic battle plan points to the need to add a new product line and, for time reasons, an acquisition is preferable to internal development. Further assume that the product will be manufactured in the target company's plant but will be managed by the acquirer's operating manager and marketed by the acquirer's sales force. Thus, each line in the P&L Forecast for the target company will reflect the anticipated changes in operations resulting from the strategic initiative. In this example, we estimate how sales would benefit an expanded sales force and show a reduction in the target company's historical headquarters expense among other adjustments. The P&L Forecast should be prepared using the accounting policies of the acquirer, for example, depreciation schedules. As will be discussed later, this adjustment methodology also applies to the Forecasted Investment Plan (Appendix E).

Shown below is the format used to develop the P&L Forecast for the target company. For further guidance in preparing the P&L, refer to the *Financial Assessment* discussion in the Critical Evaluation chapter (page 105) for questions that need to be answered when forecasting the line items.

Profit and Loss (P&L) Forecast

Line 1: SALES

Sales numbers are obtained from Section 17 of the Strategic Battle Plan (see Appendix B, page 180). Thus, the forecasted sales reflect

Profit and Loss Forecast

	Year −5	Year −4	Year −3
1. Sales			
2. Cost of Goods			
3. Gross Profit			
Gross Margin %			
4. Selling Expense			
5. Marketing Expense			
6. General & Admin. Expense			
7. R&D Expense			
8. Depreciation & Amort.			
9. Other Income (Expense)			
10. Operating Profit (EBIT)			
(3 −4 −5 −6 −7 −8 +9)			
Operating Profit Margin			
11. EBITD (8 + 10)			
12. Interest Expense			
13. Pretax Income (10–12)			
% of Sales			
14. Income Taxes			
Tax Rate			
15. Net Income (13–14)			

Year −2	Year −1	Year 1	Year 2	Year 3	Year 4	Year 5

the target company's sales as impacted by the strategic initiative
following acquisition. Therefore, it is not the target company's own
five-year forecast of its sales, but those sales as adjusted for the
strategic initiative, externalities, and other factors.

A single line is shown here, but a more detailed sales breakdown for
the target company by product line or division may be possible.
Sales information can also be tailored for the type of business being
analyzed. For example, the airline industry uses passenger miles and
revenue per passenger mile. A defense contractor that works off a
backlog could include beginning sales backlog, plus new orders, less
annual sales, to project ending sales backlog.

Line 2: COST OF GOODS

Include all costs that can be directly allocated associated with the
supplying of goods or services. Depreciation and amortization is
excluded. As with the sales numbers, segregate cost of goods by
business element when possible and reflect changes in operations
resulting from the Integration Plan, for example, plant closings or
employee reductions.

Line 3: GROSS PROFIT

Subtract Line 2 from Line 1. The Gross Margin % is Line 3 divided
by Line 1 multiplied by 100.

Line 4: SELLING EXPENSE

Include all direct selling expense during the time period such as
sales personnel, sales support staff, and associated overhead. If the
acquirer's sales force will sell the target company's products, that
portion of the selling expense should be reflected here.

Line 5: MARKETING EXPENSE

Include all direct marketing expense during the period such as
promotional and advertising costs, market research, and marketing
support staff, as well as allocated expense of the acquirer.

Line 6: GENERAL AND ADMINISTRATIVE EXPENSE

Include all direct general and administrative expense such as
corporate staff, legal expense, and accounting costs. Show any

allocation to the target company of the acquirer's corporate overhead as a separate item because it is not a controllable expense of the business unit manager.

Line 7: R & D EXPENSE

Enter all research and development costs incurred during the time period. Ongoing product support costs should be included in the cost of sales.

Line 8: DEPRECIATION AND AMORTIZATION

Enter annual depreciation and amortization of assets including increases resulting from write-up of assets allowable under purchase tax accounting. Also include amortization of intangibles (goodwill) to the extent that it is tax deductible.

Line 9: OTHER (INCOME) EXPENSE

Enter all income or expense not included above as directly involved in the business. For example, rental income from subleases, extra-ordinary severance expenses for planned work force reductions, and the cost of non-compete agreements would be included on this line.

Line 10: OPERATING PROFIT (EBIT)

Subtract lines 4, 5, 6, 7, and 8 from Line 3 and add (subtract) line 9 to calculate Operating Profit (EBIT—Earnings Before Interest and Taxes). Divide line 10 by line 1 and multiply by 100 to calculate the Operating Profit Margin.

Line 11. EBITD (EARNINGS BEFORE INTEREST, TAXES & DEPRECIATION)

Add Line 8 to Line 10 to calculate EBITD. This amount is operating cash flow.

Line 12. INTEREST EXPENSE

Enter total annual interest expense including the cost of target company debt assumed, projected amortization of debt, additions to debt, and any costs of seller notes. For divisional operations financed at the parent company level, also include an allocated interest expense.

Line 13. PRETAX INCOME

Subtract Line 12 from Line 10. The % of Sales equals Line 13 divided by Line 1 multiplied by 100.

Line 14. INCOME TAXES

Enter total federal, state, and foreign income taxes. For companies filing consolidated tax returns this will be an allocated number. Tax Rate equals Line 14 divided by Line 13 multiplied by 100.

Line 15. NET INCOME

Subtract Line 14 from Line 13.

Appendix E

Forecasted Investment Plan

The Forecasted Investment Plan projects balance sheet data and cash flow for the target company. The Investment Plan projects the assets and liabilities required to support the P&L Forecast. Historical data is as reported for Years −5 to −1. As with the P&L Forecast, the forecasted data (Year 1 to 5) incorporates anticipated changes in assets and liabilities resulting from strategic initiatives and integration of the target company with the acquirer's operations. Examples of changes affecting the Investment Plan include plant closings, asset sales, and revised actuarial assumptions for pension plans. These changes will be developed as part of the Strategic Battle Plan, as discussed in Section 15 (the Tactical Plan) of Appendix B.

The Investment Plan Financial Ratios include receivables aging (days sales outstanding), inventory turnover, sales/net operating assets, sales/net investment, and return on net operating investment. These ratios are compared with those of the acquiring company and the norm for the target company's industry to determine where improvement is possible. For example, if it appears that inventory turnover can be improved from six times per annum to seven times per annum in Year 3, then that ratio would be used to forecast inventory.

The *Financing Sources* section of the Investment Plan gives the business manager a tool to evaluate the financing implications of the forecasted assets, liabilities, and cash flow. As discussed in the *Limiting Financial Authority* section of the Integration Step (Chapter 11), you must immediately establish the lines of financial authority at closing. While we recommend that financing be done at the parent company level, the acquirer will want to relate financing to the investment plan so that the financing needs of the acquired company can be analyzed. By combining the financing needs of each division, a consolidated forecast of the sources and uses of financing can be prepared. This is the "bottoms up" approach. The overall financial guidelines of the parent company can be applied to the acquired business unit in the "top down" approach. For

Investment Plan

	Year −5	Year −4	Year −3
OPERATING ASSETS			
1. Accounts Receivable			
2. Inventories			
3. Accounts Payable			
4. Accrued Expenses			
5. Working Capital $(1 + 2) - (3 + 4)$			
6. Fixed Assets at Cost			
7. Accumulated Depreciation			
8. Net Fixed Assets $(6 - 7)$			
9. Other Assets (Liabilities)			
10. Net Operating Investment $(5 + 8 + 9)$			
OPERATING CASH FLOW			
11. Operating Profit			
12. Depreciation & Amortization			
13. Other Sources (Uses)			
14. Increase (Decrease) in Working Capital			
15. Capital Expenditures			
16. Operating Cash Flow $(11 + 12 + 13) - (14 + 15)$			
FINANCING SOURCES			
17. Short-term Debt			
18. Long-term Debt			
19. Equity			
20. Net Change Financing Sources			
FINANCIAL RATIOS			
21. Accounts Receivable (Days Sales Outstanding)			
22. Inventory Turnover			
23. Sales/Net Operating Assets			
24. Sales/Net Investment			
25. Return on Net Operating Investment			

Year -2	Year -1	Year 1	Year 2	Year 3	Year 4	Year 5

example, if a target company acquired in a pooling of interest transaction has debt to total capital ratio of 50%, whereas the acquirer's goal is a maximum debt ratio of 35%, the Financing Sources will show when that rate could be achieved given the cash flow projections. Therefore, although we recommend that the acquirer take charge of financing the target company, these financing decisions are best made in a feedback loop of "bottoms up" and "top down." The historical figures (Years −5 to −1) show how the business was financed in the past.

Shown below is the format used to develop the Investment Plan for the target company. For further guidance in preparing the Investment Plan, refer to the *Financial Assessment* discussion in the Critical Evaluation (chapter 9) for questions needing to be answered when forecasting these items. All line items are forecasted using the acquirer's accounting and reserve policies.

INVESTMENT PLAN

Operating Assets

Line 1:   ACCOUNTS RECEIVABLE

Enter accounts receivable at the end of the period, net of reserves for uncollectible accounts.

Line 2:   INVENTORIES

Enter the inventory at the end of the period, net of reserves for excess and obsolete inventory. If product lines are broken out in the sales line of the P&L, then inventory should also be broken out by product line. Thus, if there is a projected change in the sales mix of products with different inventory turnovers, this will be properly reflected in the inventory turnover ratio.

Line 3:   ACCOUNTS PAYABLE

Enter the accounts payable, net of disputed accounts, at the end of the period.

Line 4:   ACCRUED EXPENSES

Include obligations such as accrued vacation, bonus, retirement fund contributions, and severance pay.

Line 5: WORKING CAPITAL

Subtract the total of Line 3 + Line 4 from the total of Line 1 + Line 2. Working capital is the net current operating assets of the business, excluding cash, short-term investments, and short-term financing. We advise controlling the latter items at the corporate level.

Line 6: FIXED ASSETS AT COST

Enter the cumulative dollar amount of fixed assets acquired including the value of capitalized leases.

Line 7: ACCUMULATED DEPRECIATION

Enter the total amount of depreciation taken against the fixed assets included in Line 6.

Line 8: NET FIXED ASSETS

Subtract Line 7 from Line 6.

Line 9: OTHER ASSETS (LIABILITIES)

Include those other assets or liabilities required to operate the business. Include assets to be disposed of and net assets of business lines to be discontinued as a separate item on this line.

Line 10: NET OPERATING INVESTMENT

This is the net amount of operating assets employed in the business before subtracting financing claims on these assets. It is calculated by adding Line 5, Line 8 and Line 9 (excluding assets to be disposed of and discontinued business lines).

Operating Cash Flow

Line 11: OPERATING PROFIT

Enter Operating Profit (EBIT) from Line 10 of the P&L.

Line 12: DEPRECIATION AND AMORTIZATION

Enter total Depreciation and Amortization for the current time period, calculated by subtracting Line 7 (Accumulated Depreciation) for the prior time period from Line 7 for the current time period.

Line 13: OTHER SOURCES (USES)

Enter other sources and uses of cash. Examples include sale of
assets and payments of extraordinary legal claims.

Line 14: INCREASE (DECREASE) IN WORKING CAPITAL

Enter the difference between the current period Working Capital
(Line 5) and Line 5 for the prior period.

Line 15: CAPITAL EXPENDITURES

Enter the difference between the current period Fixed Assets at Cost
(Line 6) and Line 6 for the prior period.

Line 16: OPERATING CASH FLOW

Calculate cash flow from operations by subtracting from the sum of
Line 11, Line 12, and Line 13, the total of Line 14 and Line 15.
This is sometimes referred to as "free cash flow." If the number is
positive, it shows that the business is self-financing; if negative, it
indicates that the shortfall will have to be made up from financing
sources.

Financing Sources

Note: The forecasted items (Years 1 to 5) will include the debt of the
target company assumed in the acquisition and debt incurred to finance
the acquisition. For acquired companies subsequently financed at the
corporate level, short-term debt, long-term debt, and equity will be an
allocated amount including changes in the forecasted financing of the
acquired business. For example, in a pooling of interests transaction,
acquired long-term debt may be refinanced at a lower interest rate by the
parent company.

Line 17: SHORT-TERM DEBT

Include bank debt, commercial paper, and other sources of short-
term financing including current maturities of long-term debt.

Line 18: LONG-TERM DEBT

Include senior debt, subordinated debentures, capitalized lease
obligations and seller notes.

Line 19: EQUITY

For a pooling of interests transaction, the amount in Year 1 will be the shareholders' equity at closing plus net income (loss) for Year 1 (Line 15 from the P&L). For a purchase acquisition, the amount in Year 1 will be the purchase price, less the amount of debt assumed, plus net income (loss) for Year 1 (Line 15 from the P&L). To calculate Equity in subsequent years, net income (loss) for the current year will be added to the amount for the prior year. Include any cash infusions into the business from the parent that are not associated with short-term or long-term debt.

Line 20: NET CHANGE FINANCING SOURCES

Subtract the sum of Line 17, Line 18, and Line 19 for the current accounting period from the total of Line 17, Line 18, and Line 19 for the prior period.

Financial Ratios

Line 21: ACCOUNTS RECEIVABLE (DAYS SALES OUTSTANDING)

Divide Accounts Receivable (Line 1) by Annual Sales (Line 1 of the P&L) and multiply the result by 365.

Line 22: INVENTORY TURNOVER

Divide Cost of Goods Sold (Line 2 of the P&L) by Inventory at the end of the current accounting period (Line 2).

Line 23: SALES/NET OPERATING ASSETS

Divide Sales (Line 1 of the P&L) by Working Capital (Line 5).

Line 24: SALES/NET INVESTMENT

Divide Sales (Line 1 of the P&L) by Net Operating Investment (Line 10).

Line 25: RETURN ON NET OPERATING INVESTMENT

Divide Line 11 by Line 10 and multiply the result by 100.

Appendix F

Valuation Models

A business manager needs to know how much to pay for a strategic acquisition and how much to ask for a divestiture. These basic pricing questions are answered by using the **Comparables** and **Discounted Cash Flow** Valuation Models. The **Liquidation Model** provides a worst case estimate of the downside risk should the acquisition turn out to be a mistake and provides an estimate of the minimum likely proceeds if a business to be sold cannot be sold as a going concern and has to be liquidated.

Our valuation objective is to arrive at an acquisition price for the entire target company as a going concern—what we call "Enterprise Value." Although legal control of a target company is ultimately gained by payments, directly or indirectly, to selling shareholders, we need to know the total cost of the acquisition (Enterprise Value) including the cost of equity securities plus the cost of debt securities (the latter either assumed or redeemed at closing). For example, when you buy a house, the cost includes not only your initial equity, but the principal amount of the mortgage, and any seller financing. The same is true when acquiring a business.

Detailed instructions are given for each model. Financial data from the P&L and Investment Plan are used as input for the models. To estimate the probable proceeds from a divestiture, the business unit to be divested is substituted for the target company in the valuation models. Potential buyers for the divested company will likely go through similar valuation exercises to arrive at a purchase price.

In a typical strategic acquisition or divestiture, you are advised to seek information from investment bankers and business brokers as to current valuations of businesses similar to the target company. This intelligence will provide a comparison for results produced by the valuation models.

COMPARABLES MODEL

The basic assumption underlying the Comparables Model is that market prices provide a reliable measure of acquisition value because there is a sufficient number of knowledgeable buyers and sellers to establish an efficient market for mergers and acquisitions. At any point in time, a business is worth something between the price a seller wants *and* the price a buyer is willing to pay. For a deal to take place, there must be a meeting of the minds. The seller's position can be compared to a securities investor who thinks his stock is worth $30 per share when the market price is $20. It may or may not be worth $30 in the future, but if the holder wants to sell immediately, the price is likely to be closer to $20 per share.

For the Comparables Model to be workable, you must find companies similar to the target company—either recently acquired companies or ones that are publicly traded. As a buyer, you want to know that you are not paying more than a fair price and that, as a seller, you are not getting less. Thus, if the asking price for one target company is too high, you search for a similar company at a lower price. Similarly, if your bid is too low, the target company management will search for another buyer willing to pay a higher price. In economics this model is called the theory of substitution. The Comparables Model gives us an insight into what these hypothetical prices might be for the target company.

The instructions that follow will be illustrated by the following hypothetical target company, averages for comparable acquisitions, and averages for comparable public securities.

	Target Company	Average Comparable Acquisitions	Average Comparable Public Securities
Financial Data			
Sales	$5,000,000	$10,000,000	$8,000,000
EBIT	500,000	1,500,000	800,000
EBITD	600,000	1,600,000	960,000
Market Capitalization			
Debt Securities	1,000,000	3,000,000	2,000,000
Equity Securities	NA	7,800,000	3,900,000
Total Market Cap	NA	$10,800,000	$5,900,000

NA–Left blank because target company is privately held.

Comparables Model

	Target Company	Comparable Acquisitions Company A to Company X	—(A)— Average Co. A to X	Comparable Public Securities Company A to X	—(B)— Average Co. A to X
1. Sales					
2. EBIT					
3. EBITD					
Market Capitalization					
4. Debt Securities					
5. Equity Securities					
6. Market Cap (4+5)					
Valuation Ratios					
7. Market Cap/Sales (6/1)					
8. Market Cap/EBIT (6/2)					
9. Market Cap/EBITD (6/3)					
Target Company Valuation					
10. Market Cap/Sales			7(A) × 1		7(B) × 1
11. Market Cap/EBIT			8(A) × 2		8(B) × 2
12. Market Cap/EBITD			9(A) × 3		9(B) × 3
13. Average			10 + 11 + 12		10 + 11 + 12
Target Company Acquisition Price					
14. Enterprise Value—Comparable Acquisitions (Line 13 Col. [A])					
15. Enterprise Value—Comparable Public Securities (Line 13 Col [B])					
16. Acquisition Price—Enterprise Value (Line 14 + Line 15)/2					
17. Acquisition Price—Equity Securities (Line 16 − Line 4)					

INSTRUCTIONS FOR COMPLETING
COMPARABLES MODEL FORM

Step 1. *Select Comparable Acquisitions and Public Companies*
The first step is to select a representative sample of comparable acquisitions and publicly traded companies. Separate data will be filled out for
each comparable company under either the column heading "Comparable
Acquisitions" or "Comparable Public Securities," as applicable.

As part of your ongoing strategic acquisition program, you should
develop a competitive intelligence database, which includes financial information and acquisition prices for companies in targeted industries, as
well as financial data on principal competitors. This information is found
in trade publications, the financial press, company annual reports, SEC
filings, and due diligence on target companies that have not been
acquired. When an internal database is not available, deal intermediaries,
such as investment bankers, are good sources for this information. If the
target company has engaged an investment banker or broker to sell the
business, the Selling Memorandum will usually contain financial and
valuation data for comparable companies.

Comparable companies for inclusion in the Model will be obtained
from the following sources:

(A) The target company's principal competitors in each of its major
     served markets, as identified in the Market Battlefield Summary.
     These competitors are segregated into three categories: com-
     panies that were acquired by a third party within the last five
     years, publicly traded companies, and privately held companies.
     The latter are not included in the model because the required
     financial data is not available. However, when a private com-
     pany has been acquired by a public company there may be
     sufficient worthwhile information disclosed to be useful as a
     crosscheck against model results. For example, if you learn the
     target company's principal competitor with annual sales of $5.0
     million has been acquired for $6.0 million, the price-to-sales
     ratio of 1.2 is a relevant indicator of value.

(B) Publicly traded companies in the same industry (same SIC Code)
     as the target company, which are not included in the Market Bat-
     tlefield Summary. For example, a regional supermarket company
     would include competitors within its trading area in the Market
     Battlefield Summary, but not chains in other regions of the country.
     Corporate financial reference manuals, such as those published
     by Standard & Poor's, Moody's, and Dun & Bradstreet, contain

listings of publicly traded companies broken down by SIC Code. These same manuals will contain financial statements and histories of the company, including major acquisitions. Select up to ten companies from this list, including those companies most comparable to the target company in terms of annual sales. Note which companies were acquired within the last five years.

From the foregoing list of companies, select a representative sample. How many companies should be included in the comparables model? We believe that a representative sample would generally include five comparable acquisitions and five equivalent publicly traded companies. If more companies are available, first use all competitors included in the Market Battlefield Summary and then select those companies most similar financially to the target company. For example, if the target company is a private supplier of automotive parts with $25 million in annual sales, a publicly traded company with sales of $200 million that was recently acquired is not going to provide a meaningful comparison.

In searching for comparable companies, you may find only a few that can be included in the sample. There may be no comparables when the target company is truly unique, such as a start-up company developing a new technology. We recommend using whatever data is available, but the validity of the model will be limited with only one or two comparables.

Step 2. *Target Company Financial Data*
The next step is to fill in Financial Data for the target company (under the column heading—Target Company) using the P&L and Investment Plan, as shown in the table below (Year −1 is used, i.e., the latest reported fiscal year):

Financial Data	Name of Form	Line No.
Line 1. Sales	P&L	1
Line 2. EBIT	P&L	10
Line 3. EBITD	P&L	11

Step 3. *Comparables Financial Data*
Lines 1 to 3 of Financial Data are filled in for the selected comparable companies. Include a separate column for each company under the applicable heading, "Comparable Acquisitions" or "Comparable Public Securities." Columns (A) and (B) on the form are averages for the comparable companies. Financial data is obtained from company annual reports, SEC

filings, and financial reference services such as Standard & Poor's, Moody's and Value Line. This data should be compiled at the same time Step 1 is being completed.

Step 4. *Market Capitalization—Target Company and Comparables*

If the target company is publicly traded, Lines 4, 5, and 6 are filled in; otherwise only Line 4, which is derived from the Investment Plan (Line 17 plus Line 18, Year −1), is completed. A divestiture is treated like a privately held company—Line 4 is completed.

In completing the Market Capitalization data for comparable acquisitions, debt securities are included at face value at the date of acquisition. Equity securities are included at the acquisition price paid shareholders, which is equivalent to the price paid per common share times the number of shares outstanding at the date of acquisition.

In filling in the Market Capitalization data for comparable public securities, you must adjust common stock prices for a "control premium." Shareholders of a public company will not relinquish control unless they are paid a premium over the pre-acquisition price of the stock. Thus, the control premium equals the acquisition price paid equity holders divided by the market price of a target company's common stock prior to the acquisition announcement, expressed as a percent. For example, if a target company's common stock is selling for $10 per share and the acquirer pays $15 per share, the control premium is 50%. Since market capitalization data for Comparable Acquisitions are based on prices paid, the control premium is already reflected and no adjustment is necessary.

The control premium is derived from an analysis of comparable acquisitions. For each comparable acquisition it is necessary to know the price of the stock prior to the merger announcement and multiply this price by the number of shares outstanding. We advise using the stock price fifteen days prior to the date of the merger announcement to eliminate increases due to pre-announcement speculation. For example, shareholders of comparable acquisition company X with one million shares outstanding were paid $50 per share for their stock, which sold at $40 per share 15 days prior to the merger announcement. The pre-merger market value of the company's Equity Securities was $40,000,000 ($40 per share times one million shares outstanding). The control premium was 25% $\left(\frac{50-40}{40}\right)$.

The pre-merger equity values thus calculated for each comparable acquisition are totalled, and the total is divided into the amount on Line 5, Col. (A). The resulting ratio will be used to adjust market prices of publicly traded securities (Line 5, explained below). Pre-acquisition stock prices can be obtained from back copies of financial newspapers. The date of the acquisition announcement can usually be found in financial reference manuals or SEC filings. In addition to control premiums calculated in this manner, investment bankers and deal intermediaries are sources of information on control premiums. As a general guide, control premiums typically range between 25% and 50%.

Line 4 for comparable Public Securities includes the total of Short-term Debt (commercial paper, bank loans, other borrowing, and current maturities of long-term debt) and Long-term Debt. Debt securities are shown at market value if publicly traded; bank debt and other private debt issues are shown at principal (face) value.

On Line 5, for Comparable Public Securities, first determine the current market value of the comparable company's equity securities, which is calculated by multiplying the total number of shares outstanding for each class of stock by the relevant market price per share. Then multiply this amount by the control premium ratio as calculated above. Enter the result on Line 5, Column heading "Comparable Public Securities." For example, if comparable acquisitions involved a control premium of 25% over the pre-acquisition values, this premium would be used. If a public company has privately held equity shares outstanding, such as a redeemable preferred stock, include these at the redemption price and add to Line 5.

For example, a comparable publicly traded company has one million shares outstanding selling at $12 per share and has publicly traded subordinated debentures selling at a 10% discount from face value. For this company, the following amounts will be shown on Lines 4, 5, and 6:

	Face Value	Market Capitalization
Debt Securities		
Bank debt	$ 1,000,000	$ 1,000,000
Sub. debt	$ 5,000,000	$ 4,500,000
Line 4 (Debt Securities)		$ 5,500,000
Equity Securities		
Common Stock	$10,000,000	$12,000,000
Control Premium		×1.25
Line 5 (Equity Securities)		$15,000,000
Line 6 (Market Capitalization)		$20,500,000

For Line 6, Market Cap, enter the total of Lines 4 and 5.

Step 5. *Valuation Ratios*

Lines 7, 8 and 9 are calculated as shown in the parentheses. For example, Line 7 equals total Market Cap (Line 6) divided by Sales (Line 1). These ratios are left blank for a privately held target company. Columns (A) and (B) are averages of Valuation Ratios calculated for each comparable acquisition company and comparable publicly traded company.

The Valuation Ratios are interpreted as follows:

(A) Market Cap/Sales—The target company's sales represent the gross amount of operating income that will accrue to the acquirer. It measures the amount the market says you will have to pay for each dollar of revenue generated by the target company. The acquirer can compare this amount with how much it would cost to develop a dollar of revenue using internal resources. For example, a defense professional services company evaluating the acquisition of a similar company may essentially be buying a contract backlog. As an alternative, the company could bid on new contracts in an attempt to build a similar backlog. The acquirer would weigh the relative costs versus the chances of successful bids.

The Market Cap/Sales ratio is particularly useful when the comparable company is operating at a loss or nominal operating profit, which will produce meaningless results for the Market Cap/EBIT and Market Cap/EBITD ratios.

(B) Market Cap/EBIT—This is a measure of how much the market is willing to pay for a dollar of operating earnings. Think of it as a measure of return on the strategic acquisition before financing the acquisition and paying income taxes. In our hypothetical example, comparable companies were acquired at an average of 7.2 times EBIT. If you were to pay a comparable price for the target company, the cost would be $3,600,000 (7.2 times EBIT of $500,000). The reciprocal of this ratio, expressed as a percent, is the preinterest, pretax current return on your investment—in this example 13.9% (1/7.2 × 100).

Although the denominator in this ratio is the comparable company's reported EBIT for the latest available fiscal year, it will not be meaningful if EBIT was artificially depressed or inflated in the latest year. Therefore, compare the comparable company's operating profit margin for the latest year to the average for prior years. Where the margin is out of line, use average EBIT for the last three years to calculate this ratio.

Market Cap/EBIT ratios will vary according to the forecasted growth of EBIT, the nature of the industry, the level of interest rates and stock prices, and operating profit margins (EBIT/Sales). Thus, at any point in time there is no absolute ratio that is too high or so low it indicates a bargain price. It has to be interpreted relative to comparable companies.

(C) Market Cap/EBITD—This ratio provides a measure of how much is paid for a dollar of operating cash flow (EBIT plus depreciation and amortization) before payment of interest costs and taxes. This ratio will be important in industries where a significant investment in fixed assets is required to produce a dollar of revenues, for example, oil, cable TV, and forest products. It must be interpreted relative to comparable companies, not on an absolute basis, and provides a simple measure of the payback period—the ratio equals number of years required to get back the purchase price. A company selling at five times EBITD would take five years to earn back our investment, *before* interest costs, taxes, and new investments in fixed assets. Although depreciation and amortization are non-cash charges, they have to be evaluated relative to future requirements to maintain the company's plant and equipment in competitive condition. If EBIT for the latest year is adjusted as discussed, then a similar adjustment should be made for EBITD.

Step 6. *Target Company Valuation*

We now use the average Valuation Ratios calculated in Step 5 for Comparable Acquisitions (Column A) and Comparable Public Securities (Column B) to calculate the Target Company Valuation.

Lines 10, 11, and 12 for the target company are calculated by multiplying the target company's financial data (Lines 1, 2 and 3) by the average valuation ratios for the comparable companies (Lines 7, 8 and 9—Columns A and B). The resulting values for Lines 10, 11, and 12 are placed in either Column A or B. Refer to the formula in the appropriate block on the Comparables Model form. For example, the amount on Line 10, Column A will be the product of Line 7, Column A times the target company's sales from Line 1. Thus, for our sample target company, the amount on Line 10, Column A is $5,400,000 (1.08 times $5,000,000). Each of the other blocks in Columns A and B are calculated similarly. Line 13 is the average of Lines 10, 11, and 12.

Step 7. *Target Company Acquisition Price*

The Target Company Valuations calculated in Step 6 determine the Target Company Acquisition Price (or the selling price for a divestiture). We first calculate *Enterprise Value* (the total value of the target company).

Line 14, Enterprise Value—Comparable Acquisitions, is the amount shown on Line 13, Column A. This is the total amount you would expect to pay for the target company based on actual prices for acquisitions of comparable companies.

Line 15, Enterprise Value—Comparable Public Securities, is the amount shown on Line 13, Column B. This is the total amount you would expect to pay for the target company based on current prices for securities of comparable publicly held companies, adjusted for a control premium.

Line 16, Acquisition Price—Enterprise Value, is the average of Line 14 and Line 15. It is the total Acquisition Price to pay to holders of the target company's debt and equity.

Line 17, Acquisition Price—Equity Securities, equals Line 16 minus Line 4. It is the total acquisition price to be paid to the target company's shareholders.

Whether the Acquisition Price on Line 16 or Line 17 is applicable will depend on the structure of the acquisition. In a pooling of interests, or common stock exchange transaction, the acquirer will exchange common stock, cash, or other consideration for common stock of the target company. In this case, Line 17 would be the price to pay the target company's shareholders. For transactions involving the purchase of assets, Line 16 is the acquisition price to use.

For our hypothetical target company, the valuations and acquisition prices are summarized below:

		Column A	*Column B*
Line 10		$5,400,000	$3,500,000
Line 11		3,600,000	3,700,000
Line 12		4,050,000	3,660,000
Line 13		4,350,000	3,620,000
Line 14	4,350,000		
Line 15	3,620,000		
Line 16	3,985,000		
Line 17	2,985,000		

Summary—Comparables Model

The target company acquisition price derived from the Comparables Model gives you an *estimate* of the price you are likely to pay for a strategic acquisition or receive for a divestiture. Rather than think of it as absolute price, consider it the midpoint in a range of outcomes. There will undoubtedly be characteristics of the target company that differentiate it from the sample of comparable companies. The comparables acquisition price provides a benchmark to evaluate a seller's asking price.

Comparable acquisitions have the advantage of being based on actual transactions. The disadvantage of comparable acquisitions is that the current market for acquisitions may be significantly different than that which existed when the comparable transactions closed. Comparable publicly traded securities offer the advantage of reflecting current pricing conditions in capital markets. For comparable publicly traded securities, a hypothetical control premium has to be calculated.

The main drawback of the Comparables Model is it does not allow a determination of whether the estimated acquisition price should be paid, or, if you pay the price, what your financial return will be. These questions can be answered by using the Discounted Cash Flow Model.

DISCOUNTED CASH FLOW MODEL

Discounted Cash Flow Models are widely used as a basis for establishing the value of an acquisition. This involves forecasting future cash flow from the acquired business to determine if the amount you are paying is less than the present value of those future cash flows, the concept being that you should never pay more than the net present value of those future cash flows because it *establishes* your *maximum purchase price*.

Discounted cash flow valuation models tend to be complex both mechanically and theoretically and will mislead users unless applied with careful attention to their proper use and limitations.

Discounting Future Cash Flows

Why discount future cash flows? If you invested $100 today in the bank you would expect to receive 5% interest on your investment. This would give you $105 a year from now. The $105 would then have the same value to you as $100 today. The 5% is the discount rate that must be applied to future amounts of cash received ($105) to give you the present value ($100) of those funds. If you invested the same $100 today in the stock market, you may expect to receive $120 at the end of one year in dividends and stock price appreciation since it is a more risky investment. Your effective rate of return would be 20% on your stock investment. The $120 received a year from now is the financial equivalent of $100 today for this risk class of investment. The 20% is the discount rate that must be applied to future amounts of cash received ($120) to give you the present value ($100) of those funds. In each case the future receipts must be adjusted by your expected earnings to determine their present value equivalent. That is, comparisons between funds received in the future and funds received today must be discounted by the investor's *expected* rate of return on investment. *What discount rate should you use?* Why do expected rates of return vary from 5% to 20% in our example? As investments become more risky, investors expect higher potential returns to compensate them for risk. In the investment world, short-term U.S. Government treasury bills are considered virtually risk free, carrying an interest rate of 3.48% as of March 31, 1994. Investors expect to be compensated for the additional risk they take over the short-term (risk free) treasury bill rate. But risk is a subjective assessment of a financial investment's returns. How can you get a risk/return calibration? Develop your own risk return calibration chart based on public information.

The example shown on the next page shows three-month treasury bills at 3.48% with no investment risk. The other end of the risk return chart shows venture capitalists expecting to get 35% to 50% returns with 35% to 45% risk of a failed investment. Telephone and municipal bonds are commanding 6% to 8% returns while subordinate debt (subordinate to bank debt) is commanding 10% to 20% returns. The bank prime rate is 6% to 6.5% as the rate charged to secure corporate investors. Publicly traded stocks are expected to generate returns from 13% to 25%. As you can see, higher returns correspond to higher risk by investors. If you invest in an acquisition, you must adjust the rate at which you discount future cash flows by a discount rate that reflects the riskiness of investment to get its equivalent present value.

For example, if you acquire a gold mine in Africa, you may expect to receive a 50% rate of return on your equity investment. If you acquire a

Risk Return Chart

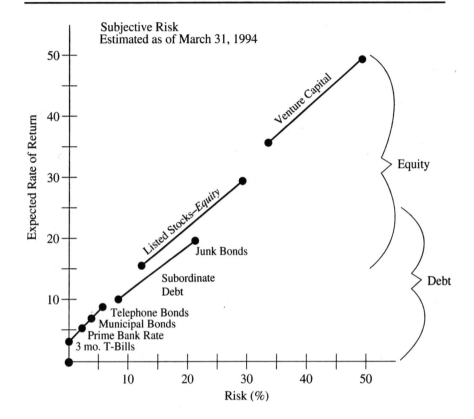

mature distributor of your products, you may expect to receive a 20% rate of return on your equity investment. The rate is determined by your equity investor perception of risk.

However, in acquisitions you may have a combination of this risk adjusted equity investment and debt in the financing of the transaction. You must then use a weighted average of these two rates to determine the appropriate rate to discount future cash flows.

The weighted average discount rate applied to the discounted cash flow model is called the "weighted average cost of capital." This takes into account the different discount rates applicable to the Debt and Equity portions of your investment in an acquisition. It is calculated by the following formula:

$$Weighted\ Average\ Cost\ of\ Capital = \left(\begin{array}{c} Expected \\ Return\ on \times \begin{array}{c} \% \\ Equity \end{array} \\ Equity \end{array} \right)$$

$$+ \left(\begin{array}{c} Required \\ Interest\ Rate \times \begin{array}{c} \% \\ Debt \end{array} \\ on\ Debt \end{array} \right)$$

where:

$$\%Equity = \frac{Equity\ Investment\ \$}{Total\ Investment\ \$}$$

$$\%\ Debt = \frac{Debt\ Investment\ \$}{Total\ Investment\ \$}$$

For example:

	Weight	Return	Weighted Cost
Debt	.3	.05	.015
Equity	.7	.20	.140
Weighted Average Cost of Capital			.155

This example shows a financing composed of 30% (.3) Debt at a 5% (.05) interest rate and 70% (0.7) Equity at a 20% Expected Return on Equity that yields a weighted average cost of capital of 15.5% (.155). This is the appropriate discount rate to use in discounting future cash flows in this example.

Note: When combining two companies, it is theoretically more appropriate to use the cost of capital for the combined businesses. This is beyond the scope of this text but may be explored by reading Al Rappaport's text *Creating Shareholder Value*.

Forecasting Future Cash Flows and Terminal Value

Future cash flows are forecasted based on your strategic plan as shown in the Forecasted Investment Plan. These cash flows are a result of your estimate of what will happen in the competitive market and how it will drive your business opportunity. We have chosen five years as the forecast horizon period for the purpose of developing strategic plans and cash forecasts. You may be able to forecast a business's performance for a longer period of time or perhaps you can only forecast future cash flows for less than five years. At the end of your forecast period, the acquired business usually has some residual cash value or **terminal value.** There are many methods of estimating this terminal value. It should represent the cash value of the business at the end of the forecast period in case you were to either liquidate the business or continue its operation in perpetuity. Each of these methodologies is fraught with potential errors and may add considerably to the uncertainty of the discounted cash flow valuation.

The first approach, the "Going Concern Model," is to assume the terminal year's cash flows continue on into perpetuity. This method calculates terminal value by dividing the last year's cash flow by the weighted average cost of capital (capitalization rate).

The second method, not recommended for going concern valuations, is to estimate the cash flow from liquidating the business at the end of the forecast period. It is usually the most conservative measure of residual value and involves estimating the value of selling off all assets at the end of the forecast time period, and paying off all operating liabilities. This should leave you with cash representing the liquidation value of operations at the end of the forecast period.

Terminal Value Risk

As pointed out, the residual value or terminal value calculation adds considerably to the uncertainty of the discounted cash flow. It is the most speculative portion of the forecasted future cash flow. If the terminal value represents more than half the maximum investment, the Discounted Cash Flow Model indicates you should understand that the DCF model is highly speculative. If the terminal value represents 10% to 20% of the maximum investment the Discounted Cash Flow Model indicates, the Model is more realistically based on operating cash projections during the five-year (or other) forecast period.

DCF Model Summary

The Discounted Cash Flow model can be used to establish the maximum amount you should pay for an acquisition. It lets you establish this price based on your perception (or your investors' perception) of the equity risk to be taken with the acquisition. It also takes into account the amount and cost of debt financing.

However, you should be cautioned:

1. The forecasted cash flow is only as good as your Strategic Battle Plan and your understanding of the market battlefield.
2. The forecasted financials are subject to your understanding of the financial characteristics of the acquired company and your ability to implement financial controls after the acquisition.
3. The forecast period cash flows become more uncertain with time.
4. The discount rate is often based on a subjective assessment of equity risk.
5. The residual valuation or terminal value calculations are speculative, at best.

But, as long as you recognize the sensitivity of the maximum purchase price (total investment in the acquisition) that results from this analysis to the input data assumptions, this model can give you guidance in pricing an acquisition.

Recommended Additional Reading on Discounted Cash Flow Models

1. Marron, J. H. *Mergers and Acquisitions, Will You Overpay.* Irwin, 1993.
2. Cornell, B. *Corporate Valuation.* Irwin, 1993.
3. Rappaport, A. *Creating Shareholder Value.* Free Press, 1986.

DEVELOPING THE DISCOUNTED CASH FLOW (DCF) MODEL TO DETERMINE MAXIMUM PRICE

Line 1. Enter the % of debt you expect to be included in the purchase price (include debt assumed), expressed as a decimal equivalent (i.e., 0.xx) and multiply times the decimal equivalent rate of return your lenders require. If you have more than one type of debt, calculate the weighted average interest rate as follows:

$$\begin{aligned} \text{\textit{Debt Rate}} \\ \text{\textit{of Return}} \\ \text{\textit{(Interest)}} \end{aligned} = \left(\begin{array}{c} \textit{Interest on} \\ \textit{Debt A} \end{array} \times \% \textit{ of Debt A} \right)$$

$$+ \left(\begin{array}{c} \textit{Interest on} \\ \textit{Debt B} \end{array} \times \% \textit{ of Debt B} \right)$$

$$\dots \text{etc.}$$

Discounted Cash Flow (DCF) Model (To determine maximum price)

Weighted Average Cost of Capital (WACC)						
	% of Total		*Expected Rate of Return*		*Weighted Cost*	
1. Debt	_____ (A)	×	_____	=		
2. Equity	_____ (B)	×	_____	=	+	
3. Weighted Average Cost of Capital (WACC)						

Notes: (A) % of total debt $= \dfrac{\text{Debt}}{\text{Debt} + \text{Equity}}$

(B) % of total equity $= \dfrac{\text{Equity}}{\text{Debt} + \text{Equity}}$

Going Concern Discounted Cash Flow		*Start*	*YR 1*	*YR 2*	*YR 3*	*YR 4*	*YR 5*
4. Forecasting Operating Cash Flow from Acquisition	(Inv. Plan, Line 16)						
5. Residual Value 5th Year	(Line 4, 5th Yr) (WACC Line 3)						
6. Total Future Cash Flows	(Line 4 and Line 5)						
7. Discount Factor	$(1 + WACC)^{YR}$	1.0					
8. Pres. Value of Each Yr Cash Flow	(Line 6/Line 7)						
9. Max. Inv. in Acquisition	(Sum of Line 8 Items)						
Fifth Year Termination Discounted Cash Flow		*Start*	*YR 1*	*YR 2*	*YR 3*	*YR 4*	*YR 5*
10. Forecasted Operating Cash Flow from Acquisition	(Inv. Plan) (Line 16)						
11. Residual Value 5th Year	(Liquidation Value per text pg. 228)						
12. Total Future Cash Flows	(Line 10 & Line 11)						
13. Discount Factor	$(1 + WACC)^{YR}$	1.0					
14. Pres. Val. of Each Yr Cash Flow	(Line 12/Line 13)						
15. Maximum Inv. in Acquisition	(Sum of Line 14 Items)						
Terminal Value Risk							
16. Going Concern % Residual Value	(Line 5/Line 9)						
17. Fifth Year Termination % Residual Value	(Line 11/Line 15)						

Multiply the % of total debt times the % rate of return (decimal equivalents) to get the weighted average cost of debt.

Line 2.   Enter the % of equity you expect to be included in the purchase price. (Note: % debt + % equity = 100% of purchase price.) Multiply that decimal equivalent (i.e., 0.xx) times the decimal equivalent rate of return you (or your shareholders) expect to achieve on similarly risky equity investments to get the weighted average cost of equity.

Line 3.   Calculate the weighted average cost of capital (WACC) by adding together the weighted average cost of debt (Line 1) and the weighted average cost of equity (Line 2). This cost of capital is the discount rate you will use to calculate the present value of future cash flows.

Line 4.   *Forecasted Operating Cash Flow from Acquisition:* Enter operating cash flows from Investment Plan Form, Line 16. If there are any extraordinary cash flows (fees, severance costs, cash balances, etc.) not included in your purchase price, enter these cash flows in the Start column.

Line 5.   *Residual Value 5th Year:* Divide the 5th year cash flow from Line 4 by the weighted average cost of capital (decimal equivalent) of Line 3. Place value in year 5. Put zeros in years 1–4.

Line 6.   *Total Future Cash Flows:* Add Line 4 to Line 5 for each period.

Line 7.   *Discount Factor:* Calculate each year's discount factor (or look up in a table or on a computer) using the formula:
Discount factor for year (N) = $(1 + WACC)^N$ where WACC is on Line 3.

For the 5-year forecast period the formulas are as follows:
Start discount factor = 1.0
End of Year 1 discount factor = 1 + WACC
End of Year 2 discount factor = $(1 + WACC) \times (1 + WACC)$
End of Year 3 discount factor = $(1 + WACC) \times (1 + WACC) \times (1 + WACC)$
End of Year 4 discount factor = $(1 + WACC) \times (1 + WACC) \times (1 + WACC) \times (1 + WACC)$
End of Year 5 discount factor = $(1 + WACC) \times (1 + WACC) \times (1 + WACC) \times (1 + WACC) \times (1 + WACC)$

For example: If the weighted average cost of capital were 15.5%:

Start discount factor = 1.0

End of Year 1 discount factor = 1 + .155 = <u>1.155</u>

End of Year 2 discount factor = (1 + .155) × (1 + .155) = 1.155 × 1.155 = <u>1.334</u>

End of Year 3 discount factor = (1.155) × (1.155) × (1.155) = <u>1.541</u>

End of Year 4 discount factor = (1.155) × (1.155) × (1.155) × (1.155) = <u>1.780</u>

End of Year 5 discount factor = (1.155) × (1.155) × (1.155) × (1.155) × (1.155) = <u>2.055</u>

As you can see, cash received at the end of five years is discounted by a factor of 2.055 (i.e., it is worth half as much as cash received today) in this example.

Line 8.   *Present Value of Each Year's Cash Flow:* Divide the cash flow for each period in Line 6 by the corresponding discount factor of Line 7.

Line 9.   *Maximum Investment in Acquisition:* Add together each period of Line 8 to obtain the total discounted cash flow, which should be the maximum amount you are willing to pay for the acquisition as a going concern.

Line 10.   Same as Line 4.

Line 11.   *Residual Value 5th Year:* Estimate the liquidation value as per the liquidation value calculation on page 228 of Appendix F for the Fifth Year Balance Sheet shown in Appendix E investment plan. Place value in year 5. Put zeros in years 1–4.

Line 12.   *Total Future Cash Flows:* Add Line 10 to Line 11 for each period.

Line 13.   Same as Line 7.

Line 14.   *Present Value of each Year's Cash Flow:* Divide the cash flow for each period in Line 12 by the corresponding discount factor of Line 13.

Line 15.   *Maximum Investment in Acquisition:* Add together each period of Line 14 to obtain the total discounted cash flow, which should be the maximum amount you are willing to pay for the acquisition, assuming liquidation at the end of the fifth year.

Line 16. *Going Concern % Residual Value:* Calculate the terminal value risk by dividing Line 5 by Line 9 to obtain the % of residual value in the maximum investment in the acquisition when considered as a going concern.

Line 17. *Fifth Year Termination % Residual Value:* Calculate the terminal value risk by dividing Line 11 by Line 15 to obtain the % of residual value in the maximum investment in the acquisition when considered as part of a fifth-year liquidation analysis.

LIQUIDATION VALUE

As discussed in the Perspectives on Value section chapter 6, the reason for calculating Liquidation Value is to estimate the worst case loss should the acquisition prove to be a mistake or, in the case of a divestiture, the minimum price to be received.

Liquidation Value

	(A)	*(B)*	*(A) × (B)*
Liquidation Value			
1. Accounts Rec.			
2. Inventory			
3. Net Fixed Assets			
4. Tax Saving			
5. Oper. Cur. Liab.			
6. Value (1+2+3+4)−5			
Potential Loss			
(Acquisition Price—Line 6)			

Liquidation Value Form

The amounts in column (A) are from the Forecasted Investment Plan (Appendix E). Line 5, oper. cur. liab., is the sum of Line 3 and 4 from the Forecasted Investment Plan. Liquidation factors (decimal equivalents) are placed in column (B). Liquidation values equal (A) × (B).

The liquidation factors are estimated by an analysis of the assets and the nature of the business. As a guide, asset-based lenders will usually lend 75% of accounts receivable, 60% of inventory, and 50% of fixed assets. If appraisals of real estate, plant and equipment or other assets have been obtained, these can be used in calculating the appropriate liquidation factor. Line 4, Tax Saving is an estimate of the tax benefit that would result from the loss created by liquidating assets for less than the cost basis. This will vary according to the tax attributes of the acquiring corporation.

Potential Loss is acquisition price (price paid minus cash in the target company) minus liquidation value. This is the worst case loss because a target company that does not produce the expected strategic benefits may still be saleable as a going concern.

Note that the asset values are those at the time of acquisition. If any major expenditures or asset sales are planned during the first year or two of an acquisition, these should be included in the analysis. For purposes of calculating the Terminal Value in the Discounted Cash Flow model, the values in year 5 are used.

Index